TRUE AND FALSE

RELIGION

EXAMINED;

THE

CHRISTIAN RELIGION DEFENDED;

AND THE

PROTESTANT REFORMATION VINDICATED:

IN A SERIES OF

DISCOURSES,

DELIVERED AT GENEVA.

BY BENEDICT PICTET,

FORMERLY PASTOR AND PROFESSOR IN THEOLOGY THERE.

TRANSLATED FROM THE FRENCH,

BY A. BRUCE,

MINISTER OF THE GOSPEL.

WITH AN

INTRODUCTION, containing some account of the

LIFE and WRITINGS of the AUTHOR

Berith Press
P.O. Box 861, Kansas, OK 74347
(918) 896-2055
www.berithpress.com

True and False Religion was first published in English in 1797, translated by A. Bruce. It was initially published in French as *Huit sermons sur l'examen des religions* in 1701. In this Berith Press reprint, spelling, grammar, and formatting changes have been made. Printed in the U.S.A.

978-1-963516-29-6

BERITH PRESS

AN ACCOUNT OF THE LIFE AND WRITINGS OF THE AUTHOR.

After the light of evangelical truth had arisen at the Reformation, and spread its happy influence through various parts of Europe, the church of Geneva early appeared in youthful beauty and vigor, and continued long distinguished among the other Reformed churches. By the labors of some of her eminent doctors the Scriptures were greatly elucidated, and from that exuberant source the streams of pure doctrine were diffused around. Her academy was long resorted to by those who wished to become proficients in theological learning, as Athens of old had been by philosophers. To her assistance and advice, as well as example, several other churches were greatly indebted, in settling their reformation—that of Scotland in particular. Since the days of her Viret, Calvin, and Beza, she continued to enjoy a succession of eminent pastors in the church, and teachers in her chairs. The names of Diodati, Mestrezat, Spanheim, the Tronchins, and Turretins are familiar to the learned, and will be long remembered with honor.

Our author, Benedict Pictet, though following after a train of such eminent men, yet appeared with no diminished luster. He obtained a name among the first of these for his extensive acquaintance with ecclesiastical learning, his pious labours, and his instructive writings. He was born at Geneva in 1655, of a distinguished family, some of which since his time have been known in the world for attachment to literary studies, as well as for the offices of honour they have filled; particularly J Louis, Pictet, Counsellor, and Syndic of Geneva, who died in 1781. Mr. Benedict Pictet, after he had prosecuted his studies for a considerable time with much success, traveled into Holland and England. Upon his return to his native city, he was soon called to teach theology, having been appointed to succeed his uncle Francis Turretin in 1687, whose funeral eulogium he pronounced for his inaugural oration, according to the custom of that university. It may be found prefixed to Turretin's *Theological Works*. The University of Leyden, after the death of

Spantreina, solicited him to come and fill his place, but this he declined, thinking his own country had the best right to his services; and for this generosity he received its thanks by the mouth of the members of council. He was ever ready to lend his assistance for promoting the public interests of religion, and the peace of the church. He had much sweetness in his disposition and affability in his manner. The poor found in him a father and a comforter. He was chosen correspondent member of the society at London for reformation of manners; and afterwards of that for propagating the gospel among the Indians. He published a great number of works both in Latin and French, which have been much esteemed in Protestant countries, and by which he may be best known. "All of them," says Sennebier, author of a history of Geneva, "show evident marks of piety and good sense." He intermitted not his labors, until a languishing disorder, occasioned by too much fatigue, hastened his death; which happened on the 9th of June, 1724, at the age of 69 years.

His principal work is his *System of Christian Theology*. This appeared first in a compendious form in Latin, being chiefly intended for the use of students at the university. It is drawn up in a more plain and easy manner than books of this kind often are, as he avoided as much as possible the use of scholastic terms, and omitted a number of the nicer controversies, which had been discussed at large in the questions of Turretin. This has been admitted as a textbook in several universities, particularly those of Scotland; and it is still retained for this purpose in that of the capital. The larger system was published in the beginning of this century, in two quarto volumes, to which a third was annexed by way of supplement, in the more correct and enlarged edition published by the author in 1721, a few years before his death. This elaborate work is written in French, and contains a rich fund for those who read that language. It is executed in an easy perspicuous manner, and is one of the completest and most regularly digested books of the kind that the Protestant churches have as yet been furnished with, though no work of such extent, and treating on such a variety of subjects, can be equally well executed, and free from blemishes in every part. It may of itself, and still more if taken in conjunction with the system of his uncle and predecessor in office, be sufficient to give candidates for the ministry, a competent idea of the principal heads of divinity, and of the most useful branches of ecclesiastical learning. Besides an exposition of the doctrines, it contains a refutation of the opposite errors, a historical account of many of the more remarkable controversies and errors in different ages of the church, the sentiments of fathers, and the opinions and arguments of modern writers, interspersed, and an abridgment of what is most considerable in sacred and profane history. The third volume gives a short account of ecclesiastical writers and doctors, ancient and modern; an index of the history of popes, heretics, and sects; a list of councils, an abridgement of general history, and of Jewish antiquities. He had formed a design of publishing a fourth volume to consist of answers to objections, explication of difficult passages, reconciliation of apparent contradictions in Scripture, letters or questions of criticism and history, etc.; but they were deferred for separate publication. Some, if not all of them, were afterwards published.

As he had bestowed particular attention on the study of ecclesiastical history, he undertook the continuation of *The History of the Church and Empire* begun by Le Sucur, at the desire of a synod of the French church, and brought down by him to the tenth century. The original work bears marks of care and judgment, and was done with exactness and fidelity; but too rigid an adherence to the form of annals, and the mingling continually the secular affairs with those of the church, interrupts too much the thread of narration, and renders the reading of it rather dry and disagreeable. Mr. Pictet added the two following centuries, published in two quarto volumes in 1713, which some have reckoned preferable to the former volumes.

He compiled another useful work, entitled, *La Morale Chrétienne*, or *Christian Morality*, printed in eight volumes, duodecimo at Geneva, in 1710. It was also published in quarto. He wrote a number of other tracts on moral and religious subjects: among these was *The Art of Living and Dying Well*, in

1705, duodecimo. He published a *Syllabus Controversiarum*, for the assistance of those engaged in the study of divinity; besides other controversial treatises that appeared from time to time. He is a fair and dispassionate reasoner; while he states candidly the opinion and arguments of adversaries, he fails not to give concise yet very forcible replies. He has the art of selecting the principal topics of argument, and of exhibiting briefly the substance of what has been written on the subjects of which he treats. A number of his sermons were also published, at different times, from 1697 to 1721, which make four volumes in octavo; but they are very rarely to be met with in Britain.

The *Discourses* now offered to the public in English appear to have been delivered in the end of last century. They were published in a volume by themselves, as they all relate to the same general subject, and pursue throughout one leading and important design. Soon after they appeared abroad, an edition of them was published at London, bearing the dates 1702 and 1704, from which the translation was made. They have never before been translated (so far as the writer knows) though it deserved this mark of distinction much more than hundreds of books in that language which have received it. The original itself is become exceeding scarce, and is now known but to few. The translator—though long attentive to books of that sort—has never seen another complete copy but that which he used; nor has he observed more than one or two copies at any time offered to sale, either in Scotland or in London. Some time after the publication of these discourses, the author resumed the consideration of some of the heads of them, by bringing them under academic discussion, particularly the right of judging and examining in matters of religion, the criteria of true and false religion, with the principles and proof of natural religion. These were cast into a new, enlarged and more scholastic form, which he published in Latin, under the title of *Theses Theologicae de Examine Religionis*, etc.; which may be read by scholars with profit.

But the discourses delivered in the pulpit, as they embrace a more extensive plan, so from the manner of execution, they were calculated for more general usefulness. Much attention has been bestowed in the composition of them: they are evidently the result of reading and mature reflexion. Few books indeed have ever been written that comprised, in so small a compass, such copious matter, or so much useful instruction, adapted to the various classes of readers. The learned—especially studious youths, who may be beginning their enquiries into these matters—may be pleased to find here some of the capital articles of religion clearly stated and defended; and many voluminous controversies summarily discussed; not in a dry contentious manner, but in a perspicuous order, with a serious desire to discover the truth, and to direct the consciences and practice of men in reference to it. Common people while they are here instructed in the right they have to judge for themselves in matters of religion, they are at the same time directed and assisted in the proper exercise of it, in opposition to levity and scepticism on the one hand, or bigotry and implicit faith on the other. The unlearned Christian may see his religion satisfactorily though briefly defended, and many of the most common cavils of infidels obviated, whereby he may be ready to give an answer to those who attack it, or may ask a reason of the hope that is in them. Something of this kind adapted to ordinary capacities executed in a pious as well as rational strain, is rendered but too needful, in our land, from the infectious poison and creeping gangrene of infidelity that has begun of late to appear among the lower classes of people, for which the long indifference and growing ignorance as to religious concerns, both among high and low, have been gradually preparing the way, and made them an easy prey; while a false glare of modish wit or learning, the abuse and false pretext of liberty, and the parade of some modern improvements of another kind, impose upon the unthinking, fill novices with pert conceit, and make them assume insolent but contemptible airs of superior wisdom.

The Protestant may here see the principles and grounds of the Reformation stated and vindicated, the horrid idolatries and corruptions of the Romish establishment exposed, and the necessity for a total separation in judgment and practice, from such a communion clearly proved, in opposition to the many pleas that have been urged for abiding at least in external union with it. The intelligent may easily discern that the reasons adduced on this head, and the answers to objections, may with little variation be applied to the question of communion with or separation from other corrupt churches, though bearing the Protestant name, in many of which the genuine doctrines of the gospel, and all the valuable interests of Christianity, are almost as completely destroyed, and the souls of men in connexion with them in as great danger of perishing, as they were formerly in the Antichristian communion. The original maxims and spirit of the Reformation scarce any more appear in any of them; and while a public reformation in these degenerate churches is become demonstrably as needful as the former was, it seems to be as effectually precluded, and its warrantableness or necessity as really denied, by the high violent strains of authority, civil or ecclesiastical on the one hand, in support of whatever has been once established or introduced into a nation, which is often but another name for abuses and corruptions, and the blind and tame compliance with them; and no less, on the other, by the loose system of principles, and latitude of practice, in reference to external communion with almost any church, whatever errors or corruptions be prevalent therein, in a way of discarding the duty of a public and consistent testimony against them, and abandoning the term of contending for reformation. In either way, as all former reformation in Protestant nations is virtually condemned as unlawful or unnecessary, so everything of the kind in future must be considered in the same light; the invaluable privilege of trying all things by the Scriptures, and the duty of discriminating the false from the true in religion, the pure from the corrupt, must be rendered of no effect, or if retained and used, must only tend to make persons the objects of political or religious persecution, either as disobedient subjects, or as bigots and schismatics, for declining such an indiscriminate communion. If there be no important difference between the various communions of Christians, or if the commands of human authority, custom, vague general professions of unity, or personal piety, be sufficient to secure persons against the sin or danger that may arise from connection with them, and to make religious conformity a duty, then surely to be at pains to enquire into true and false religion, or the right or wrong constitution of particular churches, would be only so much unnecessary trouble. To close with that which first offers, or as many as afterwards may come in our way, without further enquiry, must be the wiser course and the general rule: for whether men enquire, or not, the result, in that case, must be precisely the same.

It were to be wished that there were less occasion for still displaying to the view of professed Christians, and of Protestants themselves, the wicked tenets and shocking superstitions of the Romish church, and for inculcating the heinous guilt and danger of continuing to adhere to them, or of participating therein. Perhaps at no time since the retreat was first sounded from idolatrous Babel, was there greater necessity for this than at the present juncture; though almost all descriptions of men have got nearly every apprehension on this head banished from their minds. While multitudes from sottish ignorance, and by the arts of imposition, are still detained in the old errors and grossest superstitions of Rome, many who profess to have renounced them are ready to afford them patronage, and the most direct and effectual support; some from political views or particular interests, others from absolute indifference about every species of religion. What our reforming ancestors strove to abolish, what the true church of Christ has been incessantly praying heaven to destroy, and what God has declared to be above all other things most abominable in his sight, and against which his indignation shall burn most fiercely in this world, and in the lowest hell, that is what even modern Protestants scruple not to maintain, or labour to restore, by furious wars, or negociations for peace. The fall of idolatrous altars, the overthrow of image-worship, the abolition of monkery, the degradation of mass-priests, the destruction of the usurped jurisdiction and tyranny of prelates, the alienation of the abused wealth, and secularization of the immense estates, belonging to the papal establishment, whereby its force and vital spirits are drained: these are now bewailed, even by the clergy of Reformed churches, as the most dreadful events and serious evils, equivalent to the abolition of the institutions of the true God and Redeemer. Thus the true religion and holy institutions of Jesus are blasphemously confounded with the abominable interests and constitutions of the *Man of Sin*, and his zeal and glory are represented as equally concerned in the preservation and vindication of both. Terms of the most opposite signification have lost all proper and distinct meaning in their mouths. Christ and Antichrist, the kingdom of the Lamb, and of the dragon, the temple of God and of idols, the worship of God and the worship of creatures, instead of being totally and diametrically opposite, are, it seems, but different names for one and the same thing. "Be astonished, O ye heavens, at this! be horribly afraid." Our fathers could not have believed such a thing possible, and posterity will hardly credit it. The native import of such language is that the Glorious Reformation was a sacrilegious farce, or a lamentable tragedy of outrage, spoil, and robbery. Such men, while they may pretend to laugh at popery as an antiquated absurdity, are in fact engaged in defence of the very life and substance of it, as really as any people formerly were, or presently are. They are not content to receive again the mark of the beast, only in their right hand, but they are not ashamed to bear it in their forehead. Those ministers who can preach, and fast, and pray, and learn the use of arms, to such an effect, or the nations who can deliberately make war and peace of such a tendency, deserve no more to be called Protestant: they have forfeited the very profession and name.

Whoever look into the following *Discourses*, or indeed into any of the noted writers since the Reformation who have handled the same argument, will find a very different doctrine, and a different spirit breathing in them; such as may make all tremble to think of partaking of the sins and plagues of that apostatical church, and excite such as have escaped to try "to save others with fear, plucking them out of the fire." As a number of zealous adherents to the old superstition, both priests and laity, have lately sought refuge in the bosom of Protestant nations, it would be well if the professors of the gospel would show their compassion and kindness to such, by imparting to them something better than external protection and the means of a temporal life—even the knowledge of salvation, and "the true riches;" and were these emigrants disposed to improve that freedom, and the means of information they now enjoy, when they have no longer the terror of laws and authority to deter them, or the splendor of a worldly establishment to fascinate them, from the impartial enquiry after truth—would they seriously compare the two religions together, open their eyes on that mystery of iniquity in which they have been involved, and cordially profess the truth as in Jesus, the event would be happy, and their losses and exile they might then account their unspeakable and eternal gain. Besides this production of our author, they may be abundantly furnished with assistance in such an enquiry, in a variety of writings, in their native tongue; as those of Du Moulin, Daille, Jurieu, Claude, Allix, La Roche, etc.; besides innumerable others in the Latin.

In these sermons, the author has employed no pomp of diction, nor the swelling figures of oratorical declamation; as some of the celebrated preachers in that language have done. He expresses native sense, and clear reason, in a style distinguished for its simplicity, conciseness and energy, which is best adapted to the purpose of didactic instruction, and discriminating truth from error. The translator, while he was above all things careful to express the sense, has also endeavoured to retain the manner of the author, so far as the different idioms of the language would permit. His translation is for the most part rather literal than otherwise. It is possible in some instances he may not have happily expressed the import of some of the original phrases; yet he hopes these instances are but few, or of the more trivial kind. He may sometimes too—by following too closely the idiom and structure of sentences in the French—have introduced what a critic in language would call Gallicisms. But as this is not a work of taste, but of piety, designed solely for serious instruction, anything of this kind will readily meet with indulgence, especially as his leisure permitted him not to transcribe the greater part of the copy. In a few places the author's manner of expression displeased him; but if he has varied from it, and in one place has omitted a sentence or two, he has accounted for it in the notes. The few notes that are added by the translator, are carefully marked below as such, to distinguish them from those of the author.

May 1, 1797.

THE
CONTENTS.

THE
NECESSITY AND DUTY
OF
EXAMINING THE RELIGION
OF WHICH MEN MAKE PROFESSION.

The first discourse, on 1 Thessalonians 5:21.
Prove all things.

N ancient father of the church, in one of his writings, speaks of five sorts of people in the world; the first are those who have found the truth, and consequently are happy; the second are those who search for it with care, and by a sure and safe way; others seek it not at all, because they falsely believe they have found it, and imagine they know what they are ignorant of; others again, though they believe not they have found it, yet do not seek it in a proper manner: Others, *in fine*, though they want it, yet give themselves no trouble to find it.[1]

These last are most blameable, and they are to be met with in great numbers. There are persons innumerable who have never examined the religion which they follow, nor have they so much as thought of it; as if it were of very small importance to them to know, whether they can be saved in the religion which they profess. Run through the whole circuit of this

---

[1] "Duae personae in Religione, sunt laudabiles: una eorum, qui jam invenerunt: quos etiam beatissimos judicare necesse est. Alia eorum, qui studiosissime et rectissime inquirunt. Primi ergo sunt etiam in ipsa possessione, alteri in via, qua tamen certissime pervenitur. Tria sunt alia hominum genera profecto improbanda et detestanda. Unum est opinantium, id est, eorum qui se arbitrantur scire, quod nesciunt. Alterum eorum, qui sentiunt quidem se nescire, sed non ita quaerunt ut invenire possint. Tertium eorum, qui neque se scire existimant, nec quaerere volunt." Aug. *de Utilit. credendi* c. 11.

lower world, and ask those you meet with, why they are Pagans, or Jews, or Mahometans, or Christians; the greater part will tell you, it is because they were born or educated in one of these religions, without pretending to offer any reason for their belief; and you will find but very few of them, who have embraced a religion from knowledge and from choice, or who have taken care to examine what has been taught them from their infancy.

It is this that keeps so many people in error; and is the cause why truth has not so many followers as it ought to have, and would doubtless have, if it were known. As this conduct of the greater part of mankind is highly blameable, and entirely unworthy of a creature who has the use of his reason; we propose at present, to show the necessity and the manner of examining that religion of which persons make profession. And it is with this view that we have made choice of the words of the apostle Paul which you have heard read, *Prove all things*.

This holy apostle had recommended to the Thessalonians not to despise prophesyings, nor, by consequence prophets; but seeing as it might very possibly happen that many pretending to divine inspiration, and boasting of the gift of prophecy, might seduce their hearers, Paul warns the faithful, to whom he writes, to be on their guard against them, and not to receive blindly whatever they might utter; but to examine carefully all prophesyings. "Prove," says he, "all things."

In order to profit by the exhortation of the apostle, we intend:

I. To prove that it is needful to examine all that is proposed to us, whatever may have influence either upon our faith or manners; and consequently, that every one should examine the religion he professes.

II. To show that all sorts of people are obliged unto this, that this examination is not impossible, and how it ought to be performed.

III. To inform you what are the characters whereby a man, of whatsoever religion he be, may know whether his religion be good or not; and what is the particular rule according to which Christians, who acknowledge the divinity of the holy Scriptures, may prove their religion.

IV. Finally, to evince to you that of all the religions in the world at present, the Christian religion alone is the true, and that which ought to be adhered unto; and that of all those religions which are called Christian, there is not one, which is equally pure as that which we profess.

Here is a rich and copious subject, my brethren. Pray God that he may perfect his strength in our weakness, and grant us a religious attention.

POINT 1

That whatsoever is proposed that may affect faith and manners ought to be examined.

It must be acknowledged that man cannot sufficiently praise his Creator for having formed him so different from and so much superior to other animals; in enduing him with a spirit which thinks and reasons; which is capable of conceiving the most sublime truths; having a power of self-reflection, which can apprehend what his senses do not discover; which recalls back things past, and penetrates into those to come; which elevates itself from earth to heaven, and descends again from heaven to earth, with a velocity incomprehensible.

But it must also be acknowledged that the principal use which man ought to make of his understanding and reason, is to examine that which is proposed to him, that so he may not take errors for truths, and allow himself to be imposed upon, and seduced.

This is the grand counsel inculcated by philosophers: they advise that in the sciences, a man should never give his assent to any proposition until after he has examined it carefully, and found it so evidently true that one cannot refuse to admit it, without incurring the severest reproaches of his reason. What obliges them to give this advice is their observing that the greater part of mankind take for true what is scarcely probable, and follow their senses, their imagination, their natural inclinations, and their passions, rather than reason. This is the cause of their falling into so great errors. To avoid them, therefore, it is necessary to prove all things.

Those who choose not to examine what is said to them do not make that use of their understanding which God would have them to do; they act as mere animals, or at least as fools. For what would be said of a man who should buy for diamonds, without examining them, all stones which might be offered him, under pretence of their being brilliant? Certainly nothing could be said of such a man, which might not justly be applied to those who receive blindly whatever impressions any may incline to give them. Therefore, as we may not act as unreasonable creatures, we must examine whatever is taught us, but especially those things which may influence our faith and manners. In truth, a wise man ought to believe nothing lightly, but ought to be extremely cautious and upon his guard, when that which is said to him may corrupt his heart, or spoil his understanding. It is of small importance, if he should be deceived in philosophical speculations, about the laws of motion, the nature of comets, the effects of the loadstone, the flux and reflux of the sea; about the seat of the soul, the colors of the rainbow, and other things of a like nature. One is no less happy in abandoning the knowledge of things of this sort than in knowing them, or in imagining that he knows them. But it is of the highest importance to him that he be not deceived in things which may render him more or less agreeable to his Creator; in matters belonging to his salvation, on which his eternal happiness or misery depends.

All such things ought therefore to be examined with care. If any example be proposed for our imitation, we must consider whether that be a proper model to follow, or whether that which we are desired to imitate deserves indeed to be so: for otherwise we should imitate a Noah in his drunkenness, a Lot in his incest, a David in his adultery, a Solomon in his debauchery, or a Peter in his denial of his Lord. In like manner, if we meet with any who teach us any doctrine, or who would have us to practise any worship, or observe any ceremony, whether it be by word or writing; whether they be private doctors who speak and write to us, or doctors assembled in a council, we must still examine. If they say they are infallible, we must examine whereupon they found their infallibility, and whether it be true that God has spoken by them. Though they were angels from heaven yet we should not be obliged to receive blindly their decisions; "Try the spirits," says John, "whether they be of God; for many false prophets are come into the world." (1 John 6:1) "Judge ye what I say," said Paul to the Corinthians; and here again to the Thessalonians: "Prove all things." But from hence it clearly follows that we must examine that religion which we profess: this is what we proceed to prove.

The necessity of this will be evident, if we consider that it is absolutely necessary that every one be assured his religion is good; for how can he be assured of this without examining it? I say that it is absolutely necessary that everyone be assured of the goodness of his religion; for if he is not assured of this, it will happen, either that his attachment to that religion which he professes will be very weak, and he will not acquit himself as he ought, in performing the duties which it prescribes, and thus he cannot be saved in that religion; or if he attach himself to it with ardor, that will be nothing but mere obstinacy, destitute of reason; so that he might have had the very same ardor and the same attachment for every other kind of religion, if it had been his lot to have been born in them. Besides, if one is not assured of the truth and goodness of his religion, he will not know whether he is in the way to heaven, or in the road to hell. Strange uncertainty!

Indeed, a man needs not too anxiously perplex himself about his religion, if men may be saved in all religions. But this cannot be asserted without extravagance and impiety.

In order to maintain such a position, it will be necessary to prove either that religion is only the invention of politicians, or that there is no providence, and that God does not concern himself with what passes on earth, so that a man may be saved whatever he believe and whatever he do; or that all religions are equally true or false; or that there is nothing true or false in its own nature, or that there is nothing right or wrong, so that it may be allowable to embrace whatever religion agrees best with men's interests; or that it is indifferent to God in what manner they serve him, or in what manner they live; or that God takes as much pleasure in being honored by different kinds of worship and ceremonies, as in being glorified by a prodigious number and variety of creatures, whose different beauties proclaim his power; as a Barbarian king, in this present age, is said to have spoken; or at least, that God has never made known to men that religion, which he would have them to follow. But nothing like this can ever be proven.

1. It cannot be proven that religion is the invention of certain politicians. For before this can be done it must be made to appear that previous to the birth of these politicians, the people were ignorant of the being of a God and that they rendered him no sort of homage; that these politicians were themselves destitute of any sense of the deity; and that these politicians could deceive all mankind, even those who were most improved and enlightened: three things which never can be made good.

2. It is no less false that there is not a providence. This sentiment is contrary to the light of right reason, and to the idea which we have of God as a being most perfect. For how could we consider as the most perfect being, a God who should keep himself shut up in heaven, without taking care of that which he has created, and without taking account whether it attains the end which he proposed in creating it, or whether his creatures do that which they ought to do?

3. It cannot be proven that all religions are equally true or false. To talk in this manner, is to shock every principle, and the most common notions. It is not possible that contradictory propositions should be equally false or true: of necessity one of them must be true, and the other necessarily false. But it

is certain that there are religions which contradict one another almost in everything.

4. It is false that there is nothing true. Those who dare advance this ridiculous paradox, acknowledge, in spite of themselves, certain truths, which they cannot deny, without feeling remorse; and according to their principles, they ought at least to own that there is one truth; that is, according to them, that there is nothing true. It will be said that the passions, the habits of infancy, and the prejudice of education, render our search after truth very painful and difficult. I grant it; but they do not render it impossible. When a choice is to be made on which our eternal salvation depends, we ought to resist the violence of our prejudices, of our passions, and habits, as we often do when our temporal interests require it.

5. To dare to say that there is nothing just and unjust in itself; is to contradict all the light with which every human mind is furnished. What? Can any believe that virtue and vice are only chimeras? That perjury, treason, assassination, poisoning, parricide, are indifferent actions? That it is an act equally good to kill a father as to obey him? To destroy the innocent, as to pardon enemies from a spirit of charity? Surely one must be delivered up to a reprobate sense, before he can adopt such detestable maxims; and I am persuaded that even those who advance them are forced to acknowledge that there is a real difference between virtue and vice, which depends not on the will and caprice of men.

6. Neither can it be imagined that it is indifferent to God, whatever be the manner in which men serve him, or in whatever manner they live, as if it were matter of indifference, whether they adore him under the figure of a golden calf, as the Israelites, or worship him as a Spirit, as the Christians do; whether they ascribe to him a thousand imperfections, or consider him as the most perfect of beings: whether they follow the light he has afforded them, or the contrary; whether they act according to their own conscience, or oppose it! To attribute such indifference to God, is to form an idea of him the most false and extravagant imaginable.

7. It is also impiety to maintain that God takes as much pleasure to be honored by different kinds of worship and ceremonies, as to be glorified by the prodigious variety of his creatures. Should God take pleasure in those kinds of worship and ceremonies which strike against his perfections, and expose him to the contempt of his creatures? Can he think himself honored by those who attribute to him the most shameful qualities, and who bestow his name upon his enemies? Where is the prince who would take it well that the greater part of his subjects should compliment away his titles, and render the homage which they owe him to his most inveterate enemies, and his rebellious subjects? It will be said, if God did not take pleasure herein, he would have inspired all men with the very same sentiments about the religion which they ought to follow; and should have caused all nations be born under the same law. But this is to assert the greatest of all absurdities, seeing by the same reasoning it might also be proven that God takes pleasure in the crimes which men commit; because they may say that God could have given, had he seen meet, the same sentiments for virtue. To support such reasoning, a principle must be supposed, which is absolutely false, namely, that God would have inspired all men with the same sentiments about religion, if he had not delighted in that diversity, as if he could not have had other reasons, besides this, worthy of his wisdom. The Deity is not obliged to make himself equally known to all the human race; he is most free in the whole of his operations. It will perhaps be said that "Men being entirely insignificant before God, he does not trouble himself with their worship." But is it credible that God—infinitely wise, holy and good, who was pleased to create men, and still preserves them—should care nothing whether he be honored, or despised and affronted by them?

8. *In fine*, it is false that God has never discovered to men the religion which he would have them to follow. Right reason allows us not to believe that God, who is most wise and good, has not communicated himself to his creatures, nor given them laws, nor made known to them his will; and we need only to read the Scripture to be convinced that it is the book wherein

God has revealed to men, what he has done, and what he is about to do for them, and what he would have them to do in order to please him.

It is therefore clear that a man cannot be saved in all religions, but only in that which bears all the characters of being derived from God. And hence it follows that he must examine whether he be of that religion which is possessed of such characters. *Prove all things.*

POINT 2

That all are obliged to this examination.

But to whom is this commandment addressed? *To all men*: to all those to whom Paul had said, "Despise not prophesyings"; and to whom he afterwards says, "Abstain from all appearance of evil;" to those whom he had exhorted to "pray without ceasing, and in everything to give thanks;" and for whom he prays God to sanctify them, that their soul, body, and spirit may be found without spot or blemish at the coming of our Lord Jesus Christ. In the same manner does John enjoin all to prove the spirits, for he gives this injunction to all those to whom he writes; but he writes unto all. "I write unto you fathers, because ye have known him that is from the beginning. I write unto you young men, because ye have overcome the wicked one. I write unto you, little children, because ye have known the father" (1 John 2:13). Thus all are obliged to examine their religion of whatever sex, age, and condition they be, provided they are capable of reason.

Indeed, it belongs not to teachers alone to have the truth at heart, but to all indiscriminately; and it is with regard to teachers particularly that Paul and the other apostles wish to put persons on their guard. Paul—addressing himself to the elders of the church of Ephesus—says, "Even from among yourselves shall men arise, speaking or teaching perverse things to draw away disciples after them" (Acts 20:30). And he tells the Thessalonians that Antichrist should sit in the temple of God (2 Thessalonians 2). Peter warns the Christians to whom he writes that there should be false teachers among them, "who privily should bring in damnable heresies, denying the Lord that bought them, bringing upon themselves swift destruction" (2 Peter 2:1-2). And we have already heard the apostle John, who speaks of false prophets which should come.

How is it possible that men should have the interests of God and eternal salvation so little at heart, as not to enquire and look after them themselves? "When you are about to receive money," said one of the fathers, "You take care to count it yourself; to weigh it, and examine whether it be good and current coin. When you would purchase an estate, you take all the precautions in your power; and should you take none at all in the business of salvation? Would not this evidently show that you make less account of your salvation, than of a piece of money or an estate?"

To prove that private persons ought not to examine what is proposed to them, it must be made evident: either that God would have us resign ourselves absolutely to the direction of our masters and teachers, or that our teachers are infallible, or that no bad consequences can arise from our putting unlimited confidence in our guides, or that more may ensue if everyone is allowed to examine, or that private persons and simple common people are incapable of this examination, and that it is impracticable for them. But none of these four things admit of proof.

1. It is not true that God would have us to abandon ourselves absolutely to the direction of our masters and teachers. "Take heed," said Jesus Christ to his disciples, "of the leaven of the Pharisees and Sadducees," who were the doctors of Israel. And under the Old Testament, God said to his people, "Hearken not to the words of the prophets that prophesy unto you; they make you vain: they speak a vision of their own heart, and not out of the mouth of the Lord: for both prophet and priest are profane" (Jeremiah 23:11, 16). "Though we," said Paul, "or an angel from heaven preach any other

gospel than that which we have preached unto you, let him be accursed" (Galatians 1:8). And lest you should entertain a persuasion that God will not punish men for having followed their teachers, hear what the Saviour of the world said of the Jewish doctors: "Let them alone; they be blind leaders of the blind: and if the blind lead the blind, both shall fall into the ditch" (Matthew 15:14).

2. He must also be wilfully blind who believes that the teachers of the church are infallible. This can neither be proved by natural principles, nor by revelation, nor by experience; on the contrary, reason tells us that they are men, and consequently liable to err; revelation teaches us that there are many false teachers and false prophets, and foretells that there shall always be such; the experience of every age and every day confirms the same thing.

3. It is easy to perceive that more evil is to be apprehended from trusting implicitly to pastors of the church, to which one belongs, than from examining what they say. If all Jews and Pagans had followed the direction of their teachers, no Jew or Pagan would have become Christian. If the Pagans and Mahometans, at present followed their teachers, not one of them would embrace Christianity. And is not this an evil of great magnitude – even the greatest which can be dreaded?

It will be said that: "It is disorderly that every one should claim the power and right of judging in the church." I answer: 1. That were it indeed a disorder, this evil would not be comparatively so great as that of which we were speaking; and of two evils the least ought always to be chosen. 2. A distinction must be made of a twofold judgment, namely: a private judgment of discretion, and a public judgment, to which others are required to be subject. It would be a disorder for every private person to assume to himself the authority of judging others, and to pretend to regulate the sentiments of another; but it is no disorder for everyone to examine what concerns his own salvation, since it is said, "The just shall live by his faith." Of this judgment, no private person can justly be deprived; and there is no sect but inclines that the private individuals, which are in its communion should judge that they ought to prefer it to all others. There is only this difference: there are some communities who would have every man to make this examination with knowledge, and there are others who choose that they should only inform themselves what the church to which he belongs, says: which is, as I have already observed, to oblige all people never to quit the religion in which they are born.

If it is alleged that: "There is less danger of being deceived in examining the doctrine, which is proposed to us by the authority of the church, than by the Scripture itself;" this is a gross mistake. There is but one danger to fear in examining the truth by the Scripture, that is, lest we deceive ourselves, for we know that the Scripture will not deceive us; whereas in examining the truth by the authority of the church, we are in danger of being deceived by the church, of whose infallibility we have no evidence; and also of deceiving ourselves by not apprehending aright the sense of the church.

It will also be objected that: "If everyone examines, there will be as many religions as men; that there will be no longer any means left for keeping persons in the unity of the faith; and this would open the door to all manner of heresies."

But why may it not be supposed that many in making such enquiry should coincide in the same sentiments; as it often happens that many doctors interpret in the same manner, a great number of passages of Scripture? Further, why should it not be supposed that God who presides over events will prevent such confusion by his providence and Spirit?

One must be grossly mistaken who imagines that in following blindly his pastors, he cannot depart from the unity of the faith. This would be true on the supposition that pastors are infallible; but if they can fall into error, as without doubt they may, of course those who shall follow them may become the heretics, and those who do not, shall continue in the unity of the faith.

To this reflection, we may add that there is no human means which can actually hinder the extravagancies and heresies incident to the mind of man. For in order to retain men in the unity of the faith, it is not only needful to teach them the truth, but also to give them a right spirit to follow it. But there is none but God alone, who can bestow such a spirit, and this he imparts to the faithful; with regard to others, he permits their wanderings.

Once more it will be said, "If the people, in this manner, try their pastors, they will not render them that respect which they owe them, seeing as they will become their judges."

I answer that this will by no means diminish that respect which of right belongs to pastors; because they can only claim this as their due when they act as true pastors, and teach the truth in purity, and not when they depart from it. To obey pastors blindly is nothing else than idolatry. Besides, it is not to be accounted an evil that pastors, who ought to judge the controversies which arise among private persons, should be judged by them. They judge with a public authoritative judgment; whereas private persons judge only with a private judgment.

Those who plead for this right of examination, do nothing more, on the matter, than what Paul recommends to them: *Prove all things.* Will any say that the church now is in a better condition, or possessed of greater security against false prophets, than the church was in the time of Paul? And if the Bereans are praised for having examined what was said by the apostle, why should not those be commended who examine what is taught them by their doctors?

That this examination is not impossible.

4. But since it may be objected that: "Private persons are incapable of such an examination, and that it is to them impossible," it is necessary here to make some reflections.

And first, I ask why private persons should be less capable of examining the doctrines of religion than other truths? Does not Christ expressly say, "Whosoever doth the will of him that sent me shall know the doctrine whether it be of God, or whether I speak of myself" (John 8:17)? And David said: "The secret of the Lord is with them that fear him, and he will show unto them his covenant" (Psalm 25).

Second, is it probable that the Spirit of God should so often recommend to us to examine all things, if it were true, that such an examination were absolutely impossible, even by the grace of the Holy Spirit, which God has promised to give to those who ask him? We use the same reasoning to prove that we may know whether we have true faith, because Paul exhorts us to prove our own selves, whether we be in the faith (2 Corinthians 13).

Third, is it credible that God, who gives us the means of discerning what is hurtful to our bodies, has not furnished us with the means of discerning what is prejudicial to our souls? Is this likely that God—who has established laws, advertising man when he ought to approach or keep at a distance from objects by the sense of pleasure or pain, of which he has made him susceptible in the proximity of certain bodies, for the preservation of the animal life—has not granted to him the means of discerning what is proper for the spiritual life?

"But is it not necessary for a person to be very learned, in order to engage, with success, in such a task? Does not this examination suppose great degrees of knowledge and of light? Is it not requisite to understand the languages; to know the objections which are made against his religion, as also how to resolve them; and even to be acquainted with all the variety of sects."

My brethren, this reasoning would prove that a man must, therefore, remain always in that religion which he professes, because, they say, he is incapable of examining his religion, but must submit himself to the authority of his teachers. Thus if he be a heathen he must continue a heathen; if a Mahometan, he must still remain a Mahometan. Strange divinity!

But I answer further that a distinction is to be made of a twofold examination. There is a simple examination, to which nothing more is requisite than a close and vigorous application of the mind to the doctrine which is taught, and to the reasons by which it is supported. But there is an examination of discussion, respecting all that can be said for or against a religion. This examination of discussion is impossible to the ignorant, and, in some sense, even to the learned: for where is a man so learned or wise as to know all that can be said for or against different religions? But the simple examination is sufficient for our salvation: such a one as the faithful of Berea employed themselves in. To reject an error in which one has been educated, it is sufficient if the absurdity of it be discovered by one single argument; so likewise in order to embrace a truth, which formerly a man did not know or opposed, there is need but of one good proof. The knowledge of all the objections which may be produced against a religion, and of all the sects which are within or without the pale of Christianity, is of very great advantage to those who can apply themselves thereto; but what is useful for some, is not necessary for all. A simple believer who has one solid evidence of the truth, may have his mind at ease. A man may be assured that there is a God by the strongest reasons, adapted to the capacity of all, although he may not be able to reply to all the arguments of atheists. A plain illiterate Christian may be assured by many clear and evident passages that Jesus Christ is God: *the true God and eternal life*; although possibly he cannot resolve all the difficulties which the enemies of the divinity of Jesus Christ may propose to him. It is not therefore necessary that a man should know all languages, all sects, all objections, in order to examine his religion.

To have the mind satisfied and at rest about that religion which one professes, he must perceive that all the characters are to be found therein, which, right reason informs, ought to be in a religion that is true, and which we shall afterwards point out; even all that is necessary for the instruction, consolation, and sanctification of our soul; so also, to discover the falsity of a religion, it is sufficient that he finds therein some doctrines which are false, though he should not be capable of judging of them all. If he should remain in suspense, and defer coming to any determination, until he had examined all, with the utmost precision, and answered to all objections, and removed all difficulties, in a manner fully satisfying, the most learned man in the world could not be assured even of the demonstrations of geometry; and one, perhaps, could not admit any truth whatever, because he knows not all that might be advanced in opposition to that truth.

It will be said that: "Many are even incapable of that simple examination;" that: "There are multitudes who cannot read, or who have their understanding so confined, that they can scarcely conceive the plainest and easiest things."

To this I answer:

1. That those who have sagacity sufficient to learn what is destructive to them without being able to read, may have enough of it, for learning the truth which should save them.

2. Though there are indeed some whose understandings are so weak, as to be incapable of themselves, to form reflections; yet they may be led to the knowledge of the truth, and be brought to acknowledge the error in which they have lived, by a very little assistance. There is no person whatever, but who, upon hearing these words read to him, "Thou shalt not bow down thyself to any graven image," but may be able to conclude of himself, that a religion that teaches men to render religious worship to images, is not good. There is none so simple or stupid as that, after having read or heard so many passages wherein Christ is said to be God, he may not draw the conclusion of himself that those who deny the divinity of Christ are in a gross error; and if some heretic should attack him by producing the passages which affirm that Jesus Christ is less than the Father, it will be no difficult matter to convince him that there is no reason why he should be astonished at these passages, seeing as Jesus Christ is not only God but also man; and that he is, in that respect, less than the Father.

In fine, it will be alleged that: "All private persons are *the sheep*, and it belongs to the shepherd to feed their shepherds."

It is true that private Christians are the sheep, but they are sheep of the rational kind; such sheep as Jesus Christ speaks of (John 10): "My sheep hear my voice and they follow me; and a stranger they will not follow, but fly from him, because they know not the voice of strangers." Sheep eat not of poisonous herbs; and why will they not allow that the faithful should do, by reason, for the nourishment of their souls, what sheep without reason do every day for their preservation?

It appears then that this examination is not impossible. Let us now see how it is to be performed.

If God had given to all of us the gift of discerning the spirits, which he bestowed on certain Christians in the beginning of Christianity, of which Paul speaks (1 Corinthians 12) so that we could know instantaneously, by inspiration, whether a doctrine were good or not, and whether those who speak to us deliver the words of God, we should have no kind of trouble in proving all things. But these times are no more: a man must therefore use his endeavours to make this examination.

In order to perform it properly, it is necessary:

That his mind be under a deep impression that he is engaged about a matter the most important in the world, and in which it is infinitely dangerous to be deceived.

To employ his best judgment and apply the whole power of his understanding in this enquiry.

To take all the precautions and receive all the instructions that are necessary to enable him to a right examination.

To divest himself of the prejudices which persons have for that religion in which they are born; and to consider it as if he had been educated in another religion.

To keep free, also, of the prejudices, which persons often entertain for what is new, and of that dislike which things old and common may be ready to create. For there are many that adopt errors and heresies only because they are weary of following the beaten tracts and the antiquated route of their fathers: the novelty alone makes them embrace opinions, which otherwise they would have rejected.

To avoid also a certain fondness for, and affectation of singularity, whereby persons are inclined to distinguish themselves by something or other.

To avoid listening to his passions, or consulting his temporal interests; for if these are hearkened to, it will often happen that a good religion will be forsaken, and a bad embraced; or one that is evil continued in, while a good one will be rejected.

Not to pay regard to those who make profession of that religion in which he is born, on account of their being the grandees, the learned, and the wise of this world: for God has not always been pleased to reveal his secrets to such.

To retire from the hurry of the world, and disengage himself for a time from the affairs of this life.

To consult those who may be able to aid and assist him.

To evite the company of those who might turn him away from such a good design as the examination of the truth is, or hinder his embracing it.

Finally, to demand of God the aids of his grace.

"But where is the man," (it will be said) "who will choose to be at so much pains?" Those who wish to be of the true religion with knowledge; those who wish to be saved; all those who are hearty in their regard to truth.

If they loved truth as much as they love silver and gold, or worldly grandeur, all men would make such an examination; but this is what few in reality do:

Because they love not the truth as they profess to love it.

Because they are afraid to discover, or acknowledge the falsehood of a religion in which they are at their ease.

Because they are extremely slothful in what respects their soul and their salvation.

Because they are unreasonably ashamed to consult those who might be able to enlighten them.

Because the multiplicity of other affairs in which they are engaged, and which they are not disposed to relinquish, hinders them from bestowing due time in such an enquiry.

Because they often suffer themselves to be blinded and dazzled by a false splendour and pomp of certain religions.

Because they allow themselves to be carried away by the stream of fashion, and the torrent of a multitude of persons who choose to live in security; and because they have too eager an attachment to the world and its pleasures.

Other reasons besides might be adduced; but these are the principal.

To aid you then in this examination, we proceed to inform *you, what are the characters whereby a man, of whatsoever religion he be, may know whether his religion be good or the contrary.* This belongs to the discussion of the following characters.

POINT 3

I suppose then a person to be inclined to examine his religion. In proceeding to this, he must, before all things, search within himself for that which right reason tells him ought to be found in a religion which is true. But certainly, if he rightly consults his natural light, he will find that in order to be assured whether a religion has God for its author, it ought to have the following characters:

1. It ought to exhibit the most perfect idea of God, which can be conceived, and attribute to him no sort of imperfection, or what is acknowledged to be such. For good sense dictates that a religion which has God for its author, ought to represent him such as he is; and seeing as he is a being infinitely perfect, it ought to describe him to us in this light.

2. It must ordain nothing but what is holy; and must prescribe the practice of all goodness; it must stand in opposition to all our vices, and all

our passions in which there is any irregularity. For if it favour vice in the smallest degree, it cannot be the production of the most holy of all beings, of him who is holiness itself.

3. It ought to discover to us, with clearness and precision, what it highly becomes us to know; such as, what we are by nature, what we ought to be that we may be pleasing to the Deity, and what we shall become after our death. For none but God alone can rightly inform us of these truths.

4. It ought to debase man utterly before God, and exalt God infinitely above man. For this is the natural order of things; as also it ought to place man in an absolute dependence upon God, and direct us to consider God as the sovereign Lord of all things.

5. There should be an entire and wonderful agreement between all the parts of that religion, without any inconsistency or contradiction. For otherwise God, who cannot possibly be contrary to himself, cannot be its author.

6. There should be a striking agreement between that and the first notions, or the natural knowledge impressed on the heart of all men. For as it is God who has implanted that knowledge, he cannot contradict himself.

7. Nothing should be contained in this religion, but what a conscience, that is not erroneous, must approve. Nothing should be promised therein, but what such a conscience desires. For this marvellous congruity of the maxims of this religion with conscience will be an evident proof that it has for its author the Author of conscience.

8. It ought to satisfy all our real wants and necessities. For none but God understands these fully or can remedy them.

9. It is necessary that it refers all to the glory of God, and lead us always to that supreme being.

10. *In fine*, it must not only bring us to the knowledge of the manner in which we have offended him, but also point out the true way of reconciliation with him, and of procuring us his favor and protection.

If this religion is further supported by miracles, certainly, none can avoid confessing that it must be truly divine.

Such are the characters whereby a person who is yet ignorant of revelation may come to know whether his religion be good or not.

Here a difficulty presents itself that merits our consideration. It may be said, "Since one may know by natural light the characters of the true religion, will it not be very possible for a man, possessed with acuteness of understanding, to form upon the ideas wherewith he is furnished, a system of religion proper to satisfy all reasonable minds?"

To this I answer that one may very well know in general, by natural light, the characters of a true religion; but yet it is not possible for any man to form a system of religion, which has all these characters. A man may draw a beautiful plan of a work, which he shall never be able to execute. There is none but God who can speak worthily of the Deity; or can know the necessities of men, and provide a remedy for them: and when we look into the Scripture, we are obliged to confess that the human mind could not have proceeded to such a pitch.

If it is enquired: "But how shall a man, who acknowledges the divine authority of the holy Scriptures, be ascertained of the excellence of his religion, or whether the contrary quality belongs to it?", then it is not very difficult for any to understand this. These holy Scriptures shall be his rule, even as they affirm themselves to be, and as the ancient fathers style them. These are a rule both certain and infallible, a rule which is entrusted into the hands of all sorts of persons; a rule to which God remits us: "To the law and to the testimony." I shall say nothing more of it here, because we have but lately discoursed to you on this subject. Such a man therefore must search:

If his religion teach nothing but what is drawn from the Scripture, either in express terms, or by just consequence.

If it makes God known no otherwise than as he wills to be known, namely, as a spirit, and as a spirit most perfect; and if it require no other worship than that which he ordains, namely, that which is in spirit and in truth.

If it parts not the glory of God between him and the creature, for God is so jealous of his glory that he will not suffer it to be alienated or divided; as he says by Isaiah: "I am the Lord, and my glory I will not give to another."

If it does not exalt man too highly, whom the Scripture takes care to abase, by representing to us his emptiness, his impotence, his corruption and his frailty; and if it does not, on the contrary, debase God; whom the Scripture always celebrates and exalts infinitely above all creatures.

If that religion does not lead him to reject the truth, which the Scripture establishes, under the pretence that it surpasses the comprehension of his reason.

If it teaches us to have recourse to Jesus Christ, as the alone "name given among men whereby they must be saved" (Acts 15): to him, as he describes himself, as "the way, the truth, and the life" (John 14), who has declared that no man can come unto the Father but by him (1 Timothy 2), in one word, to him as our only mediator; as he is called by the apostle Paul.

If there is nothing in that religion, but that which tends to promote the interests, and the practice of true holiness.

In fine, if it is capable to allay our fears, and calm the agitations of our conscience; for this is the characteristic of the true religion.

By these marks, one may ascertain the true religion, when he enjoys and is convinced of the divinity of the Scriptures.

We should now, according to the plan which we have laid down, proceed to show that by these characters, it may appear that of all the religions in the world, there is none that can deserve our attachment but the Christian; and that of all the religions which are called Christian, there is no other so pure as that which we profess. But as this would carry us too far at this time, we shall here finish this discourse, after subjoining some reflections.

APPLICATION.

We have shown to you that it is necessary that everyone should examine the religion of which he makes profession. It is our duty then to obey the injunction of the great apostle, or rather Spirit of God, who spoke by his mouth.

It is a notion that passes current in the world, that errors and ignorance do not render us criminal before God. But this is a very great mistake. In the Old, and also in the New Testament, God condemns the incredulous and idolaters, for their errors. Nothing but an ignorance which is absolutely invincible, can excuse. The greater part of the errors, into which men fall, are the effects of their negligence, of their pride, their sensuality, or some other vice: of these some flatter our reason, as those which overthrow the mysteries of our faith; others flatter our senses, as those which lead to superstition, forming a gross religion, the splendor of which dazzles the eyes of the vulgar, and transports with admiration the simple. But both the one and the other are productive of the greatest evils. It is our duty then to be on our guard, lest we be infected with any error, and to search after the truth with all care.

Do you ask me here, "Whence is it, that God, who is the God of truth, permits the spirit of error to seduce men?"

My brethren, it is not for us to attempt to penetrate into the counsels of the Almighty. He has not seen meet to reveal to us, why he had permitted sin and all its consequences. We ought to be silent, and adore with submission, his unsearchable ways. We shall only say that God cannot be the author of sin, so neither is he the author of errors: error being a moral disorder, an abuse of reason, and an effect of the corruption of our heart, it cannot without blasphemy, be ascribed to God. This would be to despoil him of his divinity, and of the glorious name he bears, *the Father of Truth.* But though errors have not God for their author, God, by his admirable providence, brings light out of this darkness; as physicians, by their skill, convert even poisons into remedies. Errors serve to manifest the justice of God, which lights upon the miserable souls who suffer themselves to be entangled therein. They serve to keep in exercise, the faith of believers. They serve to excite the minds of Christians to a more attentive and accurate study of the truth; as the error of Pelagius was the cause of their informing themselves more exactly than they had done before, of what the apostle Paul teaches about the grace of God, and its efficacy. They serve, *in fine*, to discover and distinguish the true disciples of the Lord Jesus.

Do not ask me, "Whence it comes to pass that God does not make himself equally known to all men?" I will make no other reply to this, than what Paul says: "He will have mercy on whom he will have mercy, and whom he will he hardeneth;" and what our Lord spoke on a certain occasion: "I thank thee, O Father, Lord of heaven and earth, because thou hast hid these things from the wise and from the prudent, and hast revealed them unto babes: because it so seemed good in thy sight." (Matthew 11). Let us be content with knowing that such is his will and pleasure; but let us not attempt to pry into the reason, or enquire why he has so willed. Let us rather labor to distinguish the truths which God has revealed to us, from the errors which the devil has disseminated in the world, and for this purpose: let us prove all the doctrines which are proposed to us: *Prove all things.*

If Paul had been persuaded that God would bestow on the church a visible and infallible head, to whom they might entirely refer the concernments of their faith; if he had believed that at least, there would be councils and assemblies, which should possess the gift of infallibility; I scarce think he would have required the faithful to be at the trouble of examining whatever was proposed to them. He would rather have said, "There shall be a visible and infallible head, whom you may consult; and a sovereign tribunal, to which you may apply, for the decision of controversies;" or: "There shall be venerable assemblies, which shall make canons, to which you must blindly submit, and which shall constitute the rule of your faith." But neither Paul, nor any other apostle has told us any thing like this; and it does not appear that the primitive Christians, after the death of the apostles, were persuaded of the infallibility of the See of Rome. On this account, when any speak to us of the canons of this or the other council; and of the decisions of pontiffs, we think we have a right to examine them, and to reject them, if we find them contrary to Scripture; and this by the authority which the apostle here gives us: *Prove all things.*

But do not think that it is sufficient only to examine the religion which we follow; we ought also to examine ourselves: "Prove your own selves," said Paul, "whether ye are in the faith; Know you not your own selves, whether Christ be in you?" Truly, what will it avail us, to have attained to the knowledge and persuasion, that the doctrine, which is announced to us, is of God, if we have not received it into our hearts for our sanctification? What will it avail us, to have escaped from the seduction of false teachers, if we suffer ourselves to be seduced by our own lusts. Let us prove then our own selves.

Let us examine if we are truly what we profess to be: we make our boast of being the sons of God; let us consider, if we live as his children, and if we study to imitate his divine excellencies?

Whether instead of a true faith of which we boast, we have only perhaps the appearances of it; or, whether it may possibly prove to be only a temporary faith, so that the smallest storm arising shall be able to overthrow us?

Whether we are fully persuaded of what Jesus Christ has done for us; of the sufferings he endured for our salvation, and whether our gratitude is proportioned to the love which he has shown us?

Let us examine and search our hearts, that we may discover what passes there; the passion which rules there; and the principles which influence our actions.

Whether it is not with us, as it was with the angel of the church of Laodicea, who said, "I am rich and stand in need of nothing; who yet was poor, blind and naked" (Revelation 3).

Whether, after having so frequently offended God, we feel a real and hearty sorrow for having thus sinned against him?

Let us examine, whether after so many tokens of his love as he has given us, we love him in return, as we ought to love him?

Whether we be as jealous of his honor as of our own; and whether we have the interests of his truth as much at heart as our personal interests?

Whether we be in good terms with God; whether our peace be made with him; and whether we are in that state in which he would have us to be, in order to render us happy.

Whether we render to him the due tribute of his worship; and whether we discharge, with care, the duties which he demands from us?

Let us further examine if we make any progress in sanctification, and whether we find as much joy in having performed a good action, as in meeting with success in our worldly affairs; or, if we are as much displeased for having offended God, as for the loss of some temporal good?

If we abstain from such crimes, as even natural men condemn, on account of the horror we entertain at sin, and the love we bear to God; or if it be not from considerations purely human.

If, in the best actions we have done, we have rightly proposed the glory of God as our end?

If that which is called virtue in us, be not a false virtue?

If we are not under the power of some habitual sin, sufficient to bring us into a state of damnation?

If we love our neighbour as ourselves, and acquit ourselves of the duties of charity?

If we—every one of us—attend upon and fill up the duties of our several callings and offices; as magistrates, pastors, heads of families, merchants, artisans?

Let us examine, in a word, if we be in that condition, in which we would wish to be, when we must die, and when Jesus Christ shall come to judge the quick and the dead?

How many persons would be displeased with themselves, if they should, make this search! Alas! We should all find but too much reason to be dissatisfied with our hearts and our conduct. However, let us not defer making this trial, although we should meet with nothing but what tends to afflict us.

It is often too late, at the hour of death, to examine our hearts; for then it is but rare to possess sufficient composure of mind and distinctness of judgment. How wise, and at the same time, how happy, should we be, if every day we did sound our heart! If, in the evening, before we resign ourselves to sleep, we surveyed and retraced the actions of the day, and took measures to prevent our falling again into the faults and sins we have committed. We would, in this way, make considerable progress in sanctification. We would render ourselves agreeable to our Creator, who searches the hearts, and the reins, and beholds all our actions. We should draw down his blessing upon our persons and our affairs; and we should hereby put ourselves in a suitable condition for meeting death comfortably. Why do we not attempt it? My brethren, our salvation and our interest engages us to it. Let us seriously think of it. May God grant his grace to enable us to think aright of it; and to make us perfect in every good work. Amen.

THE DIFFERENT
RELIGIONS
OF THE
WORLD
EXAMINED

The second discourse,
on 1 Thessalonians 5:21.
Prove all things.

My brethren,

God, in order to engage his people to reformation without their princes and teachers, and in opposition to them, addresses them, by his prophet Jeremiah, in this manner, "Stand ye in the ways, and see, and ask for the old paths, where is the good way, and walk therein, and ye shall find rest to your souls" (Jeremiah 6:16). By these words, God clearly intimates to the Jews three things: First that they ought not implicitly to receive whatever their priests, or even their prophets taught them. Further, that they were obliged to enquire after the course which they ought to pursue with the same care and earnestness, as travelers would do, who are afraid of wandering, and falling over precipices. Finally, that as soon as they have discovered the right way, into which they should enter, they must walk therein constantly, otherwise their souls should not find any rest.

What God enjoined upon his people, under the old dispensation, is what he also prescribes to us all, under the new economy. We have not more reason to acquiesce blindly in the sentiments of our teachers than the Jews had to follow their prophets; and our interest engages us, no less than theirs, to examine the path which we ought to walk in. Those who never reflect upon the religion they profess, can have no experience of solid comforts; because they know not whether they be truly in the way of salvation; and whether they be not multiplying their offences against God, in multiplying the acts of their devotion. Those only who are assured that the religion they adhere to, is derived from God, are possessed of true rest, because the knowledge of the truth, and of that alone, can afford a joy constant and perfect. Hearken, then, O ye sons of men! And ask for the good path; prove and examine all things. This is the exhortation tendered unto us by the apostle Paul, in the words which we have read for the second time.

In our first discourse, we showed you the obligation lying upon all men to examine whatever is proposed to them, which may influence their faith and manners, from whence we drew this conclusion, that we are therefore obliged to examine the religion of which we make profession. Afterwards, we proved that all men were bound to make this enquiry; and that it was not impossible for them to do so. After this, we proceeded to tell you how this examination ought to be made; and what are the characters whereby one might know a religion that is true and good.

We must now examine by these characters the several religions in the world, and demonstrate that the Christian deserves the preference above all others. May God aid us in this great design, and grant us grace powerfully and forcibly to maintain his truth!

I. OF NATURAL RELIGION.

IN entering upon the subject, it is necessary that you should first remark that God has furnished all men with light, which may serve to lead them to the knowledge of many truths, which compose, what is called **Natural religion.**

These truths are the following:

1. That there is a God, and that there is but one only.

2. That this God is not any of those things which we see, and that are corruptible; but that he is a being more perfect than all others.

3. That he is just, holy, good, wise, blessed, eternal, almighty.

4. That he has created whatever exists, and governs all by his providence.

5. That he ought to be honored, feared, loved; that he only ought to be adored; and that all praise and thanks are to be rendered to him, for all the good things which men possess.

6. That there is a real difference between good and evil, virtue and vice, and that there are some things in their nature just and honest, and others which are not so.

7. That it is unwarrantable for a man to act contrary to his light, and against the dictates of his conscience.

8. That father and mother are to be honored; and none ought to do to others what they would not that others should do to them.

9. That those who commit wicked actions are worthy of death.

10. That God, being infinitely just and holy, cannot be offended with impunity, but that his justice demands a satisfaction.

11. That the soul is immortal; and that there shall be a judgment.

12. Finally, that in order to happiness, the deity must be rendered propitious.

This is a summary of what they call Natural Religion.

You will ask me, if this then be the true religion by which we must abide?

No, my brethren. I grant there is nothing but what is good in this religion: and all the truths which it teaches ought to be firmly believed. But it is very imperfect, and insufficient to conduct us to salvation. It informs us clearly that God wills that he be honored and served; but it tells us not how he chooses to be worshiped.

It informs us that men cannot be happy unless the Deity is propitious to them; but it teaches not how he may be appeased; and consequently, it cannot compose a soul, disturbed by the sense of its crimes; which the true religion ought to do.

It furnishes us with no consolation against the fear of death, or the miseries of life. It instructs us not as to what we shall be after death; or whether our soul, which is immortal in its nature, shall not be annihilated, by him that created it, at the same time, that the body is reduced to dust; nor yet what shall become of that body, whether it must always remain under the dismal and fatal empire of death.

Therefore, another religion must be sought for. And the first which presents itself is the **Pagan.**

II. OF THE PAGAN RELIGION.

It will not be difficult to show that the Pagan religion is not the true religion which proceeds from God; whether we consider the Pagan religion of the ancient Egyptians, Persians, Chaldeans, Greeks, Romans,[2] and others; or consider that religion, as it now reigns among these people who acknowledge neither Jesus Christ, nor Moses, nor Mahomet for the head of their religion, and of which we find the description in innumerable historical accounts.

Indeed, if one were to judge of the truth of a religion by its antiquity, he would be greatly prejudiced in favor of the Pagan: and it is by this test that Symmachus, governor of Rome, would have it judged, in a book which he addressed to emperors Valentinian, Theodosius, and Arcadius, wherein he

---

[2] See upon the Paganism of the Egyptians, Kirch. in *Copt. Prodromo*; Vossius *de idol.* Upon that of the Persians and Arabians, Jul. Cæs. Auleng. in *Eclog. ad Arnob.* Pocock, in *Notis ad Georg. Abulfaraeum.* Upon that of the Chaldeans, Syrians, etc. Selden, Vossius, etc.

introduces Rome supplicating, "that they would venerate her years and her hoary hairs."[3] But it is long since it was observed that error is not the less error for being ancient; and that there is no prescription against the truth.

If we likewise were to judge of the goodness of a religion by the multitude of its professors, we could not hesitate to decide in favour of Paganism; but everyone may readily perceive that it is not by this that any religion ought to be judged.

To convince you of the falsity of the Pagan religion we shall content ourselves by making three or four reflections.

Among the characters which we have laid down of a true religion this is the first, "that it ought to give us the most perfect idea of the Deity that can be conceived, and that it ought not to attribute to him any known and acknowledged imperfections." Let this character be applied to the Pagan religion, and we shall immediately discover its falsehood and absurdity.

If we consult our reason ever so little, the idea which we naturally form of God is, that he is a being spiritual, almighty, all-wise, most good, holy, unchangeable, and faithful; in one word, most perfect; and that there can be but one. But when we read the writings of the Pagans, or the accounts given us of modern Paganism, we shall soon find that they are far from keeping to this idea. What idea did these people form of the Deity, who had gods of all sorts, gods great and small; whereof some had their residence in heaven, some on the earth, others in the sea or in the rivers, and some in hell?

---

[3] "If great antiquity," said he, "ought to authorize a religion, we should retain the belief which has been confirmed by so many ages, and we ought to follow our fathers, who had so happily marched in the footsteps of theirs. Suppose Rome should just now appear, and address herself to you in the following terms: Most excellent Princes, I ask of your clemency, not any advanced wealth, or honours, but only my pious customs. Allow me to observe the ceremonies taught me by my ancestors, and of which I have had no cause to repent. Let me live as I have been hitherto accustomed. It is this divine service that has subjected all the world to my law. This is the religion which chased Hannibal from my walls, and the Gauls from the Capitol. Have I been preserved for so long a time, that I might be contemned and cast off in my old days?"

People who adored all creatures from those that are most excellent even to the vilest; angels, men, the stars, planets, animals even the most base?[4] People who changed the glory of the incorruptible God into the likeness and the image of corruptible man, and of birds, and four-footed beasts, and creeping things" (Romans 1)?

People who adored for gods, men to whom themselves imputed the most horrible crimes; who were, on this account, so very far from being worthy of adoration, that they deserved to be regarded with execration, and as objects of punishment?

People who worshiped the devil, even as not a few Pagans continue to do to this very day?[5]

People who ranked among the objects of their worship the fever and fear? What extravagance: that reasonable creatures should adore what is even void of sense!

What idea did these Pagans form of God, who, for the most part, believed that the divinity did not at all interfere, in the events and transactions, which took place on earth?[6]

In fine, what notion must these people have entertained of the Deity, who rendered to those, whom they accounted their gods, a worship the most extravagant, the most ridiculous, and often the most infamous and cruel which can be conceived?[7] As those who sacrificed to their idols human victims, and sometimes their own children, or those who prostituted

---

[4] *Quicquid humus, pelagus, coelum mirabile gignunt.*
Id dixere Deos, colles, freta, flumina, flammas.
They had divinities whom they made to preside over everything. See Augustine, *The City of God*, Book 5 Chapters 8 & 11, and Book 21 Chapter 16.

[5] As those of Calcutta, on the coast of Coromandel; the Chinese, and many other people. They say that God has committed the empire of the world to the devil, in order to punish men according to their desert; and temples are built by them for his honor.

[6] Such were the Epicureans, and certain Brachmins in the Indies.

[7] See Lactantius Book 1 Chapter 11. Augustine, *City of God*, Book 6 Chapter 10. Arn. B1 *Cont. Gent. Cæs. Comment.* B6, Eusebius *Preparation for the Gospel* B4 C7.

themselves in their temples to all sorts of impurity,[8] imagining hereby to please their fictitious divinities.

It will perhaps be alleged here that: "The wisest among the Pagans believed not a plurality of gods; and that the sentiments they had of the Supreme Being, whom they adored, were very different."

But it is easy to answer: 1. It is foreign to the present purpose to enquire, what certain philosophers have believed, but we speak of the form of religion which was established, and publicly allowed among the Gentiles. 2. Further, the greater part of these philosophers, entertained sentiments of the Deity, very extravagant and most injurious to that Supreme Being, such as those who denied his providence, those who exalted their sages above their gods, those who considered the universe as a deity, and those who maintained that their great god—content with having made the heaven and the stars—did not deign to employ himself in the formation of this lower world, but left it to the agency of subaltern beings; and that man, though born to know him, because he was mortal, was not a piece of workmanship worthy of his hands.

This first reflection might suffice to convince you of the falseness of the Pagan religion; but we shall subjoin to it some others which will confirm you more in the same opinion. "The true religion ought to prescribe nothing but what is holy; it must be in opposition to all irregular passions, and give no manner of encouragement to any vice." Try the Pagan religion by this character. Who knows not that it deified all the passions of human nature, and gave occasion and full licence to commit all sorts of vices, by proposing for objects of adoration, men who had rendered themselves infamous by their debaucheries, their incests, their adulteries, and a thousand other disorders? It is true that Paganism also deified *Virtue*, and pretended to set it forth as the last end of man. But this also was nothing but pure idolatry; for virtue is indeed an image of the Deity, but is not itself a deity. It is one of

---

[8] This is still practised in the Indies. See Linoch. Roger Martyr. *comm. de Inf. nuper. repert.*

the means of pleasing the deity, but yet it is not the last end of man: to which we might add that there were virtues unknown to the Pagans, and left out of the system even of their sages, such as true humility and true patience.

"The true religion also should instruct us as to the state of our souls after death." But this information is not to be met with in the writings of the Pagans, in any way that can prove satisfactory to a reasonable person. I grant, they had a knowledge of a life to come, of the immortality of the soul,[9] and of a future judgment.[10] But what absurd fables did they not advance upon these subjects? And is it not well known that the wisest among them, when dying, have acknowledged that they did not know what should become of them; as Socrates himself did; not to speak of the emperor Hadrian?

Finally, for I choose not to enlarge further on this subject, if it be true, as was said in the former discourse, and as the thing itself testifies that "the true religion should discover to us the mean of appeasing the Deity, whom we have so highly offended;" who knows not that the Pagan religion discovers not this means? It appointed indeed a variety of propitiations, purifications, and sacrifices; but its most enlightened followers acknowledged that the death of beasts was incapable of appeasing the anger of God; that as the beasts had not committed the trespass, so neither could they bear the punishment of human crimes; that if their blood had the virtue to make

---

[9] The greater part of the heathens have believed the immortality of the soul, and do so still, if we except some libertine sects in the Indies, in China, and Japan. Rather than admit that souls perished utterly, they chose rather to believe that they subsisted from all eternity, or that, on quitting the body, they passed into other bodies; or that they were reunited to God, as the waters to the ocean; or that they should be born anew; or that they are transformed into angels or demons; or that they shine in the air, or mix with the water: the Druids, according to the testimony of Cæsar, believed that souls were subject to death, but that they passed into other bodies. *Com.* l. 6.

[10] It is a very beautiful account which Plato, in his *Republic*, puts into the mouth of one designed *Armenius*, whom he makes to return to the world, twelve days after his death, to report to men whatever passes in the infernal regions; he tells them that: "The judges before whom the souls appear after they are departed out of their bodies, cause the just to be placed on their right, and the wicked on the left hand; and that the first are made to ascend into heaven, and the latter to descend."

expiation of sins, the rich would then be most happy, who had it in their power to offer whole *hecatombs*; and that it was the greatest folly to believe that water could cleanse the conscience.[11]

It would be easy to add other reflections if we were inclined here to repeat all that has been written against Paganism.[12] But what we have said is sufficient to evince that the Pagan religion is not that which we search after; and this examination may be easily performed by persons of the most ordinary understandings. Does it require much intelligence and penetration to discern the blindness and stupidity of the people who continue in such a religion as this?

We shall only here remark two things, which must be carefully attended to, in the matter of examining:

1. When we assert that a private person can try his religion, we do not mean that he can, without any assistance, discover the absurdity of all the tenets or practices belonging to his religion; but we are persuaded that he may of himself discover enough of them to be able to say that his religion is false. For example, there is no Pagan whatever but can know that it is absurd to adore gods which are more criminal than the most wicked and abominable of men, or to pay adoration to animals.

2. We must further remark that although there are certain things which a man, not accustomed to meditation, can hardly discuss of himself, yet he may be able to do so, if his mind be but a very little opened. For example, I suppose an ignorant Pagan is at a loss to believe that God knows all things

---

[11] *Ah minimum faciles, qui tristia funera cædis,*
Tolli flumineâ putatis posse aquâ!   OVID.
Ah credulous! who think, when blood is spilt,
The running stream can wash away the guilt.

[12] Many have written against the Gentiles: Justin Martyr, Athenagoras, Theophilus, Tatian, Clement of Alexandria, Tertullian, Minucius Felix, Origen, Cyprian, Arnobius, Lactantius, Eusebius, Julius Firmicus, Gregory Nazianzen, Prudentius, Chrysostom, Augustine, Raymond of Sebonde a Spanish divine, Jerome Savonarola, Peter de la Cavalleria, Marsilius Ficinus, Lewis of Grenada, Philip de Mornay, Peter Charron, Hugo Grotius, Joannes Micrelius, and others.

that can possibly be known. Is it not obvious that he might be brought easily to acknowledge that truth only by proposing to him two simple questions; the one, whether it is not true that when he thinks of a God, he does not think of a being more perfect than any other, and who must be possessed of all perfections; the other, whether it is not an imperfection to be ignorant of something.

After having examined the Pagan, let us see whether we shall have cause to be better satisfied with the *Mahometan* religion.

III. OF THE MAHOMETAN RELIGION.

If one should judge of the truth of a religion by the conquests and victories of its author, he would be much prejudiced in favour of the religion of Mahomet; but for the same reason he would also have great prejudices in favour of the religion of those conquerors who have gained such glorious victories and founded powerful and flourishing monarchies.

We have no intention to give you the history of Mahomet. That infamous prophet deserves not that we should entertain you with what relates to him. The question here is not about what Mahomet was, but about his doctrine. If it be true it ought to be received; if it be false, it must be rejected. We shall only tell you that this impostor established his religion in the seventh century.[13]

When we look into the doctrine of Mahomet, we find therein many truths, which he had taken from Jews and Christians, which greatly advance his religion above that of the Pagans. He admitted only of one God, and asserted that his essence was simple and infinite. The Persians would define

---

[13] There are many opinions as to the year of Mahomet's birth: Some would have it to have been A.D. 570, others 580, others again place it in 620, etc. [The year 571 is that most generally adopted. *Translator*]

God to be, "a Being without qualities;" they say that "His essence is destitute of height and depth:" that is to say, that it is not corporeal.

He assigned no limits to the knowledge of God. Thus one of his followers teaches that God knows whatever can be known; that his knowledge embraces all objects from the utmost boundary of the earth to the highest heaven; that nothing can escape his knowledge, not even the minute dimensions of an ant; that he knows the motion of an atom in the air, as well as the thoughts of the mind; and that, by a knowledge ancient and eternal, and not natural and acquired in time.

He held that nothing comes to pass in the world but by the will of God, that he governs all things by his providence, and that all things are subject to his empire, even those which we call fortuitous, and the motions of the mind of man. He enjoined humility, contempt of the world, patience, alms, justice, liberality, constancy in friendship, obedience to parents and superiors. On the contrary, he forbade calumny, lying, perjury, avarice, dishonest gain, ingratitude, hypocrisy, envy, and even whoredom.

He believed that God would reward virtue and punish vice. He extolled the mercy of God, which invites men to repentance. He taught that men should rise again, and should be judged at the end of time.

Thus far his doctrine is good: these are truths which that impostor drew from the books of the Old and New Testament. But let us proceed, and see what Mahomet further taught.

If one will be at the trouble to read his Quran, which he protests was sent him from heaven, he will find in it extravagancies and impieties without number. He owns the books of the Old and New Testament to be divine; nevertheless his Quran contains many things contrary to these books. Is not this to make God contrary to himself? When he relates the histories which Moses or the apostles have recorded, he mixes therewith things so ridiculous, so many fables and falsehoods, that one hardly knows whether he is dreaming or awake, when he reads these reveries.

In the Old and New Testament, adultery is expressly forbidden. The gospel no less expressly forbids polygamy and divorce, except for the cause of adultery. If therefore the gospel be divine, as Mahomet acknowledges, how comes it about, that he should defile himself with the crimes which the gospel condemns; and that the Quran permits polygamy and divorce?

The gospel informs us that Christ is God; Mahomet denies and derides the Trinity. It is true, we are told that there are sects,[14] presently among the Mahometans who believe that the Messiah being eternal, became incarnate; that, others among them maintain that Christ is God, and that he is the Redeemer of the world, and that others of them admit the Trinity; but this is not a sentiment general among the Mahometans.

The gospel declares that a man should eat whatever is presented before him; Mahomet enjoins abstinence from swine's flesh and the use of wine. The gospel tells us that circumcision is abolished; Mahomet reestablishes it. The gospel makes it a duty to forgive enemies and to pray for them; Mahomet allows men to revenge themselves on those who have offended them, and to kill them. Who sees not that this impostor was actuated by him who "is a liar and murderer from the beginning?"

In fine, who can read the description he gives of Paradise without acknowledging that he was a man abandoned to his pleasures, who sought nothing so much as the gratification of his lusts?

If Mahomet had been a teacher inspired by God—a prophet greater than Jesus Christ and Moses who should change the religion which God himself had established, as Mahomet confesses—is it likely that we should meet with no predictions of the coming of such a prophet in the books of the Old and New Testament? To tell us, as the Mahometans do, that Moses spake of him in Deuteronomy 18, when he said, "A prophet shall the Lord raise up unto you, like unto me, him shall ye hear:" is to assert the greatest of all absurdities: for the apostles only apply this oracle of Moses unto Christ; if

---

[14] Ricaut, *De L'Empire Ottoman.*

they do so justly, how can the Mahometans pretend that it agrees to Mahomet? If the gospel falsely applies this prophecy to Jesus Christ, how then does Mahomet say that the gospel is of divine authority? Certainly, if the gospel be a revelation of God, Mahomet is an impostor. I think it not worthwhile to mention the other passages, which they also cite to prove that Mahomet was promised.[15] One needs only to read them to see that they are quoted for this purpose without any manner of foundation.

To tell us further that "The name of Mahomet was written in the Old Testament, but that it has been effaced by the Jews and Christians," is also a plain and wilful imposition. For who was he that blotted out the name of Mahomet from these books? Did this happen before Mahomet was born, and before his doctrine was in vogue? No: for neither the Jews nor the Christians had any interest to erase from the sacred books the promise of a great prophet. If they have preserved the predictions of Antichrist, who was to make such ravages, how much more would they not have preserved the predictions of the coming of a teacher who should be more excellent than Jesus Christ and Moses? But how was such a thing possible, seeing as there were so many copies of the holy Scripture spread throughout all the world, and translations of them into different languages? No; the Mahometan religion, in what is peculiar to it, and what it has not adopted from the Jewish or Christian, contains nothing but what is ridiculous and extravagant; and consequently deserves not to be regarded as a religion that is divine.

In order to give you a fuller conviction thereof, we needed only to have recited to you some reveries which are to be found in the Quran, and in a dialogue between a Muslim and a Jew, in which we have an account of a

---

[15] They apply also to him Deuteronomy 2: "The Lord came from Sinai, and rose up from Seir unto them; he shined forth from mount Paran," etc. as if this passage had a respect to Mecca, to Mahomet, and his law. They make the same application of Genesis 17:20 where Ishmael is spoken of, not Mahomet. They abuse in like manner Daniel 2:24 and Psalm 72:10-11, wherein Christ is evidently pointed out. So likewise Joshua 15 and 16:7-8, which respect the Holy Spirit, who is our true Paraclete; as also Isaiah 21:7, where the ruin of Babylon is foretold.

pretended voyage of Mahomet in company with the angel Gabriel, and you could not then forbear to acknowledge that these books are rather the production of a man who raves than the work of God incomparably wise, as Mahometans pretend. All that can be gathered from this is that the religions from which Mahomet has gleaned the truths he taught, are good: these are the Jewish religion and the Christian. But let us examine these more narrowly.

IV. OF THE JEWISH RELIGION.

It is needful to distinguish here in the entrance, the religion of the Jews who lived before the coming of Jesus Christ, from the religion of the Jews who have been posterior to that time.

With regard to the religion of the ancient Jews, we cannot entertain a doubt of its truth, if it be examined by the marks which we have laid down, which serve for a criterion to try any religion.

If it be the property of the true religion to give the most perfect idea of God that can be conceived, and to remove all imperfection from him, then can any question the religion of the ancient prophets, who describe God, as the Lord Almighty, who has founded the earth, and stretched out the heavens; who rules over all kingdoms, and nothing can resist him; who does whatever is his pleasure in the heavens, on the earth, and in the deeps; who says to the raging sea, "Here shall thy impetuous waves be stayed!" As a God infinitely good, whose goodness endures forever; whose mercy and compassions are infinite? As a God eternal, whose days never had any beginning, nor shall ever have any end; before whom there was no God, and after whom there shall not be any? As a God whom the heaven of heavens cannot contain, who has the heaven for his throne and the earth for his footstool; from whose presence it is impossible to escape, whether we ascend into heaven, or descend into hell, though we should take the wings of the morning and fly beyond the sea? As a God who knows the hearts of all the sons of men, and searches them, to whom the darkness is as light? As a God invincible, whose face or similitude none can behold? A God, whose wisdom is unsearchable, whose thoughts are not as our thoughts, nor his ways as our ways, who doth great things past finding out? A God whose justice is like the great mountains, whose truth reaches even to the clouds, and his mercy is in the heavens? A God glorious in holiness, before whom the angels cry, "Holy, holy, holy Lord of hosts!" A God full of majesty and glory, terrible to avenge the contempt of his laws? A God governing all by his providence, who keeps even the hearts of kings in his hand, and turns and inclines them as the courses of waters, who calls all the hosts of heaven by their names; who makes the winds his messengers, and the flames of fire his ministers! As a God, who at last shall judge all the world! *In fine*, as the God who only is to be feared and adored! Is it possible to give a grander or more sublime representation of the Deity?

If it is the character of the true religion to prescribe nothing but what is holy, then can any doubt of the truth and divinity of the religion of the ancient Jews? Was there ever a more perfect system of morality than the law of Moses, which contains in *ten words*, or sentences, unspeakably more wisdom than can be collected out of all the Pagan philosophers and orators, or all the laws of a Lycurgus, a Draco, or other famed legislators? What Pagan did ever forbid the first motions of concupiscence which arises within us? "I had not known lust," says Paul, "except the law had said, Thou shalt not covet."

Should the true religion make known to us what we wish naturally to be informed of, from whence we spring, and whether we go, the origin of the world and of the creatures in it, the cause of the miseries and evils to which human nature is subject, the greatness of our corruption, what we have merited, what shall become of us after death, what shall befall our bodies, after having been some time in the dust? Can we doubt of the truth of the religion of the ancient Jews, which informs us that our body was taken from the earth, and that our soul is derived from God, and that this returns to God who gave it, while the other returns to the earth, which is its element? Which instructs us, how the heavens and the earth were formed, and how sin entered into the world, the ravages it has caused therein, and the judgments of God it has drawn down upon men; and which discovers how the faithful shall behold the face of God in righteousness, and how those who sleep in the dust of the earth shall awake, some to everlasting life, and others to eternal infamy!

Ought the true religion to abase man before God, and exalt God infinitely above men? Can any doubt of this religion we speak of, which represents men before God as a shadow, as dust and ashes, as a drop of water, and as nothing? And which represents God to us, as he alone who can say, I AM; who can do all things, who does all, and to whom all is subjected?

If the true religion ought to accord with the natural knowledge which God has implanted on the minds of men, and with the dictates of conscience, then can any doubt of the truth of the religion of the ancient Jews, in which there is nothing shocking or contradictory to these common notions? It acknowledges but one God, it ascribes to him all perfections, it teaches the immortality of the soul and a judgment to come, the precepts which the moral law contains are the same with those taught us in natural religion, and there is nothing in that law but what conscience approves; even as there is nothing in the promises which it makes to men of eternal life, which conscience does not desire.

Is it requisite that there should be a marvelous agreement between all the parts of a religion which proceeds from God? And can the divinity of that ancient religion be a matter of doubt, seeing as it is in nothing self-inconsistent? It is contained in many books, which were written at different times, and by different men, but the same spirit appears to have animated the whole.

True religion should also raise us towards God, and this the Jewish religion does. Its chief design and tendency is to make us admire the greatness and perfections of God, to oblige us to love him supremely, to submit absolutely to his will, never to murmur against his orders, to bestow upon him all our desires and affections, to make an entire sacrifice of ourselves to him, to refer all to his glory, to invoke him in all our necessities, and to glorify him by all our thoughts, words, and actions. If it relates any victories to have been gained by the Israelites, it declares that it was to God alone they owed the victory; if they were defeated in battle, it tells us that it was because God would thereby correct them. Whatever is great, excellent, and beautiful is therein ascribed wholly to God.

Ought the true religion to satisfy all the wants of our soul, and calm its agitations; and shall we not acknowledge the religion of the ancient Jews to be true, seeing as in it we are furnished with consolation against the miseries of life, against the fears of death, and against the conscious sense we have of our sins.

In fine, if the true religion should discover to us the true mean of reconciliation with God, does not the Jewish religion inform us that the Messiah was "wounded for our transgressions and bruised for our iniquities, that the chastisement of our peace was upon him"; that it is by the knowledge and faith of him that men are justified? And further, that we ought to cease to do evil and learn to do well, that we should pursue what is good, and practise virtue, being assured that, though our sins should be red as crimson, they shall be white as wool.

Add to all these reflections: 1. That the books which contain the Jewish religion include admirable prophecies, which have had their accomplishment, and which cannot be suspected to have been written after the event has come to pass. 2. That this religion was confirmed by surprising miracles.

The truth of the facts recorded in the books, in which this religion is taught, cannot be doubted. Can it, for instance, ever enter into the mind of a reasonable person, that Moses has imposed on mankind by the books which bear his name? Is it possible that he could have dared to tell the people of

Israel things false, of the falsehood of which they could easily have convinced him, and thereby covered him with confusion, or that he would have taken more than 600,000 men for witnesses of his lies? Is it probable that no person would have been found to contradict and expose his impostures? Is it possible, upon supposition that the accounts given by Moses are fabulous, that the monuments of those things whereof he has written, should have been seen, for so long a time, among the people of Israel; as the rod of Aaron, the manna preserved in a golden urn, the brazen serpent, which remained even to the days of Hezekiah; the ceremony of the Passover, which recalled to the remembrance of that people the departure of their fathers from Egypt; the ceremony of Pentecost, which was a commemoration of the manner in which God had given them their law? Is it likely that a people so difficult to govern, that the Hebrew people would have submitted themselves to this law had they believed it to have been only the invention of a man? *In fine*, is it credible that Moses, if he were such a great impostor, would have given a law so perfect, which condemns all sort of criminal desires?

I know very well that it is alleged that there are facts in these books which can hardly be believed, as that a serpent and an ass did speak; and that a man could live in the belly of a great fish for the space of three days. But what is there incredible in the assertion that the devil had borrowed the organ of a serpent to speak to our first parents? Does this exceed the powers of the devil? Or that God made an ass to speak, to reprove a false prophet who would not obey his orders? Is it impossible for God? Is it more difficult for him to make brute animals to speak, than to enable men to speak? If it is true beyond doubt that there are fishes capable of swallowing a man, what difficulty is there in conceiving that God might preserve Jonah in the belly of that sea monster? Is this more difficult than to preserve alive an infant for nine months in the belly of a woman?

It would be very easy to justify the other facts, which the profane treat with ridicule, by showing that the facts themselves are very possible; that what appears surprising to us at this time might not appear so to the Jewish people formerly; and *in fine*, that there were reasons, very worthy of the wisdom of God, for which he has permitted certain things should have taken place which appear so strange to us. But what has been said is sufficient to oblige us to conclude that the religion of the ancient Jews was divine, and that it was the only one, at that time, which men were bound to follow.

"Must we then," you will say, "become Jews, receive circumcision, and offer to God sacrifices?" No, my brethren, but that you may not be surprised that, after we have extolled the Jewish religion so highly, we do not desire you should embrace it, we entreat you to remark:

1. That the Jewish religion not only contained the truths we have described, but a multitude of ceremonies besides, which were to be practiced.

2. That the books which contain this ancient religion, inform us that the Messiah behoved to come at the end of a certain number of years marked by the prophets, that God should then establish a new covenant, that the ceremonies should then be abolished, and the Gentiles called.

3. *In fine*, that the Messiah which the prophets promised, and who was described by them in all his characters, is actually come: and that he came at the time marked out, at the end of the seventy weeks of Daniel (Daniel 9) after the scepter had departed from Judah, as Jacob had foretold (Genesis 49:10). While the second temple was yet standing, according to the prediction of Haggai; in Bethlehem, as Micah prophesied; of a virgin, according to the oracle of Isaiah (Isaiah 7), and that the Messiah is not only come, but the Gentiles have also been called. Hence it follows:

1. That we ought fully to believe all the truths taught in the ancient religion of the Jews above delineated, but that we ought no longer to practice all the ceremonies which this religion prescribed, because they are no longer of any use, having been instituted only to prepare men for the coming of the Messiah; and Jerusalem itself, where the greater part of these

ceremonies were to be performed, having been long since entirely destroyed.

2. It follows, further, that we ought no longer to expect the Messiah, as the Jews formerly expected him, but ought to be persuaded that he is already come.

This is what the Jews, in these last times, will not admit; and this makes it evident that we ought no longer to adhere to the religion which they profess, but to a religion which—teaching the same truths the prophets taught—informs us that the Messiah is come, to discharge us from the heavy yoke of ceremonies, which ought not to continue beyond the coming of the Redeemer of Israel and of the world.

Many reasons induce us to reject the religion of the present Jews.

How can we receive a religion which allows not to acknowledge for Messiah him who has all the characters of that divine and promised Savior? A religion which will not admit that God has fulfilled the promises he had so solemnly made, and which were absolute? A religion which does violence to the clearest passages which respect the time of the coming of the Messiah, and his sufferings? A religion which proposes another rule of our faith than that which God gave to their fathers, and which vends the most foolish traditions as if they had proceeded from the mouth of God? A religion which teaches a thousand absurdities, which the ancient Jews never believed; things unworthy of God, and even impieties, which we would not dare to repeat in this place. So a celebrated rabbi[16] among them said that, with the losses his nation had sustained in the captivity of Babylon, it had lost *wisdom* among the rest. *In fine,* a religion which is so different from that of the prophets, that these holy men would not acknowledge any more their posterity? Surely such a religion cannot be owned as a religion authorized by God.

---

[16] Abarbanel

What then must we do? And to what hand shall we turn ourselves? Let us see, if the Christian religion, which is the only one remaining, be that we search for.

V. OF THE CHRISTIAN RELIGION.

When we reflect on the marks which we have given of the true religion, we may perceive, at first view, that the Christian religion has all the characters of a religion that is divine.

1. Is it possible to give a grander idea of God than that which it exhibits? It represents him to us as a spirit pure and infinite, as a being infinitely simple, who exists through all, who sees all that is concealed in the abyss of ages to come, who is immutable, and above all the revolutions of time, who is only wise, and only good, who does whatever is his pleasure, who needs only to will, and the thing that he wills is done; whose power extends to nothing itself, whose justice is inexorable against sin, whose compassions are infinite with regard to sinners repenting, and whose word is more firm than heaven and earth?

2. Is it possible to give precepts more holy than those which the gospel contains? It not only would have us to abstain from all appearances of evil, but also to practise goodness in the highest degree to which creatures can possibly attain: teaching us to renounce ourselves, love our enemies; lay down our life for our brethren, and that we should be perfect as God is perfect.

3. Can more powerful motives to engage unto holiness be proposed to men? More excellent examples, greater and more precious promises, or more terrible threatenings?

4. May we not find in the Christian religion that which men most anxiously desire to know for the repose of their conscience? There we learn how the worlds were made, how sin has entered into the world by one man,

and death by sin, and what God has done to rescue us from that condemnation which we have merited. Would you know what shall become of the souls of the just after their death? It informs us that they shall be carried to the bosom of Abraham, and into a house eternal in the heavens, there to be with Jesus Christ; while the spirits of the wicked shall descend into hell, where there is a worm which dieth not, and a fire which is not quenched. Would you know, further, what shall become of the bodies which are consigned to the tomb; the gospel teaches us that the hour cometh when those who are in their graves shall hear the voice of the Son of God: some unto the resurrection of life, some unto the resurrection of condemnation; and that all shall appear before the judgment seat of Christ; that in heaven the just shall enjoy infinite happiness; that they shall be glorified with Christ, reign with him, and be filled with all the fulness of God; whereas in hell the wicked shall suffer inconceivable torments.

5. Can anything tend to abase man more than the Christian religion does? It represents him as a wretched slave, as one dead in his trespasses and sins, as incapable of thinking one good thought of himself, and as putrifying and stinking in the tomb of his vices. It declares that he must be created again, as if he had not a being; that he is born in sin, filled altogether with corrupt inclinations and evil desires, and that all his evils come from himself.

6. Is it possible to exalt God above creatures more than it does? It testifies that in him we live move and have our being; that all creatures are in his hand, as a mass of clay in the hand of a potter, which he forms and fashions according to his will; and that all things are of him, and to him, and through him, who is God over all blessed forever.

7. All the parts of this religion marvellously harmonize together: and what is still more admirable, it fully and perfectly accords with the religion of the ancient Jews, which shows that the same Spirit which dictated the law of Moses, and inspired the prophets, has dictated the gospel, and inspired the apostles.

8. There is nothing in this religion which is contrary to the natural notions which God has imprinted on the hearts of all men. For we shall show in its proper place that the mysteries which appear contrary to reason, are not so in reality; and we must be convinced that the greater part of the truths which this religion teaches us, are most conformed to reason.

9. There is an exact proportion between the truths of the Christian religion, and the conscience of man. It affirms and enjoins nothing but what conscience must approve. It allows nothing but what conscience desires. It delivers no threatenings but as to things which conscience fears. It applies no reproofs or exhortations which conscience finds not to be just. Therefore it has for its author, the author of conscience.

10. It satisfies all the real wants of the soul. It enlightens, it sanctifies, it comforts, it strengthens us, and fills us with joy. It produces true contentment of mind, and calms all the agitations of our consciences. If the faithful believer fear the justice of God, it assures him that divine justice was satisfied by the son of God himself. If his sins fill him with consternation, it informs him that they are expiated by the blood of the lamb of God. If he apprehend the accusations of the devil, it enables him to say, "Who shall lay any thing to the charge of God's elect? It is God who justifieth." It makes him even to raise his voice, to sing these triumphant strains, "Who shall separate us from the love of God? Shall tribulation, or distress, or persecution, or famine, or nakedness, or peril, or sword? Nay: I am persuaded that neither death nor life, nor principalities, nor powers, nor things present, nor things to come, shall be able to separate us from the love of God which is in Christ Jesus our Lord."

It comforts us in all the miseries and afflictions of this life, by instructing us that the afflictions which God sends are the chastisements of a father, by which he recovers us from our wanderings that God will still afford strength to bear them, that they cannot be of long duration, and that they are not comparable with the glory prepared for us. It animates and fortifies against the fears of death, by teaching us that death is the gate of heaven to the faithful, and that it is only dreadful to the impenitent; that it will unite the elect to God, the author of their being and felicity, and that nothing shall ever separate them from him again. *In fine*, that if death lays our bodies in the dust, they shall arise again from it gloriously, when that which is mortal and corruptible shall arise incorruptible and immortal.

11. It also leads us to God in all that it teaches, and obliges us to glorify him by all our actions, words, and thoughts. It directs us to regard him as the sovereign master of the world, as the first truth, as our great legislator, as the arbiter of all events, as the source and author of all blessings, as the judge of men and angels, as the last end of all things, and as our supreme good.

12. It discovers the way God has found out in his wisdom to reconcile us to himself, namely, the death of his son, who has suffered what was our desert, and who has appeased his anger.

13. *In fine*, it teaches us the manner wherein we are to endeavor to render the deity propitious, by having recourse to that dear son by our faith, by abiding in communion with him, by renouncing our sins, and living as he enjoins us.[17] Can any refrain from acknowledging such a religion to be divine?

We must be further confirmed in this sentiment, when it is considered:

1. That this religion informs us that the Messiah, who had been foretold under the Old Testament, is come; that this Messiah was the son of Mary, in whom we find all the characters marked in the prophets: that he has abolished all the ancient ceremonies, which were but for a time; and that he has established a worship altogether spiritual, and far more worthy of God than that of the Jews.

2. That this religion was confirmed by surprising miracles, which are attested to us by persons worthy of credit, and of acknowledged probity.

---

[17] The author's manner of expression here is inaccurate; as he had told us before the only mean of rendering the Deity propitious, that cannot be needful a second time, nor be effected by other means. [*Translator*]

3. That this religion no sooner appeared in the world than it met with reception throughout the whole world, notwithstanding great opposition, and the weakness of those who published it; and that it has had an infinity of martyrs who have sealed it with their blood.

4. That Mahomet was obliged to confess that the Christian religion had been established by God.

5. That the keenest enemies of Christianity have borne very remarkable and honorable testimonies to Jesus Christ and his apostles; insomuch that Porphyry said that "Jesus was a man pious, and most wise, that after his death he was rendered immortal in the heavens, and that persons ought to be wary not to reproach or disparage him."

In fine, that the truth of the ancient Jewish religion cannot be consistently acknowledged without being convinced of the truth of the Christian religion.

For understanding yet more the excellence of the Christian religion, compare it with Natural religion, with the Jewish, the Pagan, and Mahometan religions.

With regard to Natural religion, you will see that the Christian religion has taught the same things that were revealed by nature with far more clearness; and that it has discovered to us a great number more, of which nature gave no notice at all. For nature furnished us with no intelligence as to the mean of propitiating the Deity, but often has manifested him as irritated against men by the tragic events which have been beheld in the world. If the religion of nature instructed us that we were made for a supreme good, it left us in misery, without showing wherein our sovereign good consisted, or the way of attaining to it. But the Christian religion gives satisfactory information as to all these matters. It discovers to us God our Redeemer, a God "made manifest in the flesh, justified in the spirit, seen of angels, believed on in the world, preached among the Gentiles, and exalted into glory." *In fine*, it points out the worship which God requires; and that it is in communion with him that our sovereign good and highest felicity is to be found.

Further, you will find that, instead of the obscurity, the figures, the shadows, the laborious ceremonies, and the carnal service, which had place in the Jewish religion, the Christian causes us to behold with open face, as in a glass, the glory of the Lord, and lets us see how the figures have given place to the truth, the shadows to the substances, and the carnal service to that which is entirely spiritual.

With regard to the Pagan and Mahometan religion, you must be convinced that there is nothing good in these but what is to be found in greater perfection in the Christian, and that all the rest is either ridiculous, extravagant, or impious.

From all we have said above, we may conclude that there is no such thing as true religion at all, which cannot be affirmed without accusing God with want of wisdom and goodness with respect to men; or that all the religions in the world are equally true or false, which is contrary to all the principles of right reason; or that the Christian religion is the true religion which we seek after.

It is not at all needful that a man should be very intelligent to know this; I am persuaded there is none so very simple as to be incapable of this examen, provided he be but able and willing to make use of his reason. There are many things he will discover of himself, and others which he may easily be brought to apprehend. There is no man so rude as not to perceive that the Christian religion speaks of God in a manner admirable; that it contains precepts most holy, exhibits promises most encouraging and delightful, and threatenings most dreadful; none so simple, but he may be made to own that if he could make application of all that the Christian religion informs him of, and practice what it enjoins, he would be of all men the most happy; nor any so simple as not feel a very great satisfaction in reading the gospel, and to find most just whatever the gospel enjoins.

But you will ask: Is there nothing in the Christian religion which may make us doubt of its divinity? This we shall examine in the subsequent discourse, if the Lord will.

APPLICATION

Let us bless God that we were not born amidst the darkness of Paganism or Mahometanism, but in the light of the Christian religion, which alone is the true. Let us bless him that we are no longer subjected to the insupportable yoke of Moses, but are under grace, and that we are no more "come to a mountain that might not be touched, nor unto blackness and darkness and tempest; but to the mount Zion, to the heavenly Jerusalem, to the assembly of the firstborn whose names are written in heaven, to Jesus the mediator of the new covenant, and to the blood of sprinkling, which speaketh better things than that of Abel."

But let us take heed that we be not accused of being worse even than the Pagans. We blame these poor blinded creatures because they adored many gods, and deified their passions; let us examine if we are not guilty of a similar idolatry. When I behold a covetous man, who minds nothing but his treasures, methinks I behold a Pagan, who prostrates himself before an idol of gold or silver; and I am certain that a covetous Christian, dying such, shall be condemned to more severe pains than an idolatrous Pagan. An ambitious man who sacrifices all to his ambition: is he less culpable than a Pagan adoring Jupiter? A voluptuary who plunges himself into a thousand pollutions: is he less criminal than a Pagan who sacrificed to Venus? We need not doubt, my brethren, but that the Gentiles shall rise up in judgment against Christians. The Ninevites, who changed their course at one preaching of Jonah, shall they not rise up in judgment against you sinners, whom so many sermons never move? They had no other light besides the dusky glimmering of nature, if I may use the expression; and you are enlightened with the brightest rays of the sun of righteousness. They humbled themselves, and you cannot subdue your pride. Does not the incorruptible justice of an Aristides, an Agesilaus, a Trajan, put to shame these venal souls, who allow themselves to be influenced by corruption, and oppress the widow and orphan? May not the temperance and chastity of a Scipio reflect shame on those infamous persons of both sexes, who, even under a profession of Jesus Christ, abandon themselves to the sensuality of their lusts? The sobriety of an Epaminondas and a Fabricius: does it not shame those Epicureans who live only to eat, and to pamper themselves with the greatest delicacies? The beautiful and excellent sentiments of Marcus Aurelius Antoninus: may they not put to the blush a great number of Christians, who with all the light of the gospel, attain not to such thoughts, so that Marcus Aurelius might be taken for a Christian, while they might be reckoned Pagans?

Does not the charity of Cimon—of whom it was said that he did as much good as was in his power—reproach those people who do not so much as know what charity means? Shall not the goodness of Titus Vespasian—who used to say that he had lost a day when he had not performed some generous and worthy action—put to confusion those persons who think they have lost their day when they have not perpetrated some mischief? And what might I not say, if I were disposed to make to pass in review, before your eyes, all those among the Pagans, who have rendered their names famous by their actions.

Strange! Is it possible that the hope of a vain immortality, the hope of an empty glory after death, should have made greater impression, and had a more powerful influence on heathens than the hope of a blessed immortality, the fear of an ever during hell, or the death of Jesus Christ, and his example, produce on the hearts of those who call themselves Christians?

My brethren, we propose to you the example of Pagans in order to cover you with shame, and to excite you to jealousy. Is it not sad that those who have travelled among idolatrous and barbarous nations, who have scarce any sense of a deity, or those who have had intercourse with the Turks, should tell us that they have found more honesty and truth among those infidels than among the professors of Christianity? Is it not just matter of regret that the Pagans should have more respect for their false gods, and the Mahometans greater veneration for their false prophet than the Christians have for the living God, and for Jesus Christ? Or that we should have less respect for our churches than the Turks for their mosques? We hear of Turks who will not enter a mosque without being reconciled to their enemies, although Mahomet permits them to revenge themselves; and how many Christians who daily frequent the temples, and who can even partake of the holy supper, and yet retain their differences and animosities? What shame to us to be surpassed by people who know nothing of the gospel? Ah! We should either renounce our name and no longer boast being Christians, or else change our conduct. We need no longer insult the Jews for having crucified Jesus Christ, if we will still crucify him afresh. Amazing indeed! There is not a Jew who would not go to the end of the world and abandon all things to follow their messiah; and yet we may perceive Christians who choose not to take one step towards Jesus Christ, and who would notwithstanding reckon it a great injustice done them, if any should say that they were worse than Jews.

My brethren, seeing as we profess to be Christians, let us live as Christians ought to live; as persons who believe that they were redeemed by the blood of the Son of God; in a word, as persons who aspire to an inheritance incorruptible, and hope for a blessed immortality. May God enable us all to do so by his grace. Amen.

A DEFENCE
OF THE
CHRISTIAN RELIGION
AGAINST THE
OBJECTIONS URGED AGAINST IT

The third discourse,
on 1 Thessalonians 5:21.

"O Lord! how great are thy works! and thy thoughts are very deep! a brutish man knoweth nothing of them." Thus speaks the prophet in Psalm 92:6-7. Indeed, wherever we cast our eyes in this universe, we shall find there just cause to admire the grandeur of God's works, the wisdom and the depth of his ways; and our mind may discover so many wonders in the contemplation of them, that it will be constrained at last to adore, with religious awe, what it cannot comprehend. But what ought to fill all men with admiration, is too often regarded with indifference, and even with contempt, by those whose minds the God of this world has blinded. "The natural man receiveth not the things of the Spirit of God, neither can he know them, they are foolishness to him (1 Corinthians 2:14)." It would be easy to prove this truth by a variety of examples, but one is sufficient to convince us of it.

The Christian religion, my brethren, is undoubtedly the most complete and perfect work which has proceeded from the hands of God. It is the masterpiece of his wisdom, of his mercy, of his power, and all his other perfections, which shine there in their brightest luster. Yet—strange to tell!—there have been some to whom this religion has been an offence, and others who have regarded it as extravagant. "We preach Christ crucified," said Paul, "to the Jews a stumbling block, and to the Greeks foolishness."

And there are still some, presently to be found, so profane, as to entertain no more favourable sentiments of this divine religion, who allow themselves to be denominated Christians, but who mock at the most sublime mysteries of Christianity; who even exert all their efforts to extinguish in their hearts the impressions of a deity; who have properly speaking no other God but themselves, and no other end but to live in the present world, without minding that which is to come.

What depravity! What infatuation! These monsters at least might keep themselves concealed and under covert, without venturing to appear openly; but impiety has lifted up and thrown aside her mask. She shows herself at noonday, obtrudes herself on the view of all, and daringly attempts to maintain her tenets. To fortify true believers against this impious tribe, is the reason why we undertake, under the favourable assistance of the God of truth, the defence of the Christian religion.

In our last sermon, we showed that of all the religions in the world this is the most excellent, and that which is possessed of the most evident marks of its having proceeded from God; and we brought the matter to this conclusion: that we must hold either that there is no such thing as true religion, which is to accuse God of want of wisdom and goodness towards men; or that all religions are equally true, which cannot be maintained without the highest absurdity and inconsistency; or that the Christian religion is divine, which we maintain. But seeing as you may demand whether there be nothing in this religion which may lead us to doubt of its divinity, we intend at present to reply to the objections, which are made on this subject, in order that you yourselves may examine whether the things we have said to you be true, according to the injunction which Paul gives us in these words, which we have read to you for the third time: *Prove all things.*

May God grant that his Word may be in our mouth as a two-edged sword, piercing to the dividing of the joints and marrow, of the soul and spirit! May he grant that if there be any one here present, so unhappy as not to be a Christian from persuasion as well as by birth, he may return, not only as Agrippa, almost persuaded, but altogether convinced of the truth of the Christian religion! God grant that our preaching may confirm true Christians, and establish the weak; and that his truth may triumph today, by our ministry, over the incredulity of men. Amen.

1ST OBJECTION

The first objection which is proposed against the Christian religion, regards the facts upon which it is founded. They ask whether we must believe those who have told us that there was such a one as Jesus Christ, and that he rose from the dead; or if it should not be held for a fable, palmed upon us as a true history?

To satisfy you, my dear brethren, that there is nothing in this objection that needs in the least to disquiet us, we require nothing more than that they should show the same justice with regard to the facts, on which Christianity is established, which they show as to these historical facts, which are by none brought into doubt. For we allege that there is nothing so well proven as the resurrection of Jesus Christ, so that we must either believe no fact at all, of which we have not been eye-witnesses, or we must be persuaded that Jesus is risen from the dead.

To convince you of this, we wish everyone to examine what are the qualities which a historian ought to possess in order to deserve credit. It will be said without doubt:

- That he must have seen what he attests, without depending on the report of another.
- That he should be of known probity and virtue.
- That he should have strong reasons and inducements to examine carefully the fact to which he bears witness.

- That there be no appearance or likelihood that he might be deceived.
- That there should be no discernible motive which might have prevailed with him to lie, or affirm what he knew to be false.
- That, on the contrary, he should have had powerful reasons engaging him to speak the truth.
- That he could not give a false account without being the most wicked of all men; and that even his enemies should be constrained to bear an honorable testimony to his virtue.
- That he has confirmed his history by his death.
- That he has published his account in a time wherein it might have been very easy to convict him of falsehood, and yet none have ever done so.
- That many historians constantly attest the same thing.
- *In fine*, that what he has recorded has been believed by a great number of people of good sense, from the time that such a history was wrote, down to our days.

If a fact related by such an author, is not incontestably true, I grant I have nothing more to say; but, at the same time, we must maintain that there never will be a fact that can be reckoned certain, but those which we may have seen with our own eyes; which even those who are most incredulous in the matter of history, will not venture to assert.

Let us then see if the apostles—who have informed us that Jesus is risen from the dead—possess the qualities which we have described.

You will not have the least doubt of it, my brethren, if you choose to bestow a proper attention; you will even find that they possessed these qualifications in a very eminent degree.

1. They bore testimony to what they saw, not afar off, but nigh, or at a due distance. It was not one apostle only who saw and wrote, but several. They employed all the senses by which they could be enabled to judge of what they attest: their eyes, their ears and their hands. By these they had

opportunity to be satisfied, by repeated proofs, having been with Jesus Christ many weeks after his resurrection, during which they beheld that divine Savior move, speak, and act; they saw the features of his countenance; they put their hands to his side; they saw and touched the marks of his wounds.

2. They were of acknowledged probity and virtue. The greatest enemies of Christianity have not represented them as villains or cheats; and their morality is admirable. They condemn, in the strongest terms, lying in particular; and they are so honest and ingenuous, as not to conceal their own faults.

3. They had the greatest reason to examine well the truth of what they testified. For if Jesus Christ were not really risen, he would have deceived them. If he were not what he gave himself out to be, in that case, they could no more have regarded him as their master. It was more conducive to their secular interest not to believe this resurrection; and it was far more advantageous, in a worldly view, to say, as Peter had done of Jesus Christ, *I know him not.* Besides, there were some among them who doubted of the fact, and who would not be convinced of it, until after they had examined the matter with all the attention and exactness possible.

4. There is no appearance that they either were or could be deceived. For how was it possible? Was it because their imagination was disturbed? But nothing can be discerned in their discourse or writings which discovers a disordered imagination; on the contrary, the most admirable wisdom shines in them. Was it because they might very easily be deceived or mistake as to the fact which they attest? Not at all: for that respects not a point of doctrine difficult and obscure, but the resurrection of their master, with whom they had conversed for a long time, even for the space of some years. Was it because they were under the delusive influence of sorcery or enchantment? That could only be from the devil, who is a liar and murderer from the beginning; but, not to mention that those whom we oppose have not perhaps a very strong faith in the existence of devils, is it likely that the devil should interfere in this matter, seeing as the whole dispensation of the

gospel tends to the destruction of his empire. Besides, what reason is there to think that the devil has it in his power to impose so far upon men by his illusive arts? Moreover, is it credible that persons should persuade themselves without cause that Jesus after his resurrection had lent them his Spirit, to speak all sort of languages, and perform all kind of miracles? No; doubtless. There is not therefore any shadow of appearance that they were deceived.

5. One cannot conceive what reason they could have had to falsify. Could it be with a view to obtain riches? They forsook all they had, and lived in poverty. They even spoke of the good things of the earth with sovereign contempt. Could it be to advance themselves to honors? But these they could not expect, either from the Jews or Gentiles, to whom their preaching made them obnoxious and odious. Could it be to enjoy the pleasures of life? But they were apprised that they should reap only pains, toils, and persecutions; that they should be exposed to all sorts of disgrace, and even punishments. Could it be to acquire reputation in the world? But their doctrine was no way suited to attract applause. They never thought of tickling the ears of their hearers by eloquent harangues, nor of gratifying their passions; and according to their own doctrine, deceivers and liars had nothing to look for, but eternal punishment as their reward. Could it be the love they bore to their master that might induce them to lie? But how could they have loved him so highly, if he had deceived them, and if he was not in reality raised again? It does not appear then that they had any reason to avouch a falsehood.

6. Nay, more, they had the most powerful reasons against lying in this cause. The preservation of their life and their peace, which all men, who retain any spark of reason, solicitously regard, engaged them to tell the truth, at least not to advance such an imposture. It is easy to conceive that a man may expose himself to death for an error which he firmly believes to be a truth; but that a man, who knows in his conscience that he imposes on the world, should love his falsehood more than his life, if he were not demented, is what can hardly be imagined.

7. Let us go a step further, my brethren: the apostles cannot be charged with lying, without [being] at the same time accused as the most wicked of all men, which none ever ventured to assert. For on that supposition, they would not have deceived, but merely for the sake of deceiving; which is the highest degree of malice.

8. Nor is this all: the apostles supported and confirmed their testimony by their death, which they suffered with joy, with patience, and in giving innumerable evidences of their piety. If it were true that they were all impostors, how came it to pass that not one of them gave himself the lie, and revealed the secret, when pressed by his conscience, by the respect which a man naturally has to truth, by the majesty of the tribunals before which they appeared, by the terrible idea of procuring the hatred of all the world, and by the fear of a future judgment? Add to this, the apostles wrote in a manner the most remote from any appearance of design to impose; for they are far from accommodating themselves to the inclinations of people, and they publish mysteries which at first shock those who hear them.

9. They wrote in a time when there were many thousands of persons who could have convicted them of falsehood; even all the multitude assembled at Jerusalem at the time of the first Christian Pentecost, upon supposition that the things they committed to writing had not been true.

10. All that they delivered agreed entirely with what the ancient prophets had taught. How could that be, if their testimony were false?

11. Since their death, an incredible number of persons, of every age, sex, and condition, have confirmed their testimony. Philosophers, orators, learned and ignorant, kings themselves, have submitted their scepter to a risen Jesus. A hundred years after his resurrection, Justin Martyr counted already in the number of believers, many savage nations, and even those wandering tribes which roamed from place to place, upon wagons, without having any fixed habitation. In Tertullian's time, there were Christians through the whole extent of the Roman empire, that is, people who believed

that Jesus was raised from the dead, and who scrupled not to die for this doctrine.

"We are," said an ancient father in his *Apology* to the Romans, "but lately sprung up, and we already fill whatever acknowledges your power, the cities, the isles, the fortresses, the towns, and the assemblies of the people; we are to be found even in the armies, the military offices, the courts, the palace, the senate, the public places; we leave you nothing but the temples."[18] It is impossible to point out a single year, throughout more than sixteen centuries, in which there have not been a multitude of Christians almost innumerable, who have believed and maintained that Jesus the son of Mary is the Messiah, that he is risen, and that he reigns gloriously in heaven. After this, what room is there to doubt of the testimony of the apostles?

It will perhaps be said, "If the facts reported by the apostles were true, some monument of them would be found in the writings of the Pagans." But this difficulty ought not to embarrass us, for: 1. Granting it were true that the Pagan historians had said nothing of Jesus Christ, could it be inferred from this that Jesus Christ has not come into the world? Might not their silence be owing to another cause? The most part of the Pagan historians who have written, wrote at Rome, and Jesus Christ died at Jerusalem. Why should it be reckoned strange that they might have been ignorant of what passed in the capital of the east? The Pagans entertained a sovereign contempt for the Jews; can we then be surprised that they would not be at the trouble to inform themselves of what fell out among them; or that they would not deign to record it? How do we know, but that their fondness for their own religion might have deterred them from bearing that testimony to truth which they owed it? Besides, will any pretend that we have all the writings of that time?

But not to rest solely in this answer, it is easy to add in the next place, that it is false that we find no monument of the history of Jesus Christ in the

---

[18] Tertullian, *Apology* Chapter 47

Pagan writers. Tacitus, who wrote in the end of the first century, speaks expressly of Jesus Christ, of the time of his death, namely under the emperors Tiberius, and under Pilate; of the extent and progress of his religion, of the hatred of people against the first Christians, and in their courage of professing the name of Christ.[19] Suetonius speaks also of Christ, whose name however he seems scarcely to know.[20] Nothing can be more handsome than that which Pliny the Younger writes to the emperor Trajan, concerning the Christians; which proves invincibly that in his time, there were people who considered Jesus Christ as God, and made profession of the Christian religion. This author, who was governor of Bithynia, informs that emperor how the Christians were accustomed to assemble together on a certain day before the rising of the sun, and to sing hymns in honor of Christ as God; and how they bound themselves by oath not to commit either theft, robbery, or adultery; nor to break their promises, nor withhold the pledge.

Phlegon, the freed man of the emperor Hadrian has mentioned the eclipse which happened at the death of Christ, as also of the earthquake accompanying it.[21]

If we may credit Tertullian, Tiberius having received letters from Pilate which gave an account of Jesus Christ, proposed to the Senate that he should

---

[19] Tac. xv. 1 Ann.

[20] Claud. c. 25. "Judæos impulsore Christo assidue tumultuantes Roma expulit." This historian seems to confound the Jews with the Christians.

[21] He says that "In the fourth year of the 202nd Olympiad (which answers to the time of the death of Jesus Christ), there was an eclipse of the sun, like to which had never been known, producing such a prodigious darkness, even at midday, that the stars of heaven were seen." He adds that: "There was a very great trembling of the earth in Bithynia." It is true, he does not say that this happened at full moon, as Origen (in Mat.) remarks: but it is affirmed that in the year marked by Phlegon, there neither was nor could be any natural eclipse of the sun. Eusebius, besides Phlegon, cites other records, wherein he had found that earthquake and solar eclipse. Tertullian, in his *Apology*, affirms (Chapter 21) that this event was to be found in the Roman archives. Ruffinus also introduces these words, as addressed to the Pagans by Lucian presbyter of Antioch, who died in the year 312. "Consult your annals, and you will find that when Jesus Christ suffered in the time of Pilate, the sun ceased to appear, and the day was interrupted by an extraordinary darkness."

be received into the number of gods. And the same father writing against Marcion says that the public registers contained the names of the enrollment which was made by the emperor Augustus throughout the whole empire; and that, in that belong to Judea, the name of the whole line and parentage of our Lord was to be found.[22]

In the preceding discourse, we informed you of the favorable testimony which Porphyry gave to Jesus Christ. Celsus denied not that Jesus Christ wrought miracles, but he ascribes them to a magical power, he who doubted before whether there were any magicians. It is not therefore true that no monument of the history of Jesus Christ is to be found in the writings of the Gentiles. To the testimony of the Pagans, let that of the Jews be added, who were no less violent in their enmity against the Christians.

This may be sufficient to convince reasonable minds who are disposed to hearken, not to their passions and prejudices, but to right reason. We have been larger on this objection, because it is a capital one; and if the testimony of the apostles concerning the resurrection of Jesus Christ be true, we have no ground to doubt of the Christian religion, which is wholly founded on that resurrection.

2ND OBJECTION

The second objection comes from the Jews: "If the Christian religion," say they, "Were a religion proceeding from God, how improbable is it that our fathers would have rejected it, and even put to death him who was its

---

[22] Tertull. Ap. chap. 5. and 21. In Marc. l. 4. c. 7.

If the monuments referred to by Tertullian, be by some deemed as suspicious, there are many others which cannot be contested. This argument from heathen testimonies hath largely been discussed and illustrated by some writers of the present century: particularly Dr. Lardner in his *Credibility of the Gospel History*. The authenticity and force of Phlegon's testimony, were warmly debated between Dr. Sykes and Dr. Chapman. The arguments in vindication of it, may be seen at length in Chapman's Tracts relating to antiquity. [*Translator*]

author? Besides, Christians cannot deny that their religion was divine; whence is it then that the Christian religion is so contrary to the religion of Moses and the prophets? God gave to our fathers a ceremonial law, and commanded us to observe it forever, especially circumcision, yet Christianity has entirely abolished this law."

This objection may be very easily answered:

1. The Jews need not be surprised that their fathers rejected Jesus Christ. That rejection had been foretold. It had been declared that the chief cornerstone (by which was meant the Messiah) should be rejected by the builders (Psalm 118). Isaiah begins the chapter wherein he speaks of the Messiah, of his death, burial and exaltation, by these words, "Who hath believed our report?" (Isaiah 53). It had been foretold that the Jews should have eyes and yet should not see: and that their heart should be made fat (Isaiah 6:9-10). One needs only to read the prophets to see there many passages which expressly foretell that which has fallen out in the last times. The Jews then ought not to be astonished at what their fathers have done; but they ought to recall their attention to the manner in which God has punished them, for their having thus rejected him who was sent unto them; to that which happened a short time after they had crucified the author of the Christian religion; to the signs which preceded the destruction of Jerusalem, which had been foretold by Jesus Christ, and are attested by their own writers (Matthew 23-24);[23] to the time when their city was besieged, which was the same in which they had expressed such resentment and outrage against our Savior to the place at which the siege began, which was precisely the spot where Jesus Christ had poured out tears over Jerusalem; to what befell their nation in that fatal siege, at which time over 1,240,000 men were either taken captive or slain; to the manner in which their temple was

---

[23] Josephus' *Wars of the Jews*, Book 7 Chapter 12 may be consulted. The rabbis remark that strange things were beheld every day in the temple; which made a famous doctor to exclaim; "O temple, O temple, what is it that moves thee, and wherefore dost thou cause terror to thyself?"

burnt, notwithstanding that Titus exerted himself to the utmost to put a stop to the conflagration; to the efforts which in vain they have made to restore their commonwealth, and to rebuild their temple under Trajan, Hadrian, Constantine, Julian—*in fine*, to their sad dispersion, in which they have now remained a long time without princes, without sacrifices, without altars, according to the prediction concerning them by Hosea (Hosea 3). "What meanest thou, and what dost thou wait for, O incredulous Jew!" to the use of the words of Jerome,* "Many crimes thou hadst committed during the time of the judges; thy idolatry rendered thee the slave of all surrounding nations; but God very soon had pity on thee, and without delay sent saviors unto thee. Thine idolatries were multiplied under thy kings, but the abominations committed in the days of Ahab and Manasseh, were only punished with seventy years of captivity. Cyrus came and restored to thee thy country, thy temple, and sacrifices. At last thou wast overthrown by Vespasian and Titus: fifty years after, Hadrian made thy ruin complete; and for several ages, thou remainest under oppression! Ah! Call to your remembrance these words of your fathers: *His blood be upon us and upon our children.*" This is the first reply which we make to the objection of the Jews.

But we answer in the second place that the Christian religion is falsely supposed to be contrary to the Jewish. This is so far from being true that the apostles loudly declare that they taught nothing but what Moses and the prophets had said before them. It is true that Jesus Christ has abolished the ceremonies of the law, but the Jews have no reason to be surprised at this. Do they not know that God promised that he would make a new covenant (Jeremiah 31:31-32), and that he had said by Daniel that Christ should cause the sacrifice and oblation to cease, and that he should shut up the vision and the prophecy (Daniel 9:24, 27)? Do they not know that the Messiah should be a priest, not after the order of Aaron, but after that of Melchizedek (Psalm 110) and that the priesthood being changed, it was necessary that there should be also a change of the law (Hebrews 7:21)?

They cannot be ignorant that it was not possible to observe the ceremonies after the calling of the Gentiles, which had been foretold, and which has actually taken place: for how could it be possible that three times a year, all nations could go up to Jerusalem, and there slay victims? So God had warned that people by Jeremiah (Jeremiah 3:16-17): "In those days, saith the Lord, they shall say no more, the ark of the covenant of the Lord; neither shall it come to mind, neither shall they remember it, neither shall they visit it, neither shall that be done any more. At that time they shall call Jerusalem, the throne of the Lord, and all the nations shall be gathered unto it."

In fine, the Jews might learn from their doctors that in the time of the Messiah, almost all the feasts should cease, and that all the sacrifices should be abolished, except the sacrifices of praise; and they might see in their prophets, that God would not take pleasure in the sacrifices of goats and lambs, and accordingly, that it was only for a time that he had required of their fathers such sacrifices. They should not be obstinate, because it is said that the ceremonies should continue forever; for that manner of speaking does not always signify *eternity*, as they themselves do own, but a certain prefixed time. The Scripture employs it with regard to the Levites, who were not bound to serve beyond the age of fifty years (Leviticus 25:10), and also applies it to servants, whose service behoved to expire at the time of the Jubilee (Exodus 21, Numbers 4).

3RD OBJECTION

"But," say the Jews again, "We cannot consider your Jesus as the true Messias, which our fathers accepted, seeing as he has not the characters belonging to him. The Messiah must be a mere man, and you call him God; he ought to be a great king, who shall subdue all the world by the power of his arms, and your Jesus all along lived in poverty, and died on an ignominious cross. What! Shall we regard one crucified, for our Immanuel?"

My brethren, they must have a thick vail indeed upon their eyes, and upon their heart, who are capable of making such an objection. You affirm—O Jews!—that the Messiah should be nothing more than a mere man; whence comes it then that your fathers have applied to him the prophecy of Isaiah, wherein he is called *the mighty God*, and *the everlasting father* (Isaiah 9); the oracle of Jeremiah, where he is named *the Lord our Righteousness* (Jeremiah 23); the saying of David, who denominates him his Lord (Psalm 110), and that other in the 45th Psalm, where he is addressed in this style, "Thy throne O God, is, for ever and ever; [...] and God ever thy God hath anointed thee with the oil of gladness above thy fellows."

You say that our Jesus has not the characters of the Messiah; and what have your prophets affirmed of the Messiah which we do not find in our Jesus? Has he not come in the time marked by Jacob, by Daniel, by Haggai; in the place specified by Micah, and of the family of David, from which it was so often foretold he should spring?

You tell us that the Messiah should be a conqueror who should march forth at the head of your troops, destroy your enemies, reassemble your dispersed tribes, and lead them back triumphant to Jerusalem. Have you then forgotten what the prophets have told you, that he should have no form nor comeliness, nor any beauty why he should be desired; that he should be despised of men; that he should bear our griefs, and carry our sorrows, be wounded for our transgressions and bruised for our iniquities; that they should give him gall and vinegar to drink; that they should cast lots upon his garments and pierce his hands and his feet (Psalm 22).

After this, how comes it about—O rebellious nation! Ye obdurate people!—that the manger, or the cross of Christ, should be an offence unto you? You want a conqueror; Jesus verily was such, but his conquests were altogether spiritual; for he overcame the devil and death. You would have a king; Jesus was and still is a king, but his kingdom is not of this world. You cannot prove to us by any reasons the heavenly calling and mission of Moses, but by the very same arguments we can demonstrate to you that our

Jesus is the Messiah. Surely, the hardness of this people might fill us with unspeakable surprise, if it had not been predicted unto us. But we pray the God of Israel, who is the Father of our Lord Jesus Christ, that he may enlighten them, and restore them again.

Let us proceed now to other objections respecting the mysteries of Christianity, as these are the most weighty which its adversaries have to propose, we require of you the most earnest attention.

4TH OBJECTION

"Nothing ought to be admitted," say they, "Which is contrary to right reason. How then can the Christian religion be regarded as divine, seeing as it proposes to us doctrines which are incompatible with our natural light?"

My brethren, I grant that nothing is to be admitted that is contrary to reason. Reason and faith are never opposite, because God—who is the author of both—cannot give the lie to himself: therefore whatever is contrary to natural light, cannot be admissible in religion. But we maintain that the Christian religion has nothing contrary to that pure light. It teaches us mysteries which reason cannot comprehend, and which far surpass it, but which do not contradict it. Should anyone be surprised that there are mysteries in religion? Are there not many of them in nature?

There is not a man in the world who can comprehend how the soul is united with the body, in such a manner that by certain movements of the body, thoughts arise in the soul; and by certain things in the soul, certain movements are excited in the body. There is no person who can comprehend how a man can retain different languages, and speak in all these languages when he pleases; yet nobody ever took it into his head to deny either of these.

If those against whom we dispute acknowledge a Deity, they are obliged to own that God is a Being eternal; for a God who could have a beginning would not be God. But I beg they would tell me whether they comprehend eternity; they surely will not pretend it. Of necessity then they must acknowledge that one may believe truths which he cannot comprehend. If our reason were infinite, there might be ground for maintaining that whatever falls not within its comprehension does not exist; but as it finds itself to be very limited, and subject even to dimness of sight, when there is too great an effulgence of light, it would be the greatest absurdity to pretend that everything which it comprehends not, is a chimera. To reject mysteries because they are incomprehensible, and to be disposed to receive nothing besides what reason perfectly understands, is to impugn reason itself; for it perceives that, among those natural truths which belong to its province, and which it is indispensably obliged to receive, it meets with an infinite number which are impenetrable and inexplicable.

"But," they will say, "Would it not have been much more worthy of God, to explain all things to us with such evidence as that we might comprehend them all clearly, and without difficulty?" I answer:

1. It belongs not to us to prescribe to God, the wisest of beings, what he ought to do.

2. That it is not possible to make finite creatures, such as we are, to comprehend all that is affirmed of an infinite being, as it is not possible that infinite creatures should become infinite.

3. *In fine,* that it was not more worthy of the wisdom of God, to abate the proud reason of man, in obliging him to make a sacrifice to him of his vain reasonings; a sacrifice highly becoming, and undoubtedly due to the Deity; for, as one has well said, it is not more reasonable that we should submit our will to him by our obedience to his laws, than that we should subject our reason and our understanding to him by faith.

This may suffice for an answer to the difficulty which is raised in general with regard to mysteries. Let us enter into a more particular detail.

5TH OBJECTION

The first mystery to which men cannot be reconciled either in the Jewish or Christian religion, is that of creation, which they pretend is contrary to reason. They would rather choose to affirm, either that the world is eternal, or, that the matter of which the world was formed is eternal, than to say that God has created all things from nothing: urging against this doctrine the philosophical maxim, *Ex nihilo nihil fit! Of nothing, nothing is made!*

But those who reason thus grossly deceive themselves. The two following arguments will make you sensible of this. The first of them is opposed to those who maintain that the world is eternal. I ask them then whether they believe that motion is essential to the matter of which the world is composed? They will not venture to say so, for if it were essential to matter to move, it behoved all its parts to be in continual agitation, and matter would cease to be matter, whenever it should cease to be moved. But who knows not, and who does not see that there is not any portion of matter more determined to motion than rest? If motion is not essential to matter, it follows necessarily that some agent must have impressed on the matter which composes the world, the motion which was necessary to form the heavens, the earth, the sea, and all creatures, and consequently that the world had a beginning.

The second argument is opposed to those who believe that matter is eternal. Of these I demand whether they can conceive that matter which is so imperfect should possess the greatest of all perfections, which is to exist of itself? I ask them again, whence is it that matter does not possess other perfections? If it had no principle of its existence, it could not then have any to set limits to its excellence. Why then are its perfections so very confined? Certainly they must confess, if they were disposed to follow their light, that of necessity some principle has thus limited it; and therefore that it has a principle or cause: it is not then eternal.

But to confound entirely those who adopt such an opinion, I beg they would tell me whether it be less shocking to their reason to affirm that matter is eternal than to affirm that God made it out of nothing? To believe the eternity of matter, the understanding must admit the supposition that the most imperfect of beings has the greatest perfection of deity, which is repugnant to right reason; whereas to comprehend that God may have made something of nothing, nothing more is necessary than to admit two truths, which reason itself teaches us. These are: 1. That God has an infinite power: without which he would not be God. 2. That by virtue of this, he can do above all that we can either do or think. These two truths are incontestable. Besides, reason says not absolutely that of nothing nothing is made; but only that nothing is produced from nothing naturally; but it never affirmed that God could not make something out of nothing. It implies no contradiction that God should cause a thing that is not in this present moment to exist the moment following.

6TH OBJECTION

Let us examine another mystery: it is that of the resurrection of the body. This mystery gave the Pagans greater trouble than any other: so, when Paul declared it to be the Athenians, they treated him as a babbler and raver. The resurrection was so remote from their ideas, that they took the word for the name of a goddess, saying, "He seemeth to be a setter forth of strange gods [...] because he preached unto them Jesus and the resurrection." "What folly!" exclaimed a Pagan, as we learn from one of the first advocates for Christianity; "The Christians despise present torments, and they fear the evils to come: they are not afraid to die, but afraid of dying after their death; they say that all the world must be consumed by fire, that all the elements shall be dissolved; but as for them, they imagine that they shall revive after their death; and they believe it so confidently that it may be said already that they are raised again. What extravagance to imagine that bodies reduced to dust can be reunited!" "Where is that God which can raise the dead," said the impious and scoffing Julian, "Who cannot succor the living?" This doctrine was so insupportable to the Pagans that the history of the church informs us that they ordered the ashes of the martyrs of Lyon to be thrown into the Rhone, "to take away," said the persecutors, "all hope of rising again."

I am not at all surprised that these poor blinded people should have reasoned in this manner; but that persons brought up in Christianity should have such thoughts, this is surprising indeed! After all, in order to believe the resurrection, it is sufficient to admit three principles, which are most consonant to reason: the first is that God is a being whose power and knowledge are infinite. Who can deny it? The second, that it is not more difficult to raise a body than to create it at first. Is not this also indisputable? The third is that God, having an infinite knowledge, must know where all the various parts of human bodies are, in order to their being rejoined; otherwise his knowledge could not be infinite. Here then is all the mystery. What man who acknowledges a deity, and forms an idea of God as a being most perfect, can presume to reject these three principles?

"You ask," said Tertullian, "How it is possible that a mass of matter reduced to dust, can be brought back again? Reflect but upon yourselves—O mortals!—who make this objection, and you will find in your own person, the proof of such a wonderful phenomenon. Think what you were, before you were created, even lying in a state of non-existence. You, then, who were nothing before your creation, and who, when you shall cease to live, shall return again as it were, to nothing. What should hinder your being once again brought out of nothing, by the will of the same Creator, who was pleased to form you of nothing? Will anything new, in that case, befall you? You were not; and you have been created: when you shall be no more, God will restore to you the being which you had lost. [...] Seeing as he found no difficulty in making you what you had never been, you ought not to think that he will find any in that which may appear more easy, namely, in making you to be what you had formerly been. Can any question the power of God, who has formed this vast and stupendous body of the world of that which was not?"

I say nothing of the immortality of the soul, because this is not a doctrine peculiar to the Christian religion, but is taught by reason, and was accordingly acknowledged by the Pagans. Indeed, I can hardly believe that there are any who can be fully persuaded that their soul shall die. How can they conceive that it could be affected by death? Can it be by the dissolution of its parts? It has not any; it is a spirit: for I will not deign here to stop to dispute with those who pretend that the soul may be corporeal and that matter may be capable of thinking. Could it be by the soul effecting its own destruction? But how can those who are so averse to admit anything which they cannot comprehend, conceive that a spirit may destroy itself? Or, is it, because he who has created it will annihilate it? But how come they to the knowledge of this? Have they received any revelation of it?

On the contrary, the Scripture assures us that the spirit goes to God, while the body returns to the dust (Ecclesiastes 12). To tell us that they cannot comprehend that a soul should exist without the body, is a pitiful objection; for it is much more difficult to conceive that a soul should be united with a body than to comprehend how it can subsist without a body.

Moreover, is there anything shocking to reason in saying that God—who has prescribed laws to men, and proposed rewards and punishments unto them, but yet sees it not meet to recompense or punish them wholly in this life—should recompense or punish them after their death; and that, for this cause, it is not his will that the soul should be annihilated? And with regard to their bodies, that he has assigned a certain time in which he will reunite these bodies and souls, to render them eternally happy, or miserable?

7TH OBJECTION

I proceed next to the incarnation. "Who can believe," say they, "That a God should be made man, that the Creator should be a creature, and that the father of eternity should become an infant?"

I confess that here is indeed a mystery, and a great mystery. "Without controversy," says Paul, "Great is the mystery of godliness, God made manifest in the flesh" (1 Timothy 3:16). But that you may see there is nothing in this mystery which ought to shock you, it is needful that you consider:

1. That when we say that God became man, we do not mean that the Deity was changed into humanity, or that God has ceased to be God in becoming man. If the Christian religion should advance this doctrine, we could not acknowledge it as divine, for the divine nature is eternal and immutable. But we believe that Jesus Christ, who was God blessed eternally with his Father, united himself with a human nature, without losing anything of his divinity, of his greatness and perfections.

2. It may be proper to remark that all the religions of the world have conceived of God as united in some manner to his works, and therefore one need not be astonished if the Christian religion represents him united to the human nature of Jesus Christ in a more strict manner than with other things, for if there be a creature with which divinity may unite itself, it must be a creature holy and innocent.

3. Consider in the next place that if it be difficult to comprehend the union of the divine nature with the human, it is no less so to understand the union of the soul with the body. There appears even to be a greater affinity between an uncreated spirit, as God is, and a spirit created, such as the soul of man, than between a spirit and a body, a spirit which thinks, and matter which has extension. It will be said that the difficulty arises from the infinity of God; but this is a mistake, for as the infinitude of God is no hindrance to

his communication with the creature, neither can it hinder him from uniting himself with the creature.

In fine, let it be considered that if divinity be joined with humanity, it is in order to accomplish the greatest work which can be conceived; that is, the work of our redemption, of which we shall speak hereafter.

One great reason which makes the mystery of the incarnation appear incredible to flesh and blood is, because we want not only to know it, but would also be made sensibly to perceive it. We would make it the object of our imagination, as well as of our understanding. We want that this union of the two natures in Jesus Christ should be explained to us, although we know very well that merely the explication of the union between our soul and body, far exceeds our power.

But it becomes neither Pagans nor Jews to have the incarnation of Jesus Christ for an object of their unbelieving wonder. For with regard to the former, their most famous authors have affirmed that their gods had often descended from heaven to earth, that they had traversed it under a human form; that they had mingled themselves in the assemblies of men, and made themselves like unto them. Have they not further affirmed that the presence of the gods brought health to the sick, consolation to the afflicted, and aid to the wretched?[24] And as for the Jews, did not Isaiah predict to them, that the Messiah should be born of a virgin, and that he should be their Emmanuel, that is to say, *God with us* (Isaiah 7)?

I will not spend time here in refuting those who will not believe that Jesus Christ could be born of a virgin. He must have a very limited and unworthy idea of the power of God, who thinks that he cannot form a body in the womb of a virgin, as well as in that of a woman. The one and the other to him is equally possible, and either the one or the other is a work which requires an infinite power. But I shall content myself with directing you here to admire the wise conduct of God, who was pleased thus to

---

[24] Diod. Sic. p.1 l. 1.5. Dionys. Halye. l. 2. Curt. l. 5. Eunap. in Maxim. Polyb. l. 3.

distinguish the birth of the Savior of the world from the ordinary birth of other men.

8TH OBJECTION

"But," they add, "Is it credible that the Messiah, the Son of God, should be born in a stall, and live in such a state of obscurity?"

My brethren, you need not be surprised at this: it was not at all congruous that the Messiah, whom it behoved to die for our redemption, should be born in a palace, be clad in purple, and live in magnificence. It was proper that there should be some proportion between the birth and the death; an illustrious birth and a glorious life would not have comported with a death so ignominious as his was.

Moreover, as Jesus Christ came into the world to reestablish what the first Adam had ruined, it was necessary that he should proceed in a way altogether opposite to that first sinner. Therefore, as the earthly Adam had exalted himself above his natural condition, in aspiring to be like unto God, and more than a man; it was proper that the heavenly Adam should abase himself infinitely below his natural condition, and make himself not only lower than the angels, but even less than men; so as to say, "I am a worm and no man" (Psalm 22).

Besides, you ought to consider that Jesus Christ being what he was, regarded all human grandeur with sovereign contempt. Finally, you ought not to forget that though Jesus Christ infinitely abased himself, yet the vail or the cloud wherewith he covered himself, was at no time so thick but that there were some rays of the supreme dignity of his person always appearing. Accordingly, at the same time that he was born in a stable, a new star appeared, the angels made the air resound with their songs, and the Magi came to adore him. Hence too it was that at the time of his baptism, while he submitted to the ministry of his servant, that he might fulfill all righteousness, the heaven was opened above him, the Holy Spirit descended in the form of a dove, and the Father rendered to him this glorious testimony, "This is my beloved Son, in whom I am well pleased."

9TH OBJECTION

"But is it conceivable that a God should die? That the Son of God should have been crucified?"

This I confess, is not only the stumbling-block to the Jews, as we have already said, but also foolishness to the Greek. "What folly," exclaimed the Pagans, "To believe in one crucified? To expect life from one dead, and salvation from a man who could not save himself? Weakness, condemnation, misery, and infamy! Are these the true characters of a God?" "Many strange tales," they add, "Are told of our deities, that they descended upon earth, engaged in combats, and that they have there even shed their blood; but we never yet heard that they were dead. Indeed, they tell us that some have died that they might become gods; but that those who had been already received into the number of gods should be subject to death, this is what we have no example of, nor can our reason admit it. Add to this, the kind of death: to die as a slave, to die upon a cross; how disgraceful!"

But it is easy here to confute the Gentile, as we have elsewhere confuted the Jew:

1. It is not any difficulty to conceive how Jesus Christ could die, after it has been once established as a truth that he became man. Since therefore we have made it appear that Jesus Christ could unite himself with a human nature, it is not difficult to comprehend how, in that nature, the soul could be separated for a time from the body. If we should affirm that the divinity is dead, we would assert an absurdity and a great impiety; but we are very far from using this language. It was only the humanity of Jesus Christ which

was dead, and even of that it was his body alone that remained without vital motion, for three days.

2. The same reasons which rendered it necessary for Jesus Christ to assume our nature, engaged him also to die in it, because the end of his coming was to expiate our sins, which could not be done but by a death most painful, and accompanied with a sense of the wrath of God.

3. The punishment of the cross ought not to cause surprise to the Gentiles, for the most wise of their philosophers has determined that: "As of all wicked men, he would be the most wicked who should have the art to cover so well his wickedness, as that he might pass for a good man, and enjoy by that means all the reputation which virtue could confer; so without controversy he should be accounted the most virtuous who should procure to himself by the perfection of his virtue, the jealousy and hatred of all men, insomuch that he should have only his own conscience to befriend him, and should see himself exposed to all sorts of injuries, even to be affixed to a cross, without his virtue being able to afford him the feeble aid to procure exemption from such a punishment."[25] May we not say that God had put these thoughts into the mind of this philosopher, to prepare the Gentiles against being surprised at the cross of Christ?

4. But to silence entirely flesh and blood, and absolutely to confound impiety, reflect, I pray you, on the manner in which Jesus Christ suffered and died. He suffered, indeed, and died, but did it voluntarily, without being under any other force than that of his own love and infinite charity towards men. He had himself foretold his death and sufferings. He died after having been condemned by the Jews, but justified by the conscience of Judas, who killed himself after he had betrayed him; justified by the solemn declaration of Pilate, and by the centurion who was present at his death. How glorious to our Savior that even a conscience the most guilty, and a judge the most unjust, could not withhold a testimony to his innocence! Jesus died, but in

---

[25] Socrates ap. Plat. Dial. I. De Republ.

his death, displayed every moral virtue in the highest degree; more especially an ardent love to his Father; a tender charity towards mankind; an entire submission to the appointments of providence, patience unexampled, and an earnest desire to fulfil his offices and commission in the utmost extent. Jesus died, but at his death all nature was moved. The sun lost his light, the earth trembled, the rocks rent, the graves opened, and the dead arose. Jesus died, but at his death he satisfied divine justice, he supported the rights of deity, expiated sin, triumphed over the devil, shut the gates of hell, opened paradise, swallowed up death in victory, fulfilled the law, reconciled the Creator with the creature, restored peace to the universe, obtained for man the blessing of his God, repaired the breaches which sin had made in nature, and exalted grace infinitely above the limits of nature. Jesus was lifted up upon a cross, but that cross was the instrument of his glory, and of his triumph, rather than of his ignominy and punishment, there triumphing gloriously over principalities and powers.

In fine, Jesus died, but his death ought not to be considered but as the eclipse of the great luminary, the sun; he died, but he rose again illustriously, and ascended to the highest heavens, preceded by a band of celestial spirits, who cried before him, "Lift up your heads, O ye gates, and the King of glory shall enter in!" Collect, I beseech you, all these things together, and you will be obliged to confess that amidst so much humiliation, never was so much glory beheld. There is nothing therefore in this which ought to be an offence unto us.

10TH OBJECTION

But since Jesus Christ has done all these things for redeeming man, let us see whether this mystery of redemption be not contrary to reason: "What;" say they, "Is it likely that God should send his own Son to ransom his creatures, which had so highly offended him?"

I confess that reason would never have been capable of imagining, or discovering anything like this; these are things, "which eye hath not seen, which ear hath not heard, and which had not entered into the heart of any man to conceive;" at the same time I acknowledge that since this mystery has been revealed, reason cannot sufficiently admire it.

All men merited eternal death: yet God was not willing that they should all perish, but it was his will that sin should be punished, and his justice satisfied; he could not do otherwise without being inconsistent with himself. It was necessary therefore that someone should be found who would satisfy for men, and in whom sin might be punished, while men should be spared. But such a one could not be found either among angels or men. Men could die, but they were neither holy nor infinite; angels were holy, but they were neither infinite nor mortal. Of consequence, all mankind must have perished without resource, if God, in his ineffable love, had not sent his own Son, that he might assume human nature, and so be exposed to death. Who can refrain from admiring the wisdom of God in this manner which has discovered this marvelous expedient of pardoning sinners, and yet of punishing sin? Who but must admire his goodness and mercy, who has opened heaven for us, at the very time when we deserved to enter into hell; who has given us a Mediator, and such a Mediator, even none other than his own Son? And at the same time, his inexorable justice against sin, who chose rather that it should be punished in the person of his beloved Son, who had undertaken to suffer for us, than that it should remain unpunished?

"But is it not," you will say, "A thing contrary to reason, and to the justice of God, to make the innocent suffer for the guilty?"

I answer: No, provided that the offence be punished, that he who is made to suffer for the guilty, give his consent to it, without any manner of constraint; that he be master of himself, having power to dispose of his life; that God hereby be more glorified than he would have been by the punishment of the criminal, and that a greater good should thence result to the world. Under these conditions, there is nothing in the least contrary, either to reason, or the divine justice, in making the innocent to suffer for the guilty; but it is also evident that this could never have taken place except in the case of our Lord Jesus. Sin was punished in his person, and his sufferings had an infinite virtue. He presented himself voluntarily to his Father, to die in the stead of men. He was master of his own life: "No man," said he, "taketh it from me, but I lay it down of myself; I have power to lay it down, and power to take it again." God also was infinitely glorified by the death of this divine Savior; and this has procured to mankind, benefits innumerable.

11TH OBJECTION

But to pass to another mystery: "How is it conceivable that there is one God in three persons? Is not this a contradiction, to say that there is but one God, and yet that in him there are three?"

I grant, if we said that there is one God only, and that there are three Gods, that there is one essence, and three essences, there would be a contradiction. But the Christian religion says no such thing; it only affirms that the Father, Son, and Holy Spirit, are but one God; that they are distinguished in reality, but not in respect of essence. Here then there is not one essence and three essences; one God and three Gods; which would be contradictory.

The Jews ought not to condemn the Christian religion on account of this mystery, for the Christians maintain, as well as the Jews, that there is but one God; and they affirm nothing of the Father, Son, and Spirit, which was not affirmed by the prophets.

What makes so many to rise up against this mystery is, firstly, because they reason concerning the divine essence, as they do of human nature; not considering that the divine essence is infinite, whereas human nature is finite. Secondly, because they take the term *person*, which divines have been under a necessity of using (through the want of others) in the same sense which it bears in ordinary language, in which three persons denote three essences; whereas they ought to consider that this is not the meaning or sentiment of those who use this expression, seeing as they declare that they acknowledge but one essence in God. Thirdly, *in fine*, they want to have that explained which God has concealed from men. They would be told what it is which distinguishes the Father, Son, and Holy Spirit, seeing as they are the same essence. This is what God has not revealed, and which the understanding of man cannot discover.

There are three things which make me to receive this mystery with submission, although I cannot comprehend it: 1. Because the Divinity is a subject so grand and sublime, that we ought not in the least to be surprised that we cannot reach unto the height of it by our feeble conceptions; and we receive many things in nature, which we as little comprehend as this mystery. 2. Because I see this mystery revealed in a religion which has all the characters of being divine. 3. What persuades still more is that this mystery is so strictly connected with all the rest, insomuch that it may be said to be as it were interwoven with all the parts which compose the body of the Christian religion. For it would be impossible rightly to explain either redemption, or justification, or sanctification, or adoption, without introducing into that explication the three divine persons, and their several economies.

12TH OBJECTION

"But how is it conceivable that the Father has begotten a Son, and that the Son is eternal as the Father? Is not this a contradiction?"

It would be one, I grant, if the word *generation* were to be taken in the sense wherein it is ordinarily used, in which it implies division, separation, and inequality. But we must conceive nothing like this here. For clearing this, I desire you would make this general remark, namely: that when we employ the same expressions with respect to God, which we use in speaking of men, we ought first to remove from God whatever imperfection these words may carry in them. In *generation*, I conceive a communication of nature. I do not see that this implies any imperfection. I thus attribute it unto God.[26] But I regard as an imperfection in the generation of creatures that the effect should be separated from the cause, and that what is begotten should be posterior to that which begets it. Wherefore the Christian religion ascribes not to God a generation of this sort, but a generation wherein the Father and the Son are never the one without the other.

Although I am persuaded that the mystery of the generation of the Son has nothing like it in nature; yet do we not behold in nature effects which exist at the same time with their causes? God is called a light, and Jesus Christ is named the brightness of his glory. But brightness is as ancient as the light which produces it; and as the splendor or brightness takes nothing from the light from whence it proceeds, as it neither alters it, nor diminishes it, nor even is separated from it; so Jesus Christ was begotten by the Father without alteration, diminution, or division.

If you ask, in what consists this generation, and as to what the procession of the Holy Spirit is, we declare that we know nothing of the one or of the other; because God has not informed us of this. But the ignorance in which we remain as to the manner wherein that generation, and that procession takes place, ought not to determine us to reject the mystery, seeing as we admit many things which we know but very imperfectly. Indeed, it is intolerable pride in man to seek to comprehend all that is asserted concerning God.

---

[26] This mode of expression and explanation, however, is by many reckoned very exceptionable. [*Translator*]

13TH OBJECTION

"But," it is said, "Does not the Christian religion teach a doctrine that deprives man of liberty? For it asserts that nothing comes to pass in the world but what God has foreseen. If this is the case, how can we act freely?"

For answer to this difficulty, I ask those who urge it, whether they can deny that God has foreseen all things. They cannot oppose this truth without falling into extravagance, for if it be true that God has not foreseen all things, then he is not possessed of infinite knowledge, and by consequence is not God. It will also follow that sometime hereafter, God will be more perfect than he is now, because he will know that which he had not formerly known. What then is in the doctrine taught in the Christian religion that should cause perplexity?

But they add, "It is impossible to reconcile the liberty of man with this opinion." Although it should be so, ought we therefore to deny the doctrine? Is it not a maxim of good sense that one should never deny a truth, under pretence that he cannot see how it consists with some other known truth? Reason tells us that God knows all things; we perceive that when we act, we act freely. These are two incontestable truths which must be admitted, namely: that nothing comes to pass which was not foreseen by God; and that notwithstanding we are still free agents; although we should not embarrass ourselves by attempting to reconcile these two together.

14TH OBJECTION

"But what shall we say of the mystery of election and reprobation? May not this consequence be fairly deduced from it: that it is vain for a person to be at pains about his salvation, seeing as if one is elected and predestinated unto salvation, though he should live the most disorderly life in the world, he should be saved; and on the contrary, if one is not elected, let him do what he will, he would be damned."

None who examine well what the Christian religion teaches, will ever deduce such a consequence. It asserts indeed that God has predestinated a certain number of persons to glory; but it asserts at the same time that God will not bestow that glory but on those who are diligently employed in their sanctification;[27] and that without holiness, no man can ever see the face of God. For any to imagine that a predestinated person may be saved, do what he will, is a gross error. Paul was foreordained unto salvation, but if he had always continued a persecutor, he could never have been saved. David was one of the elect, but if he had always lived in flagitious crimes, he would have been damned. Even so, if it were a thing possible that a man who is not elected should live in continual sanctity, he would infallibly obtain salvation.

15TH OBJECTION

"But does not the Christian religion say that we are justified by grace through faith, without works? What is this, but giving occasion to men to say, Let us sin that grace may abound?"

No, my brethren, the Christian religion which teaches that we are justified by faith without works, directs us also to justify our faith by our works, and declares that without works faith is dead, and cannot save us. So very far from savoring sin, by the doctrine of justification, it gives us a just horror at it, by representing to us that God could not justify us without condemning his own Son, and exposing him to all the tokens of his vengeance. At the same time that it announces to us the pardon of our crimes, it enjoins us, not to let sin reign in our mortal body, seeing we are under grace; to crucify our flesh, to renounce our lusts, and to live in this

---

[27] *Qu'à condition qu'ils travailleront à leur sanctification.*

present world in sobriety, righteousness and godliness, looking for the blessed appearance of our great God, and Saviour Jesus Christ. Is this to savor sin?

16TH OBJECTION

But they will still continue to say, "Who would not be shocked at a religion which deprives men of courage by requiring them to suffer all sort of injuries, rather than avenge themselves; which obliges us to offer violence to our passions, deprives us of all our pleasures, and speaks of nothing but of sufferings and crosses; and which even threatens us with pains eternal to plunge us in despair?"

It is not needful to stay long in confuting such reasonings. Those who make use of them are convinced that they are impious. What! Allege that the Christian religion deprives us of courage! It is that which teaches and enables men to endure the greatest punishments, and to brave death itself unappalled. It is true that it requires us to forgive our enemies; but must not a man possess a greater fortitude of mind to pardon than to take revenge?

It obliges us, they say, to do violence to our inclinations, and to deny ourselves. But examine what it would have us to do: to love supremely the most perfect of all beings, him by whom we subsist, who loads us with benefits, and who prepares for us an eternal glory. It directs us to love one another, for the love of God. It proposes to our hope infinite blessings. It obliges us to fear him who can cast our bodies and our souls into hell. Is this to do violence to our inclinations? I grant that it is to oblige us to renounce our criminal passions; but it is also instructing us to make a right use of those which are natural.

It deprives us, they complain, of all sorts of pleasures. But why? Is it to deprive us of all pleasure, to produce in our souls a joy unspeakable, by assuring us that our sins are pardoned, and that heaven is opened for us?

They are displeased that it should speak to us of sufferings and of crosses. But should any be surprised that it prepares us to be conformable to the Prince of our salvation, to have a part in his triumph, and to be one day seated upon his throne?

They are astonished that it should threaten sinners with eternal pains; but should it be accounted strange that it condemns to infinite or endless punishments those who offend every day an infinite Majesty? Can rebellious creatures be sufficiently punished, who continually offend their Creator, their Preserver, and Benefactor; and who will offend him forever, if they shall never die? Surely not.

There is nothing therefore, contained in the Christian religion, which can make us doubt of its divinity; and this is what we meant to prove.

APPLICATION

After what we have said, my brethren, it only remains that we pray to God with all the ardor of which we are capable, to engrave on our minds and hearts the things which you have been hearing. Truly, I am not surprised that in the beginning of Christianity, there should have been many to set themselves in opposition to the Christian religion; but that at the end of seventeen centuries, there should be so many unbelievers, and that their number should every day be on the increase, is what grieves and affects me in the highest degree.

When I consider the causes of men's incredulity, I find very many. I have already pointed them out in my first sermon; but they cannot be too often repeated.

The first is ignorance, and an aversion to be instructed, through a criminal negligence. They choose neither to read what might dissipate their prejudices; nor consult those who might reclaim them; nor even to examine if their doubts are well founded.

The second is because they read not the Holy Scripture, but rather peruse all manner of bad books.

The third is an unhappy propensity to whatever is new, and an extreme disgust at whatever is common. They only bestow attention on what is levelled against the Christian religion; but listen not to that which may serve for its defence.

The fourth is a root of libertinism. The Christian religion is too much an enemy to criminal pleasures to suit the taste of libertines and debauchees.

The fifth is, an insufferable pride. They choose not to admit anything which they cannot comprehend, nor are disposed to confess their ignorance; as if our understanding were infinite, and capable of everything. They decide as confidently upon that which they know not, as on that which they know. Whenever there is any appearance of a contradiction, they instantly pronounce that the contradiction is real. But especially, they refuse to believe anything incomprehensible in religion, though it should be ever so clearly shown them; that there are, in philosophical truths, which cannot be denied, difficulties as great as those which puzzle them in the mysteries of godliness. They choose rather not to believe anything of those mysteries, than to acknowledge that they are too high for us. You proud spirits! How long will you exalt yourselves against God? You know not your own selves, and you would know God perfectly! You have but a very imperfect knowledge of your own soul, which is finite; and you want to have a perfect comprehension of a spirit uncreated and infinite!

The sixth cause of the incredulity of men is the fond desire which they have to distinguish themselves in the world, to pass for free thinkers, and persons above the vulgar. It is this cursed passion which has made, and which will still make so many heretics; which has produced, and which will still produce to the end of time an infinity of errors, both in philosophy, and religion.

The seventh is that they rather seek to associate with those persons who are capable of corrupting them, than those who might edify them, and establish them in the truth.

The last cause is they have not recourse to God, to ask faith from him, and to beseech him to impress heavenly truths upon their hearts.

There are some who say that they would wish very much to believe. But, what do they in order to this? "Faith is the gift of God," but they never request this of him. "Faith cometh by hearing, and hearing by the word of God;" but these persons neither read nor hear his word. Jesus Christ says in his gospel; "He that doeth the will of God his father, shall know his doctrine:" and David said that "The secret of the Lord is with them that fear him." How then should God give the knowledge of his mysteries to those who fear him not, and who have their heart more set upon satisfying their passions, than on doing the will of their heavenly Father?

"What then must be done," do you ask, "That we may not be of the number of these miserable unbelievers!"

We must ask of God continually that he may grant to us that the eyes of our understanding may be enlightened, and give us his Holy Spirit of wisdom and revelation. We must beseech him to produce in us that faith, without which it is impossible to please him; and that he would "help our unbelief;" that he would mortify our flesh, subdue our pride, and lead all our thoughts captive to the obedience of his Word.

Nor should we be satisfied with having made this prayer once; but we must renew it constantly, and knock at the gate of heaven, until it be opened unto us. We must hear his word, read it with care, meditate upon it, without ceasing; for it is by this that faith is not only produced, but it is also the food of faith, by which it is nourished and increased. We must also have recourse to and consult such as can inform our mind; and read the books which may help us to understand the heavenly truths. We must examine, in good earnest, and with application, if the difficulties which we raise against the Christian religion, can counterbalance so many proofs as we have of the truth of this religion. We must consider if it be not our pride, our libertinism, our sloth, the love which we have for novelty, or the desire of distinguishing ourselves, which carries us into these pernicious sentiments. I am persuaded that if we were all accustomed to act in this manner, the number of unbelievers would not be seen to multiply.

My brethren, if there be anyone among us who hath an evil heart of unbelief, we earnestly entreat him to bethink himself, and to reflect on these emphatic words of the gospel: "He that believeth on the Son hath eternal life; but he that believeth not, the wrath of God abideth on him."

As for you, Christians, who are persuaded of the heavenly truths, live as persons who feel the influence of these truths. It is not sufficient to believe that there is a God, if persons live as atheists do. It is not enough to believe that Jesus Christ is come to save penitent sinners. If a person does not in reality repent, in vain does he hope for anything from him. It is not enough to believe that he came to destroy sin, and to make atonement for it; if a man suffer sin to reign in his mortal body, he shall not escape condemnation. It is not enough to believe that he rose again; he that has no desire of rising again in newness of life, and to leave the tomb of his vices, has nothing to look for but extreme misery and woe. It is not sufficient to know and believe that he will come to judge men; such as are not preparing themselves for this judgment, by a holy life, have reason to dread the lake of fire and brimstone, which is the second death.

The faith whereby we are saved is not a historical faith, but a faith working by love; a faith which purifies us, and by which we are sanctified. Let us all request of God this faith; and that he may daily increase it in us, that so, believing with the heart unto righteousness, we may be always ready to make confession with the mouth unto salvation. The day will come when we shall no longer walk by faith, but by sight: a day in which all our doubts shall be dispelled, and we shall see God face to face; and in contemplating his glory, we shall be rendered like unto him. Amen.

THE 4TH DISCOURSE

THE

ROMISH RELIGION

EXAMINED;

THE FOURTH SERMON,

On 1 Thessalonians 5:21

Prove all things.

The prophet Daniel informs us in the second chapter of his revelations that King Nebuchadnezzar had a dream which greatly troubled him. He dreamed that he saw a great image, "the head of which was of pure gold; the breast and the arms of silver, the belly and thighs of brass, the legs of iron, and the feet part of iron, and part of clay." It cannot be doubted but that this prodigious image represented the four great monarchies which should succeed one another. This is the interpretation which Daniel gave of it, to that great monarch; and the learned believe that the head of gold denoted the empire of the Babylonians, which surpassed in glory and magnificence, all the kingdoms of the earth; that the breast and arms of silver signified the empire of the Medes and Persians, which would not yield to that of the Babylonians in greatness, power, and riches, but which should be less happy, and sooner come to a period; that the belly and thighs of brass designed the empire of Alexander the Great, and the Greeks; lastly, that the legs of iron, and the feet, partly of iron and partly of clay, represented the Roman monarchy, or the empire of the successors of Alexander, who were before the birth of Jesus Christ, the last and the most cruel persecutors of the people of God.[28]

But may we not at this time be allowed to seek for another mystery in this image, and to say that it was a very beautiful and expressive emblem of the Christian religion. In the beginning, during the apostolic age, this religion was purer than gold, or the beams of the sun itself. An ancient writer says that the church was then a virgin.[29] But after the decease of the blessed disciples of the Lord Jesus, and in the ages which followed, this religion suffered great changes. The gold was seen mixed, not only with silver, but also with brass, iron, and clay; that is, the good doctrine with vain traditions, and gross and pernicious errors. Hence arose those numerous sects which divided, and still divide, the Christian world, which tear one another, and hold sentiments so very opposite. Amidst these sects, the faithful, who know that persons cannot be saved in all religions, and who are desirous to

---

[28] Some suppose that the Babylonian empire is marked by the head of gold, because the Chaldeans greatly loved this precious metal, or because this empire was very rich, or because it should be of longer duration than the rest.

It is believed that the empire of the Persians and Medes is marked by the breast and arms of silver, because of the reunion of these two kingdoms with that of the Chaldeans in the same political body.

The Alexandrian or Grecian empire, it is thought, is denoted by brass, to signify that it was worse than the second, and as different from that of the Persians, as brass is from silver; or to intimate that it would break all by the force of its arms, because in ancient times, the best arms were made of brass.

The empire of the Romans is called a kingdom of iron, because as iron breaks all to pieces, so the Romans should destroy the three preceding monarchies. That mixture of iron and clay, pointed out the division and different factions of the state, its weakness or its strength; and that this empire, though solid as iron, should be often weakened by the inundation of Barbarians, and by the revolt and insurrection of different people, who wearied of the Roman yoke, should appoint to themselves kings. The empire of the successors of Alexander might also be called an empire of iron, because it was no otherwise established than by violence, and because it had nothing of the ancient splendor of the empires which preceded it. Their kingdom was divided into that of the Seleucidæ, and of the Lagidæ; of which the former is named "the Kings of the North," and the other "Kings of the South" (Daniel 11).

[29] Hegesippus, who was born in the beginning of the II. century, and who was the first author who composed a body of ecclesiastical history, of which we have now only some fragments remaining, which Eusebius has inserted in his history.

promote their salvation, find themselves not a little embarrassed to know on what side they ought to range themselves; and they could never extricate themselves from this embarrassment, if God had not afforded them the means of distinguishing the gold from the brass, the iron, the earth, the hay, and the stubble. It is with a view to engage all of us to employ this means, that Paul addresses these words to us at this time: *Prove all things.*

In the last discourse which we had upon these words, we proved to you that there is nothing which should make us to doubt of the divinity of the Christian religion. We are already come a great length, if we are assured of the truth of the Christian religion, but we must not stop here; for we are surrounded on all hands with people who call themselves Christians, and who notwithstanding fight together, and even damn one another. It is therefore necessary to examine what is that communion where one may find the pure Christianity which Jesus Christ and his apostles have taught. This is the task in which we are now about to engage, and in it we have need of the aid of your holy prayers.

It is not our design, however, to examine all the sects which have been, or are yet subsisting in the world. This would prove an endless task. There are many of them which have made a noise in the world, which yet ought not to be considered as Christian sects, and of which the sentiments have been so very extravagant that one can hardly believe that there have been persons so mad as to maintain them, as the sect of the disciples of Simon the magician; the sects of the Basilidians and Gnostics, the Valentinians, the Ophites, the Cainites, and the Sethians; with those of a Marcion, a Montanus, and a Manes. There are others which, after they had been in a manner extinct, are revived again in these last ages, whose doctrines we will have sufficient occasion to refute.[30]

---

[30] Laelius Socinus, in the year 1525, and Faustus his nephew afterwards, renewed, with regard to the divinity of Jesus Christ, the errors which had been taught in the 1st century, by Cerinthus and Ebion; in the 2nd by Theodotus and Artemon; in the 3rd, by Paul of Samosata, condemned in two councils of Antioch in 264 and in 272; and in the 4th century, by Photinus, condemned also in certain councils. Others have

We shall confine ourselves, at present, to the three Communions which are most numerous and flourishing, namely:

- The Romish Communion;
- The Greek Communion;
- The Communion of Protestants.

But before we enter into the subject, it is necessary to put you in mind of what we advanced, in our first discourse upon these words: that God has given us a rule by which we may examine whatever doctrines are taught; and that this rule is the holy Scripture. This is the divine fire whereby we may and ought to examine all things, which makes the pure gold to shine, and which consumes all the rest. Therefore, in order to judge of these three religions, we must put them all into the crucible of the Word of God, if I may be allowed the expression, and that which will endure this proof, will be the true.

It is true, the Roman communion—in order to discern the true religion from others—would have us to follow the way of authority, and not that of examination; and wishes that we should even submit ourselves to its own particular authority. But this is to desire us to choose, before we know what ought to be chosen; and that we should follow one of the Christian communions, as true, before we can know that it is true. It is nothing else than bidding us judge that the communion of the church of Rome ought to be preferred to all others, upon the authority of that communion; and that we should be persuaded that it is reasonable to do so, merely because she says so. Is there any justice in such procedure? Certainly not. Without having

---

renewed the errors of Sabellius, who lived in the 3rd century, and who affirmed that the three persons of the most holy Trinity were only names. Others have done the same as to those of Arius, presbyter of Alexandria, who in the 4th century maintained that Jesus Christ was but a creature, etc. Others have adopted the errors of the Semi-Arians, who said that the Son had not the very same essence with the Father, but one like it. Valentine Gentilis, in the last age, has revived the error of Philoponus, who lived in the 6th century, and who asserted that there were three gods. And it is sufficiently known that, with respect to the subject of grace, Pelagius, who appeared in the beginning of the 5th age, or at least Cassian, has still many followers.

any regard then to such a pretension, let us follow the way of enquiry, which we believe to be the most sure, and at the same time the most easy. We know that whatever the Scripture teaches us is true, but we are far from being assured that all that the church of Rome teaches must be true; we have even very strong reasons to doubt it.

Moreover, in order to be assured of the true sense of Scripture, in things necessary to salvation, and that we may know whether it contain a doctrine proposed to us, we have only to read it with attention, and to compare the passages one with another, after having implored the aid of the Spirit of God. "It offers itself to all," said Gregory, "And accommodates itself to all. In it there is a simplicity, which descends to the lowest understanding; as well as a sublimity, which exercises and elevates the highest. All may draw from thence without distinction; yet, so very far from exhausting it by filling ourselves, we always leave therein deeps of knowledge and wisdom, which we may add without being able to comprehend. But what ought to console us in this obscurity is that the holy Scripture, according to St. Augustine, sets before us, in a manner, easy and intelligible, whatever is necessary for the conduct of our life; it explains and illustrates itself, by declaring clearly in some places what it expresses obscurely in others." Thus spake he, whom they style in the church of Rome, a saint, and Pope, Gregory the Great; and many in that church, have often, after him, spoken the same language concerning the Scripture.[31]

The same thing cannot be said of the doctrine of the Romish church. In order to know that, it is needful first to read the canons of Councils, where it is pretended, she has deposited her creed. For it is not sufficient for this, to

---

[31] The author of the translation of the New Testament of Mons, quoted this passage, after he had said, speaking of his version, "It is hoped that not only those whose minds are more enlightened, but even the most simple may find therein that which will be necessary for their instruction, providing they read it in an entire simplicity of heart, and betake themselves humbly to the Son of God, saying to him with St. Peter: "Lord to whom shall we go? Thou only hast the words of eternal life; and thou alone canst make us understand them.""

consult her pastors and her bishops, seeing as it is universally agreed that they may err. If the canons of councils are not sufficiently clear, but are so ambiguous that the meaning of those who composed them cannot certainly be gathered from them, we must, in waiting for a new council, either to search the Scripture for that which ought to be believed, which is what we plead for; or else read the fathers, and the other councils, which is an endless course, that leads to no issue; a way of such excessive and tiresome length, that a person can never find the end of it, whatever diligence he may use;[32] or, we must remain in suspense. For one ought not to content himself with the explication which bishops might give of these obscure canons, for it may very well happen that they may deceive us, by teaching their private sentiments.[33] If the canons are clear, it will be further necessary for the satisfaction of conscience to examine whether the church of Rome be infallible, as is believed, and if her infallibility resides in the pope or in councils; but in order to [make] such an enquiry, it will be needful not only to read the Scripture, but also the history of the church, to know whether the popes have ever erred, or whether the councils have been infallible. Why take all this trouble? Would it not be better to consult the Scripture alone, which is a rule infallible, to see if the doctrines proposed be contained in it. If they be taught therein, without hesitation let them be received. If they are not to be found there, or if truths may there be discovered contrary to these opinions, let them be rejected. "To the law, then, and to the testimony," my brethren; to the Scripture alone. Let us see what the Lord has spoken. This is our only rule. Let us examine and prove all things by it; and let us begin by the examination of the Romish religion.

---

[32] This is what the author of the book entitled *Prejugez contre les Calvinistes* has said very impertinently of the Scripture, but which may be safely, and with better reason, be affirmed of the writings of the ancient doctors.

[33] It is something remarkable that the Bull of Pope Pius IV, which contains a confirmation of the Council of Trent, expressly forbids all sorts of persons, of whatever order, or dignity they may be in the church, the Pope alone excepted, to explain the decrees of the council, in any manner, or under any pretence whatever.

In the prosecution of our design, we intend not to stay in examining the doctrines wherein the Romish religion agrees with that of Protestants; we shall confine ourselves to those which are peculiar to that religion, and proceed in the following manner:

First, we shall hear the Scripture upon the articles in which the Romish church differs from the Reformed; and shall compare what that sacred book says with that which Rome says upon these subjects; and we shall take the sentiments of that church, from the Council of Trent, from books of public and daily use, and from the celebrated doctors of that communion, and from constant practice therein. For we think it would not be fair and just to consult only certain private doctors, who sometimes carry things too far, or who represent them only in disguise.[34]

Secondly, we shall then answer to the principal objections, which the church of Rome produces in favour of her religion.

I. Of the subject of Invocation

When we consult the Scripture upon the head of worship and invocation, we find:

1. That we are neither commanded nor counseled in it to address any religious prayer to another than God; and even to express praying to God, it sometimes reckons it sufficient to use only the simple expression, *to pray*,[35] from whence this consequence should be drawn, that since "Whatever is not of faith is sin," and as faith is founded on the Word of God, that none can,

---

[34] "These pretended expositions of faith," says F. Maimbourg in his *History of Lutheranism*, "which suppress or dissemble, or which do not express, except in terms ambiguous, or too soft, a part of the doctrine of the church, give no satisfaction, either to the one or the other side; but both equally complain that there should be any trimming or shuffling in a matter so delicate as faith, in which one cannot fail in one point without offending in all."

[35] Luke 11:1, Matthew 6:6, Romans 8:25, and 10:17

without sin, invoke any other but God, seeing in no part of Scripture has God enjoined, or intimated his will, or declared it to be agreeable to him that any other besides him should be called upon.

2. The Scripture says further that God alone must be adored and served: "Thou shalt worship the Lord thy God, and him only shalt thou serve."[36] These are the words of Jesus Christ to the devil who tempted him. "Put away the strange gods," said Samuel to the Israelites, "and prepare your hearts unto the Lord, and serve him only."[37] Here it may be noted that the version of the Septuagint makes use of the word from which those of the Roman communion have taken the term of *dulia*, so that to render these words, according to the style of the doctors of that church, they would run thus: "Render to him only the worship of *dulia*," or *service*.

3. Paul informs us that men should call upon him only in whom they believe. "How shall they call on him in whom they have not believed."[38] Whence it appears that as we believe in one God alone, the Father, Son, and Holy Spirit, and as Jeremiah pronounces the man accursed "who trusteth in man," we ought to invoke none other than God.

4. Moreover, Paul, speaking of the idolatrous Galatians, says that "when they knew not God, they served those which by nature were no gods,"[39] where the word *dulia* is again employed: from whence we draw this conclusion, that it is idolatry to render the worship of service (*dulia*) to those which by their nature are not gods, which comprehend all creatures whatever. For the teacher of the Gentiles blames not the Galatians for having served the false gods of Paganism, either because they were demons, or because they were men, or because they were creatures destitute of reason, but because these objects of their adoration were not gods "by nature."

---

[36] Matthew 4:10
[37] 1 Samuel 7:3
[38] Romans 10:14
[39] Galatians 4:8

5. The same apostle exhorts us to beware lest any man beguile us by the religious service of angels, affirming that those who practice such worship hold not the head, which is Jesus Christ: "Let no man beguile you of your reward, in a voluntary humility, and worshipping of angels, intruding into those things which he has not seen, vainly puffed up by his fleshly mind, and not holding the head."[40]

6. *In fine*, the apostle John informs us that an angel, once and again, forbade him to worship him: "See thou do it not, I am thy fellow servant and of thy brethren the prophets, and of those who keep the sayings of this book: Worship God."[41]

Such is the doctrine of Scripture with regard to the object of our worship and invocation; and one cannot read it without remarking that invocation is reckoned a spiritual sacrifice, which constitutes a principal part of the adoration which is ascribed unto God. Let us examine next by this rule, what the church of Rome practises, and what she believes as to this matter.

She says in the Council of Trent that: "It is good and useful to invoke, in a suppliant manner, the saints which reign with Jesus Christ."[42] She believes then that it is good and useful to do what God has not commanded, for though the Scripture says well that we ought to honor the memory of saints, praise their faith and zeal, imitate their virtues, and follow their steps, yet it nowhere says that we ought to invoke them.

She also condemns those who maintain that we ought not to pray to saints; therefore she condemns those who hold fast with Paul that gospel which has been preached unto us.

She believes that the worship of *latria* must be given to God; the worship of *dulia* to the saints, and that of *hyperdulia* to the blessed virgin. She

---

[40] Colossians 2:18-19
[41] Revelation 19:10 & 22:9
[42] "Bonum atque utile esse sanctos una cum Christo regnantes suppliciter invocare." Sess. 25. Concili. Trid. "Illos vero qui negant sanctos aeternae felicitatis in caelo fruentes invocandos esse, etc. impie sentire." Bell. de Sanct. Beat. 6. l. c. 12.

is therefore guilty of that which Samuel forbad to the Israelites. She renders the worship of *dulia* to another than God, and of that which Paul blamed in the Galatians. She renders the same worship to those which by nature are not gods, to say nothing of the distinction which they have devised, which is altogether groundless.[43]

She addresses prayers not only to God, but also to the blessed virgin, and the saints; and that without having any assurance whether they know our necessities, or if they can hear our supplications; consequently, she holds that persons may invoke those in whom they do not believe, contrary to what Paul has said; she puts her confidence in some other than God, and hereby subjects herself to the malediction of Jeremiah.

She appoints requests to be made to saints, and the holy virgin, for things which cannot be obtained, nor ought to be demanded, except from God, or Jesus Christ our Mediator; such as that they would not only have pity on us, but also that they would defend us, and receive us at the hour of death; that they would enlighten the blind, free the guilty from their dismal chains, break the fetters of sin which oppress us, conduct us to a happy eternity, render us pure, humble, and meek, bestow on us a chaste heart, and escort us safe in the way to heaven.[44]

---

[43] The words *dulia* and *latria* signify the same thing; and if we pay attention to the force of the terms, the word *dulia* is stronger than the other which they appropriate to the Supreme being. It is an error to believe that any kind of religious worship can be ascribed to the creature. It is true that Augustine makes use of this distinction; but he distinguishes not religious worship into that of *dulia* and *latria*. He only says that the religious worship which is paid unto God is called *latria*; and that *dulia* denotes the service which is rendered unto men, as which servants give unto their masters. Augustine *City of God*, B10 C1.

[44] The above, with other articles following, relating to the popish doctrine and worship, the author confirms by a number of quotations from their offices of devotion, and other authorities, in which we do not think it necessary literally to follow him. We shall select only some of the quotations at length, and barely refer to the others. [*Translator*]

The following passages are found in the office of the church, printed at Paris, in 1677, and dedicated to the king:

Maria mater gratie,
Mater misericordie,

In that communion, they invoke the holy virgin as the life, the hope, the only hope, and refuge of sinners,[45] the mother of grace and of mercy. They say of the apostles that they "penetrate the midnight darkness of men's hearts;" that "heaven is opened and shut at their voice;" and they beg to be "delivered from their sins, by their command."[46]

From whence it appears that the Romish church parts the worship, which is due only to God, between him and the creature, which is a striking character of a false religion, as we said in our first sermon. It is no less evident that they impose upon us when they tell us that they demand nothing more of the saints but that they would pray for us.[47]

Tu nos ab hoste protege
p. 128.
– *Solve vincula reis*
Profer lumen caceis,
Mala nostra pelle.
p. 153.
Virgo singularis –
Nos culpils solutos
Mites fac et castos
Vitam praesla puram,
Iter para tutum
Ut videntes Jesum
Semper collateuntur.
p. 500.
[45] These are the express words of the Roman Breviary.
[46] In the same office of the virgin, the apostles are thus addressed:
Vos saeci justi judicis –
Votis precamur cordium,
Audite preces supplicium
Qui caelum verbo clauditis,
Serasque ejus solvitis,
Nos a peccatis omnibus,
Solvite jussu quaesumus,
Quorum praecepto subditur,
Salus et languor omnia,
Sanate regros moribus,
Nos reddentes virtutibus.
(page 125)
[47] The celebrated Bishop of Meaux, in his *Exposition* (p.19) quotes these words of the Council of Trent: "We pray God, either to bestow blessings on us, or to deliver us

That church approves of this form of address to the holy virgin, that she would make use of the right of a mother, which she has over her Son, by *commanding* him."[48]

She consecrates churches, chapels, and altars, festival days, monasteries, and religious societies, in name and to the honor of saints. She places their images upon altars; puts persons, families, cities, and whole kingdoms under their protection; she celebrates the sacrifice of the mass in their honor; and burns incense before them; she joins the saints with God, almost every day, in her prayers, thanksgivings, confession of sins, and when any threatenings

---

from evils; but because the saints are more agreeable to him than we are, we ask them to undertake our defence, and obtain for us the things that we need. Hence it is that we use two forms of prayer very different; in speaking to God, the proper manner of address is, *Have mercy on us, hear us*, whereas we content ourselves with saying to the saints, *Pray for us*."

[48] Thus in the missal of Paris, and others:

O Faelix puerpera
Nostra pians scelera
Jure matris impera
Redemptori –

So in an old hymn, much used, Mary, though choosing to call herself the servant of Jesus Christ, is said to be his lawful lady, who has by right and reason, authority over her Son:

"*Gaude Matrona caelica!*
Tu ancillam Jesu Christi
Te vocari voluisti,
Sed ut docet lex divina,
Tu illius es Domina
Nam lex jubet et ratio
Matrem praestare filio,
Ergo ora suppliciter,
Et praecipe sublimiter,
Ut nos in mundi vespera
Ad regna ducat suprema."

Vid. Hymn. Par. ann 1677, p. 499. Et Stellar. Censoriae B. Virg. L12 Part 1. So Cardinal Damian represents the Virgin Mary as presenting herself before the tribunal of the divine Majesty, *non rogans, sed imperans; domina, non ancilla*: "not praying but commanding; as a mistress, not as a servant."

are denounced.[49] Therefore it is not true that she addresses prayers to glorified saints "in the same spirit of charity, and according to that order of brotherly society, which leads us to demand the help of our brethren, which are on the earth."[50] For it has not yet come into the mind of any to invoke the saints here below in the manner they do those in heaven; to build temples to them, and call them by their names; to raise altars for them, prostrate themselves at their feet, to make devout supplications to them, consecrate festival days, and celebrate the missal sacrifice in their honor.

Further, that church gives her approbation to books, wherein such things are spoken to the virgin Mary and the saints, as strike with horror those who read them; such as, the Psalter of Cardinal Bonaventure, which has been so often printed with authentic approbations, wherein that which David speaks of God, is applied to the holy virgin.[51]

---

[49] In praying, the *Pater noster* is scarcely ever repeated, without adding an *Ave Maria*. When people are in any danger, or at the point of death, they are taught and accustomed to cry, "Jesus Mary!" In confession this form is used: "I confess to God, to the virgin, to the apostles, and to all the saints of Paradise." The pope concludes all his bulls with the menacing sanction of "the displeasure of God, of St. Peter, and St. Paul."

So abundant has their devotion been to these false objects, that it has even far exceeded what they have rendered to the Deity. Erasmus scrupled not to say that: "Their very preachers worshipped the virgin with more religion, than they did Christ himself or his Holy Spirit." *Eccles.* B2. Others have observed that: "For one prayer put up to God there were ten offered to the Virgin Mary." Sandy's *Europ. Speculum* (pp. 4-5). In one church we have sometimes an account of no less than five altars dedicated to her service; which have been called the "spring of all graces to them that call on her name." *Chron. Deip. in Olysse's *Madness of Dissatisfaction*, etc., p. 218. The English reader may find a great variety of like instances and proofs of what is here charged on the church of Rome, in the book last quoted, or in Brevint's *Soul and Samuel at Endor*; or in *Tracts against Popery*, Fol. v. 2. and many others which might be named. [*Translator*]

[50] Bossuet, *Exposit.* p.17

[51] In this the words of the 51st Psalm are applied to her, "Have mercy upon me, O our Lady, who art called the mother of mercy: according to the bowels of thy compassions, cleanse me from mine iniquities." So also the words of the 68th Psalm, "Arise, Mary," etc., and the language of the 110th Psalm, "The Lord said unto our lady, sit thou at my right hand." Who can read such things without trembling? A fraternity was instituted under the name of *The Fraternity of the Mary Psalter*, which was confirmed by Sixtus IV. Though some blasphemies were expunged from this

On the other hand, she censures the books which are designed to confine within some limits the extravagant devotion of the people.[52]

I might here also produce what those who composed the *Expurgatory Index*, by order of the council of Trent, have done, in retrenching, from the works of Augustine, the following words, in his book of the *True Religion*, that: "The saints are to be honored by imitation, and not by adoration;" as

---

psalm-book after the Reformation, yet abundance of them were retained in the Italian editions of last century, as "Cleanse me, O Lady;" "Thou, O lady, art the beginning and end of my salvation." *Salmi di S. Bonav. Genoa*, 1606. Nay, a whole Bible has been consecrated for her honor, in which they scruple not to insert here in the place of that God or Christ, as in Proverbs 8:15. "By her kings reign"; Matthew 28:18. "All power is given to me in heaven and on earth." Philippians 2:9; "God hath highly exalted her, and given her a name above every name, etc." [*Translator*]

There are many other books equally impious; as the Stellarium Coronac B Virg., the writings of one Coster, of Alexis de Salo, a capuchin; of the Jesuit Salazar, of Bernardin de Bustis' father Crasset, etc., which contain such horrible impieties, as "that God made a decree to confer his grace on none, but through the intercession of Mary; that all things are subject to the command of the Virgin, even God himself: That we ought roundly and without hesitation to assert with Arnaud of Chartres, and Richard of S. Laurence, that she is able to do all that her Son can do, because the Son and the mother having but the same flesh, possess indivisibly the same power, the Son by nature, and the mother by grace: That the quality of mother of God renders her worthy of adoration; that the angels adore the Virgin, and adored her even before she came into the world." etc.

[52](r) They have censured the book entitled, *Salutary advices of the Virgin Mary to her Indirect Devotees*; in which the author blames those "who render homage to the virgin as an inferior divinity, and who believe that without her none can approach to God, even by Jesus Christ." He thinks it sufficient to say, "Holy Mary, mother of God, supply thy praises before the Almighty, what my weakness cannot give him, and obtain for me, of your well-beloved, grace, etc. He makes her speak thus: "Let not your heart be divided, so as to love me, without loving God, on whose account alone you ought to love me: I pretend not to take any thing away from God, nor to enter into partnership with him: God, who is infinitely good, demands all your love, and demands all your love, and would possess entire your heart." Who would have believed that such a book would have fallen under their condemnation? Yet it was censured at Rome, and in Spain, as containing propositions suspected of error, impieties, and abuse of Scripture; and as drawing away the faithful from piety and devotion to the mother of God, from the invocation of her, and from the veneration of images."

also this passage from Athanasius: "That adoration belongs alone to God, and no creature whatsoever ought to be adored."[53]

I might likewise mention the adoration which they pay to the pope, after he has been elected, when he is placed upon the altar.

But methinks enough has been already adduced to prove that the church of Rome, in the matter of invocation, has entirely forsaken the way marked out for us in the Holy Scripture, and consequently, that she has not, in this article, preserved pure Christianity. None ought to deceive themselves by vainly alleging that the Romish church "terminates all her worship upon God." For besides what we have remarked above, which may be sufficient to show that they palliate and extenuate greatly the worship of that church; even if it were truly the intention of those who make prayers to saints, to terminate their worship on God, is there any reason to think that this good intention could justify such acts? If that were the case, there is no kind of worship so superstitious, as might not be defended. Certainly, all religious worship ought to begin with God, continue with God, and conclude with God, seeing as all religious worship is due unto him; and he cannot approve of that worship which he himself has forbidden.

---

[53] *Ind. Expurg. auct. Gen. Inquisit. Hispan.* In the same *Index*, they order another passage of Augustine on Psalm 113 to be erased: "*Videntur sibi purgatorius esse religionis, qui dicunt, nec simulacrum, nec daemonium colo, sed per effigiem corporale ejus rei signum intueor, quam colere debeo.*" "There are some who fancy themselves to be of a purer religion, who say, I neither worship a graven image, nor daemon, but by the image I perceive a corporal or visible sign of that which I ought to worship." They have done the same with another passage in his book against Maximinus, where he speaks of it as sacrilege to build or to consecrate temples to angels or any creature. Tom. 6. p. 689. *Cont. Max.* The passages blotted out of Athanasius belong to his 3rd discourse against the Arians.

II. Of the Mediation and Intercession of Saints

But as the invocation of saints, by those of the church of Rome, is founded upon their pretended mediation and intercession. Let us next examine what the Scripture says upon this head, and compare it with what the church of Rome teaches. The Scripture tells us that Jesus Christ is "the way, the truth, and the life, and that no man cometh unto the Father but by him." It is Christ himself who says so, that: "Whatsoever ye shall ask the Father in the name of Christ, the Father will give it" (John 16:25); that: "There is but one Mediator, even Jesus Christ;" (1 Timothy 2:5); that if we have sinned, "he is our Advocate with the Father, who hath made atonement for our sins" (1 John 2:1-2); that he is "able to save to the uttermost all that come unto God by him, and that he ever liveth to make intercession for them." (Hebrews 7). And lest we should think that we have need of some other who might conduct us to Jesus Christ, in these Scriptures we hear the voice of the Son of God, calling us, saying, "Come unto me, ye that labour, and are heavy laden, and I will give you rest" (Matthew 11:28). Further, because we may be afraid, lest the Father should become weary of hearing our prayers, and not deign to regard or answer them, the Scripture exhorts us to "persevere in prayer" (Luke 18), and "be careful for nothing" (Philippians 4), for if we who are evil know how to give good gifts to our children, how much more our heavenly Father? (Matthew 7). *In fine*, the Scripture nowhere says that we should have recourse to the intercession and mediation of the saints who are in heaven.

Let us now hear the Romish Church:

She has plainly expressed her sentiments in these words of the Council of Trent that: "It is good and useful to have recourse to the aid, assistance, and prayers of the saints in order to obtain favors from God by Jesus Christ our Lord."[54] She believes then that it is useful to seek another Mediator than Jesus Christ, and to go to the Father by another than him.

She distinguishes between a Mediator of Redemption, and a Mediator of Intercession; and holds that Jesus Christ is the only Mediator of Redemption; but that the saints are Mediators of Intercession.[55] Yet it appears from Scripture that intercession is founded on propitiation, and that it is one of the functions of the priesthood of Jesus Christ: whence it follows that as none but Jesus Christ has made atonement for our sins, so none but he can be our Mediator of intercession.

She also approves that the virgin should be called "the gate of heaven;" and that we should say to God, "We are saved by the intercession of the holy mother of his Son."[56] Judge whether this be language consistent with that of Scripture?

She thinks it right that persons should put their confidence in the intercession of the blessed apostles,[57] which the Scripture has expressly forbidden.

On the festival of All Saints, she would have us pray God, "to grant to men the abundance of favour through the multitude of intercessors with him."[58] Is it possible to derogate more avowedly from the glory of Jesus

---

[54] "*Et ob beneficia impetranda a Dei per filium ejus Jesum Christum Dominum nostrum, qui solus noster Redemptor et Salvator est, ad eorum orationes, opem auxiliumque confugere.*" Sess. 25.

[55] Bellarmine *de Christo Mediato.* chap. 1. *De Sanct. Beat.* l. 1. c. 20.

[56] *Ave Maris stella,*
Dei mater alma.
Atque semper Virgo,
Faelix coeli porta.
Offic. Virgin. p. 153. and p. 141.

[57] In the hymn, *Protege, Domine,* etc., they say, "Protect, Lord, thy people; and let the truth which they have in the intercession of the blessed Peter and Paul, and of thy holy apostles, engage thee to preserve them by a continual assistance. [In a manual of their prayers, they make the following address: "O ye blessed apostles of our Lord [...] defend me from the pains of hell, rescue me from the power of darkness, and bring me to the everlasting kingdom." – *Translator*]

[58] Breviary. Rom. et Miss. Eugd.

Christ, our only Mediator, than to ask of God, through a great number of intercessors, the abundance of grace which according to the Scripture, is not to be found but in Jesus Christ alone?

Finally, she makes her suppliants ask of God that they may be delivered from the flames of hell, by the merits and prayers of St. Nicholas; that they may be absolved from their sins by the merits of St. Athanasius, St. Leo, and St. Basil; and that, by the merits of St. Lewis they may be made fellow heirs with Jesus Christ, the King of Kings.[59] Can greater injury be done to the merit of Jesus Christ than to associate with it, the merits of others?

Judge ye, my brethren; and let it not be said, in excuse of such impiety, that the merit of saints is founded on that of Jesus Christ; for it happens always that they join the merit of Jesus Christ to that of the saints. After all, they pretend that the merit of the saint, though founded on that of Jesus Christ, and dependent upon him, is notwithstanding proper to that saint, and that it also is extended and is communicable to other believers, to furnish them with those graces of which they have need; and is not this injurious to our divine Savior? If the merit of Jesus Christ is sufficient, why join with it the merits of men? It is said that God makes use of the sun for enlightening the world, although he could as well enlighten it without that luminary; but this comparison is nothing to the purpose: for it is the will of God that we should regard Jesus Christ as the only cause of our salvation (Acts 4:12).

You may therefore perceive that the Romish religion again departs from the holy Scripture upon this article; and that it is not the Christian religion in its purity, since it does not direct us to have recourse to Jesus Christ, as he by whom alone we can have access to the Father, which is one of the characters we formally laid down of the true religion. Let us pursue this subject of worship further.

---

[59] *Miss. Rom.* p. 338. 397. 987. 423.

III. Of the Worship of Images

Nothing can be said more express, or more strong against the worship of images, than the second commandment of the law. "Thou shalt not make unto thee," says the Sovereign Lawgiver, "any graven image, or any likeness of things which are in the heavens above, or on the earth beneath; [...] Thou shalt not bow down thyself before them, nor serve them, for I the Lord thy God am a jealous God, visiting the iniquity of the fathers upon the children to many generations." There is not a single word here but does execution. He has not only forbidden to make any graven image (as the Hebrew word denotes); but to leave no room for quibbling about the word, he adds that they should not make any representation or likeness. He forbids to bow down before them, which comprehends all external acts, and in particular that one of kneeling. He adds that they should not serve them, which comprehends under it all those acts of religion which men perform in honor of an object which they adore. He says not, *Do not esteem these images for gods; nor render service to them as unto a God*; but: *Thou shalt not serve them at all*; without making any restriction. In order to engage our obedience to him, he declares that he is mighty and powerful to maintain his glory, and represents himself as a jealous God, to teach us that if we refer the acts of religious homage to images in any manner whatever, the Lord will cause us to feel the effects of his indignation, as if we were infidels. Nay more, he threatens that those who shall violate this commandment, that their children shall be punished, and the children of their children, even to a thousand generations.

God expresses himself in terms no less strong, in the fourth chapter of Deuteronomy, "Take heed unto yourselves, (for ye saw no manner of similitude in the day that the Lord your God spake unto you in Horeb) lest ye corrupt yourselves, and make unto you any graven image, the similitude of any figure, the likeness of male or female."

We find likewise many passages in the prophecy of Isaiah, which forbid us to make any representation of God, and describe the conduct of idolaters in such a manner, as to set their folly and blindness in a striking point of view (Isaiah 40:18): "To whom will ye liken God? or what likeness will ye compare unto him?" And elsewhere he says (Isaiah 44:12): "The smith with the tongs both worketh in the coals, and fashioneth it with the hammers, The carpenter stretcheth out his rule, he marketh it out with a line; he fitteth it with planes, and he marketh it with the compass, and maketh it after the figure of a man. [...] He heweth him down cedars, and taketh the cypress and the oak [...] Then that tree shall be for a man to burn; he will take thereof and warm himself; yea, he kindleth it, and baketh bread; yea, he maketh a god, and worshippeth it, he maketh it a graven image, and falleth down unto it, and prayeth unto it, and saith, Deliver me for thou art my God." It would seem as if the prophet meant here to describe what is yet practiced every day.

Further, it is evident that the Scripture applies the name of idolaters, not only to the Pagans, who adored false deities, but also to the Israelites, because they worshipped the Lord under the figure of a golden calf, although they adored not the calf without respect unto the supreme God: for they must renounce their reason who would imagine that the Israelites believed that the calf was really their God, who had brought them up out of Egypt? How could they possibly imagine that that calf had delivered them before Aaron had melted and formed it? This is readily acknowledged by not a few learned writers of the Romish church.[60]

In fine, it is certain that the Scripture has most positively pronounced that idolaters (that is to say, those who render to the creature that religious

---

[60] So Tostatus, Bishop of Avila, on Exodus 23, and the Cordelier Ferus, who says that: "We must not think that the Israelites were so stupid as to believe that Aaron could make them a god, when they said to him, *Make us gods*." This also appears from the words of Aaron, "Tomorrow shall be a solemn feast unto the Lord." There are others who, not daring directly to avow it, yet pressed by the force of truth, own that it is a probable opinion that the Jews thought to serve the true God in their idol.

worship which is due only to God) "shall not inherit the kingdom of heaven" (1 Corinthians 6). Such is the language of the sacred books in which idolatry is represented as adultery, which dissolves our fellowship with God.

Let us hear the oracle of Rome:

The Council of Trent pronounces that the images of Jesus Christ, of the holy virgin and other saints ought to be kept and retained, especially in the churches, and that due honor and veneration is to be paid to them; and that by the images which are kissed, and before which we uncover the head and prostrate ourselves, we adore Jesus Christ, and venerate the saints, whose similitude they bear.[61] It is evident then that this council would have men to bow down themselves before images, which God had most expressly forbidden.

This council also approved of what the Second Council of Nicaea had done,[62] which required, not only that images should be venerated, but also adored: as Tarasious, Patriarch of Constantinople, declares in the fourth act of the Council.[63]

In the Romish churches, in many places, may be seen images of God the Father in the form of an old man, and of the Holy Spirit in the shape of a dove. Is not this to change the glory of the incorruptible God into the likeness of mortal man, and of birds, etc.: the very thing which the apostle condemns? Judge ye, my brethren. Pope John XXII—if we believe

---

[61] "*Imagines porro Christi Dei-parae virginis, et aliorum sanctorum in templis praesertim habendas et retinendas, eisque debitum honorem et venerationem impertiendam [...] ita ut per imagines, quas osculamur, et coram quibus caput aperimus et procumbimus Christum adoremus, et sanctos quorum ille similitudinem gerunt, veneremur.*" Sess. 25.

[62] "*Id quod conciliorum, praesertim vero secundae Nicaenae Synodi decretis contra imaginum oppugnatores est sancitum.*"

[63] His words are these. All those who confess that they venerate the holy images, and who refuse them adoration, are condemned by the holy father as hypocrites. In the Synodical epistle to the emperor, they say, "We believe, without any doubt, that images ought to be adored and saluted. Whoever is not of this mind, but is in difficulty and doubt on the subject of the adoration of venerable images, our holy and venerable council, fortified by the virtue of the Holy Spirit and the ecclesiastical traditions of the fathers, anathematizes him." (Ep. 1. Act. 7).

Aventine—reckoned this practice highly blameable; but his successors approve of it.

In the Romish church, there have been, and are still, some celebrated doctors which have maintained that the very same honor is due unto the images, to the object which they represent; and that we ought accordingly to give the worship of *latria* unto those of the Father, Son, and Holy Spirit; the worship of *hyperdulia* to those of the virgin, and the worship of *dulia* to those of the saints. And one of their most famous authors says that: "The image may be adored *per accidens*; by that sort of adoration wherewith the original is worshipped properly; that the image is to be considered as conjoined with the original, which is adored, and may be adored, on that account, by accident. And he affirms that if the image were only venerable improperly, because the exemplar is adored before it, or in it or by it, one might simply deny that images are venerable, because, adds he, that which is not affirmed of anything but improperly, may be denied simply.[64] But the Council of Nicaea has denounced an anathema on those who deny that images are to be worshiped."[65]

It is likewise a matter of public notoriety that the Romish churches are filled with images, which are saluted and kissed; before them the people fall

---

[64] Bellar. *De Imag.* I. 2.

[65] Raphael de la Torre, a Spanish Dominican, mentions five different sentiments in the Roman Catholic church with respect to images. The first of those who think that they are not adored, except in an abusive and improper sense; as Durand, Gerson, Holcot, Picus Mirandola, etc. The second is of those who would have them adored with the same kind of adoration as the originals: this is the sentiment of Thomas, and his disciples, and of almost all the Scholastics. The third is that of those who hold that they are adored on account of their relation to the originals, but with a kind of adoration far inferior: so Ambrose Catharin, etc. The fourth is the opinion of those who say that the image is worshipped along with the original, but by a different act; as the honor that is given to a king, is different from that which is paid to ambassadors; this he ascribes to Sanders, Bellarmine, Suarez, etc. The fifth and last is of those who admit but of one and the same worship of the image and the original, though they deny that the image is adorable by itself without the original being adored, and refuse that it is adored except by kissing and genuflection. *Sum. de Relig.* Q94, Art. 2.

down, with head uncovered, and hands joined; on certain solemn days, they are carried in procession and in triumph, through the principal streets of the cities, in the midst of almost an innumerable crowd of people, who accompany them with inexpressible joy. It admits not a doubt that they incense them, and sometimes undertake long journeys, merely that they may have the honor of kissing the balustrades and rails of the places where they are enclosed; wherefore it is inconceivable how any should have the daring confidence to publish of late that no service is given to images in the church of Rome.[66] But at the same time that the sentiments of Romish writers were artfully extenuated in regard to images, it so happened in the providence of God that a celebrated divine of that communion, who had been one of the approvers of the exposition of a certain learned prelate, published at Rome itself, works in which these words are expressly contained, that: "The same worship is due unto images as unto the original;" and he proves this to be the opinion of the most learned authors of that religion.[67]

Neither can it be denied that in the Romish church prayers are addressed to the images themselves, and favors asked of them;[68] wherefore it is very surprising that the Council of Trent could say that they acknowledge no virtue to be in the images. If that be the case, whence comes it to pass that

---

[66] "We do not serve images," says the Bishop of Meaux, "But we serve ourselves of images to raise us to the originals." Exposit. Avertiss.

[67] Capisucchi, *Controv. Theolog. Select.*

[68] In the prayer which they address to the image of Jesus Christ, said to be imprinted on the holy napkin given to Veronica, after having saluted "that holy face impressed on a linen cloth as white as snow" and styled it "the mirror of saints," etc. they pray it "to cleanse them from every stain of vice, to cleanse them from every stain of vice, o shed light into their hearts, and conduct them into their own country, where they may see the pure face of Jesus Christ."
Salve sancta facies nostri Redemptoris,
In qua nitet species divini splendoris,
Impressa panniculo nivei candoris,
Salve Decus seculi, speculum sanctorum!
Quod videre cupiunt spiritus caelorum;
Nos ab omni macula purga vitiorum.
Salve vultus Domini, imago beata! etc.

they make far greater account of some images than of others, such as those of Our Lady of Loretto; or of Ardilliers; and that they should still travel to such a great distance in pilgrimage to the places in which they are consecrated? If that be the case, whence comes it also that, in consecrating their images, they request that they would chase away the devils, attract the company of the angels, and protect the faithful?[69]

Further, it is a thing certain that the cross is adored by them. On Good Friday, the priests cry out: "Behold the wood of the cross, to which was affixed the salvation of the world. Come and let us adore it."[70] A prayer is addressed unto it, wherein it is styled *Our only hope*, and they request it, "to increase the righteousness of the faithful, and to grant pardon to the guilty;" and it cannot be alleged that they direct their words to him who was crucified; for the prayer is addressed to the cross itself, which they call the illustrious or glorious tree;[71] and thus Thomas Aquinas, the prince of the

---

[69] In the consecration of the image of the virgin, they pray, "O God, sanctify this form of the blessed virgin, that it may afford salutary help to the faithful, that hurtful thunders and lightnings, when they prevail, may be more speedily driven away." And of the image of St John, Baptist, they say, "*Sit haec daemonum sancta expulso, Angelorum advocatio, fidelium protectio.*" Pont. Rom.

[70] The priest on that day uncovers the cross little by little in the sight of the people, and repeatedly cries, Behold the wood of the cross, while the choir sing, *Come let us adore it*; and they fall down accordingly. When brought to the middle of the altar, the whole cross is uncovered and elevated three times, and the same words are repeated a third time, and the same acts of adoration continued. Afterwards it is carried to the place prepared for it before the altar, where it is no sooner set than the priest kneels down before it three times and then kisses it: after him the ministers of the altar and the other clerks and laity two and two, kneel three times and adore it. The pontifical orders, when any image of the cross is to be blessed, that the bishop sprinkle it with holy water, incense it, and then bowing the knee before it, adore and kiss it with devotion. Did the Jews do more to the brazen serpent, which Hezekiah broke in pieces?

[71] Arbor decora et fulgida,
Ornata regis pomparia, ——
O crux, ave spes unica;
Hoc passionis tempore,
Auge piis justitiam;
Reisque dona veniam.

Romish school, proves that the worship of *latria* ought to be paid unto the cross.[72]

I might also have added that they have retrenched that commandment which mentions images in the copies of the decalogue commonly taught among them. But we have already said enough to establish the following conclusions:

- That in the matter of images nothing can be more opposite to Scripture than the doctrine and constant practice of the Romish church.

- That the charge of idolatry may be justly brought against her, and she cannot be exculpated from the direct violation of the law of God.

- And finally, that we cannot acknowledge her for a true church, until we behold her desisting from painting God under corporeal figures; from honoring him by images, by which she desires no kind of honor nor service; and from rendering to any image whatever, a religious worship, which on no account ought to be given them.

I should have here subjoined a word concerning the worship of relics, in respect to which, the blindness not only of the people, but also of their teachers, cannot be sufficiently deplored; but we have yet more important things to treat, which also relate to religious worship, as the adoration of the host, of which we shall speak, after we have said a few things concerning sacraments in general.

---

[72] Aquin. P3 Q25 A4

IV. Of Sacraments in general, and of the Eucharist in particular.

In reading the New Testament, we will find that it makes no mention of any but two sacraments of the Christian church, namely, baptism and the holy supper; so that there is just ground of astonishment that the church of Rome should pronounce an anathema against those "who affirm that there are not seven sacraments, truly and properly so called, and instituted by Jesus Christ, under the dispensation of the gospel,"[73] for this is to anathematize those who hold exactly to that which the Scripture teaches.

We never find that it speaks of penitence, marriage, or orders as sacraments, much less as sacraments of the Christian dispensation, by way of distinction from the old. It speaks of penitence as a duty, which God has always required of sinners; and of marriage as a ceremony which has been practiced from the beginning of the world; and if God has been pleased to appoint orders in the church, yet it is not under the notion of sacraments, which, being seals of the covenant, ought to be common to all the faithful. Wherefore, one cannot be surprised that the church of Rome, should require all to receive these three as true sacraments, under the pain of an anathema.[74]

We can find as little trace in the apostolic writings of a sacrament called confirmation; and though it may be said that the apostles, in curing the sick, sometimes employed miraculous unctions, it is nowhere recorded that they anointed those who were at the point of death. Such unctions as they used, can no longer be of use, since miracles have ceased in the church. It is therefore unaccountable that the Romish church should excommunicate those who receive not confirmation and extreme unction, as true sacraments.

---

[73] The decree of the council of Trent is in the following terms: "*Si quis dixerit sacramenta nova esse, non fuisse omnia a Jesu Christo Domino nostro instituta: aut esse plura, vel pauciora quam septem, viz. Baptismum, Confirmationem, Eucharistiam, Penitentiam, Extremam Unctionem, Ordinem et Matrimonium, aut etiam aliquod horum septum non esse vere et proprie sacramentum, anathema fit.*" Sess. 7 C1

[74] If the word *sacrament* is to be taken in any other than the true and proper sense, then all the sacred ceremonies may as well be so called; and in this extensive sense Peter Damian spoke of twelve sacraments. Serm. 69.

Again, the holy Scripture informs us that Jesus Christ instituted the holy supper under two different symbols, and that the apostles celebrated it in this manner. From good authority we also know that the church, for more than a thousand years, gave the communion to the people under the two species of bread and wine. Who then can think, without consternation, of the daring boldness wherewith the Romish church has changed the institution of Jesus Christ,[75] having retrenched, by an unparalleled attempt, the cup from the people! What! Is it thus they violate the laws of the Savior of the world? He said, "Drink ye all of it;" but the church of Rome thinks proper that this command should not be obeyed. It is the will of Jesus Christ that there be two separate signs, the bread and the wine, to denote his body and his blood, which were separated upon the cross, and to teach us that in him we may find full and perfect nourishment. But the church of Rome chooses to pay no regard to the ends for which Jesus Christ thus instituted his sacraments. Who can help being astonished at this?

Further, we are told that Jesus Christ, having taken bread, said, "This is my body broken for you;" and having taken the cup, he added, "This cup is the New Testament in my blood." So that, as it cannot be said that the cup was changed into a covenant or testament, neither can the bread be said to be changed into the body of Jesus Christ. And we are confirmed in this sentiment, because the Scripture teaches us that Jesus Christ had a true body like unto ours, consequently, that it was visible and palpable, and that his body is ascended into heaven, and that the heavens must retain it until the time of the restitution of all things (Acts 3:21). That we shall have the proof always here on earth, but that we should not have Jesus Christ always (John 12), namely, in regard of his bodily presence, so as to be at any expense on

---

[75] *Itaque sancta ipsa synodus Spiritu S. qui spiritus est sapientiae et intellectus - edocet declarat ac docet, nullo divino praecepto laicos et clericos, non [conficientes], obligari ad Eucharistiae sacramentum sub utraque species sumendum. [...] Nam est Chrisit Dominus in [unima] coena venerabile hoc sacramentum in panis et vini speciebus instituit et Apostolis tradidit, non tamen illa institutio et traditio eo tendunt, ut omne Christi fideles statuto Domini ad utramque speciem accipiendam adstringantur. Sess. 21. C. 1.*

that account. *In fine*, that what we eat, in the eucharist, is bread, and what we drink is wine; as it is said, "Let a man examine himself and so let him eat of that bread and drink of that cup." Our astonishment then must continue when we hear it affirmed that: "The body of Jesus Christ with his blood and soul, is present and contained really and substantially in the sacrament; and that the substance of bread and wine is changed into the body and blood of the Lord, by transubstantiation."[76] What is this, but to oblige us if possible to believe:

- That although we see nothing but bread in the eucharist, eat nothing but bread, taste nothing but bread, and though the Scripture assures us that it is but bread, yet we ought to be persuaded that there is nothing of bread there, but only the appearance of it.

- That the human nature of Jesus Christ is not like unto ours in all things, sin only excepted, as the apostle Paul asserts; since it is in a thousand places at one and the same time, impalpable and invisible, without extension; whereas ours is tangible, visible, and inseparable from its dimensions.

- That Jesus Christ is now bodily on earth, and more so than he was formerly, seeing he was only in Judea during the time of his abode in the flesh, whereas now his body is present throughout all the earth; which can by no means consist with the words of the Saviour to his disciples that they should not have him always with them.

---

[76] "*Si quis negaverit in sanctissima Eucharistia sacramento contineri vere, realiter et substantialiter corpus et sanguinem una cum anima et divinitate Christi ac proinde totum Christum, sed dixerit tantummodo esse in eo, ut in signo vel figura, aut virtute, anathema fit. Si quis dixerit in sacro sancto Eucharistiae sacramento remanere substantiam panis et vini una cum corpore et sanguine Domini nostri Jesu Christi, negaverit que mirabilem illam et singularem conversionem totius substantiae panis in corpus et totius substantiae vini in sanguinem manentibus [duntaxit] sepeciebus panis et vini quam quidem conversionem Catholica ecclesia, optissime Transubstantionem appellat, anathema fit.*" Sess. Conc. Trid. Sess. 13 C.1&2

- Lastly, that the body of Jesus Christ which was fixed to the cross, is contained whole and entire in the smallest part of a wafer.

I say no more of this, because there is not a person among you who does not readily perceive the absurdity of the doctrine of transubstantiation. I now pass on to that which shocks pious minds still more in this matter, and that is the adoration of the host.

IV. Of the Adoration of the Host.

It is most certain that the Scripture throughout is entirely silent as to the adoration of the sacrament. Jesus Christ said to his disciples, "Take, eat, drink;" but not a word of adoring. Can we believe that, if Jesus Christ had instituted this sacrament with a view to its being adored, he should never have mentioned any such thing? The evangelists and apostles—who relate with the greatest care the history of the eucharistical institution—nowhere tell us that we should adore that which Jesus Christ ordered to be eaten; and even when the apostles communicated, for the first time, it is evident that they did it in a posture which is not very suitable to an act of adoration, for they were reclining upon one side, upon small couches, placed around the table, according to the usage of that time.

Moreover, we do not read that the sacrament was ever adored in the ancient church. Justin Martyr—who describes very fully and exactly all the ceremonies of the Eucharist practiced in his time—says nothing of this religious adoration; nor is any vestige to be found of it in the writers of his age. We meet with nothing of it in the most ancient liturgies, nor even in the writings of the pretended Dionysius the Areopagite, who has expressly treated of the celebration of the sacrament; and those who are disposed to speak ingeniously must acknowledge that this piece of homage was not established but at a very late period.

Besides, seeing as it appears clearly from Scripture that the body of Jesus Christ is in heaven; and that there is only bread and wine in the eucharist, we cannot help concluding that those who adore the host, adore bread alone, and by consequence are idolaters. For we must not believe that their declared intention of adoring the body of Jesus Christ, will justify them. If that were sufficient to justify them, there would be no idolater but might thus excuse himself; and the man who should adore the sun, believing it to be Jesus Christ, could not be charged with idolatry.

Let us now enquire into what the church of Rome teaches and practices as to this. The council so often referred to, thus expresses her judgment: "There is no room to doubt but that all faithful Christians, according to the received custom of the Catholic church, are obliged to render to the most holy sacrament, the worship of *latria*, which is due to the true God: for though it was appointed by our Lord Jesus Christ that it might be received, it is not on that account, the less venerable, because we believe that the same God, of whom the eternal Father, when bringing him into the world, has said, *And let all the angels of God worship him*, is therein present."[77] Here I beseech you to consider that the council enjoins, not only that Jesus Christ should be adored, but the sacrament also, in which they suppose him to be present.

With regard to the practice of the Romish church, it is certain that all who belong to that communion, professedly adore what our senses, our reason, and Scripture, teach us to be nothing but bread. How then is it possible to excuse them from idolatry? It is not sufficient to say that they adore that which they believe to be the body of Jesus Christ; for the question is not as to what they believe, but what it really is. A man, as was already

---

[77] "Nullius itaque dubitandi locus relinquitur, quia omnes Christi fideles pro more in Catholica ecclesia semper recepta, latriae cultum, qui vero Deo debetur, huic sanctissimo sacramento in veneratione exhibeant: neque ideo minus est adorandum quod fuerit a Christo Domino, ut sumatur; institutum; nam illum eandem Deum presentem in eo adesse credimus, quem Pater aeternus introducens in orbem terrarum, dicit, *Et adorent cum omnes angeli Deli.*" Sess. 13 C5

observed, who should adore the sun, who is the most noble of inanimate creatures, and the emblem of the divinity, because he might believe that Jesus Christ were therein contained, or that it were Jesus Christ himself, who is called the sun of righteousness, would he be therefore less an idolater?

Besides, it cannot be denied that those of communion worship what they know not; for they can have no certain knowledge whether the bread is become infallibly the body of Jesus Christ by consecration, because they are ignorant whether the priest had a true intention to consecrate, or even if the priest be truly a priest, and whether he who conferred orders upon him, had an intention to consecrate; but according to the rules of the missal, and the maxims of the council, without intention there is no consecration.[78] In this respect then the Romish worshipers are like the Samaritans, to whom Jesus Christ said, "Ye worship ye know not what; we know what we worship; for salvation is of the Jews" (John 4). By these words, our Lord would have the Samaritans to understand that they could not expect to attain salvation in their communion, but that it was to be found in the church of the Jews. What reason is there earnestly to wish that those of the communion of Rome would pay due attention to the extreme peril to which they expose themselves! For it is a thing at least very possible, according to their own confession, that they may adore mere bread, which is manifest idolatry. Let them not plead that they direct their intention to Jesus Christ: this direction of the intention was perhaps the most abominable doctrine that ever was invented, because it justifies the most horrid crimes.

Neither let it be said, again that the sacrament of the Eucharist—even supposing that the body of Jesus Christ, were not in it—is a thing most holy, and most venerable, and that it is not such a great sin to adore that which undoubtedly deserves veneration, for there is a very great difference between venerating and adoring. However holy any creature may be, it can never be entitled to adoration; God has reserved this honor alone to himself, and none

---

[78] Miss. cap. 7 de def. Conc. Trid. Sess. 7 C11

can divide it between him and another without highly affronting him, and drawing down his indignation.

It appears then on this point that the Romish religion cannot be considered as the pure Christian religion which the apostles have taught, since it is a religion contaminated with idolatry. Let us examine some other doctrines: and as the eucharist is considered in this religion as a sacrifice, let us speak a little of the sacrifice of the mass.

VI. Of the Sacrifice of the Mass.

Whoever reads the epistle of Paul to the Hebrews cannot but find there the following truths:

- That Jesus Christ once offered himself.
- That he does not repeat that offering frequently; otherwise it behoved him to have suffered often, since the creation of the world.
- That as it is ordained for all men once to die, so Jesus Christ once offered himself, and having been once offered to take away the sins of many, he shall appear the second time without sin, unto the salvation of those who look for him.
- That instead of many priests under the law, which were not sufficient to continue by reason of death, Jesus Christ has a priesthood "which passeth not unto another," as the Greek term rendered unchangeable imports (Hebrews 7:24) "because he continueth for ever."
- That the law established for priests, men having infirmity, but the word of the oath (namely, that which established the priesthood of the New Testament) has established the Son, who is consecrated forevermore.

- That Jesus Christ by one oblation, has forever consecrated them that are sanctified, or has brought them unto perfection, according to the force of the original expression; and that he has obtained eternal redemption for us.
- That where there is once remission of sins, there is no more offering for sin.
- That without the shedding of blood there is no remission of sin.
- *In fine*, that the sacrifices which were often offered could never take away sins, otherwise they would have ceased to have been offered.

These are the truths which may be collected from the epistle to the Hebrews.[79] Let us try by this rule what the church of Rome maintains. The following are the words of the Council of Trent: "Since the Lord Jesus Christ, who once offered himself as a bloody victim on the altar of the cross, is the same who is contained, and sacrificed in a manner not bloody, in the divine sacrifice which is made in the mass; the holy council teaches that this sacrifice is truly propitiatory; because the Lord—appeased by this oblation, in giving the grace and gift of repentance—pardons even the most heinous sins and crimes, for it is the same victim, and the very same person who was formerly offered on the cross, who is now offered by the ministry of the priests: there is no difference but only in the manner of offering; and the fruits of that bloody oblation are received abundantly by means of this unbloody sacrifice, so far is the latter from derogating in the least from the former. Wherefore it is offered—according to the tradition of the apostles—not only for the faithful who are alive, on account of their pains to satisfy for them and for their other necessities; but also for those who are dead in Jesus Christ, and who are not yet sufficiently purified."[80]

This declaration is confirmed by anathemas: "Whoever says that in the mass, there is not an offering to God a true and proper sacrifice, or that his

---

[79] Hebrews 7:27-28, 23-24, 9:22, 25-28, 10:1, 2, 14, 18
[80] Conc. Trid. Sess. 22 cap.11 & 3

being offered means nothing else than that Jesus Christ is given to us to be eaten, let him be anathema." Again, "Whoever shall affirm that the sacrifice of the mass is only a sacrifice of praise and thanksgiving, or a bare commemoration of the sacrifice of the cross, and not a propitiatory sacrifice, and that it ought not to be offered, either for the living or for the dead, nor for sins, nor punishments, nor satisfactions, nor other necessities, let him be accursed."[81] Agreeable to the decisions of this council, the sacrifice of the mass is offered daily.

Now let us compare the apostle Paul with the canons of this council, and the practice of Romish infidels. The apostle says that Jesus Christ offered himself once, and not often; the church of Rome says that Jesus Christ offers himself every day by the ministry of priests. The apostle informs us that Jesus Christ has no need to offer daily; the church of Rome, that there is a necessity for his offering himself, and that he actually offers himself in the mass. The apostle says that it was only under the law that many sacrificing priests were constituted; the church of Rome asserts that Jesus Christ has constituted his sacrificing priests under the New Testament, that he might be offered in sacrifice by them in their ministry. The apostle declares that only under the law, men were ordained priests, having infirmity; the church of Rome maintains that the very same thing takes place under the gospel. Paul asserts that where there is remission of sins, there is nothing further to be offered for sin. And he everywhere teaches that Jesus Christ has obtained for us the pardon of our sins by his blood; the church of Rome on the contrary holds that we need the sacrifice of the mass to be offered for us, in order to satisfy and appease God by that oblation. Paul declares that without shedding of blood there is no remission, whereas the church of Rome believes that the unbloody sacrifice of the mass is propitiatory for the living and the dead. Once more, Paul affirms that sacrifices frequently offered are destitute of efficacy to expiate sins; whence it follows that if there were any

---

[81] Can. 1 & 3

need for repeating the sacrifice of Jesus Christ, it would be void of efficacy for purging away sins; or if it be powerful to take away sins, there can be no need for its being reiterated. But the church of Rome believes that it is needful to reiterate this sacrifice every day; therefore she must believe that the sacrifice of Christ wants virtue for taking away sins, which is to be guilty of a horrible outrage against our divine Redeemer: for either Jesus Christ has not made sufficient satisfaction to his Father, or the oblation of him which is reiterated daily, is unprofitable. If the oblation made on the cross be sufficient, then the other oblations are superfluous; and if the other oblations are not superfluous, then that of the cross is insufficient. Now, is light more opposite to darkness, than Rome is on this matter to the apostle Paul?

I know very well that those who want to extenuate the obnoxious tenets of that church tell us that the sacrifice of the mass is only established for celebrating the memory of the sacrifice of the cross, and for applying its virtue.[82] But how can this accord with the council, which anathematizes those who say that the sacrifice of the mass is only a commemoration, or to use the very terms applied in the decree, "a bare commemoration of the sacrifice of the cross, and not a propitiatory sacrifice"?

Besides, what necessity is there for a new and proper sacrifice in order to apply that of the cross? Is not faith sufficient for making this application unto us? "God hath appointed Jesus Christ" says the apostle Paul, "for a propitiation through faith in his blood" (Romans 3:25). If we were to treat the subject of the sacrifice of the mass in all the extent which it might require, we might make it evidently appear that it is impossible to devise and advance a doctrine more injurious to the Son of God. Strange! How dare they assert that the sovereign of the universe, the Son of the living God, who is supremely exalted above all things, comes to put himself every day into the hands of a mortal man, and even as a victim in the hands of a sacrificer; and that, whenever a priest pronounces two or three words, there should be

---

[82] *Exposit. De la Foi* p.134

effected under his hands a real and sudden change of the substance of bread and wine into the proper body and blood of Jesus Christ, and that it should depend on his intention whether this change shall be accomplished or not? Who can refrain from trembling, who beholds them offering, as Romanists pretend, the body of Jesus Christ continually, for purposes most unworthy of the greatness and majesty of Jesus Christ; as for the discovery of things lost? And who but must be filled with surprise at the offering of the sacrifice of the mass, in honor of the saints, as the council ordains?[83] What else can this mean than that Jesus Christ might offer himself daily in honor of his creatures? What impiety! This is to desire that Jesus Christ who is God, would become as it were an intercessor and mediator towards a saint, in order to obtain his intercession in favour of a man, of whom Jesus Christ is the Creator and Savior. Can any hear such a doctrine mentioned without horror?

I say nothing of the masses without communicants, which they celebrate in the Romish church, which is one of the greatest abuses which can be committed: for this is to celebrate without any communicating, a mystery of which the essence consists in communion. We have said enough on this head to warrant us to conclude that the church of Rome, in regard to it, is absolutely departed and far off from the way marked out by Jesus Christ; and that it is not in this church, that pure Christianity can be found.

VII. Of Human Satisfactions, and of Purgatory.

The doctrine of Purgatory is one of those which the interest of the church of Rome requires her most earnestly to maintain, and which she accordingly maintains with the greatest zeal. It is the foundation of a part of her worship, of satisfactions, indulgences, and prayer for the dead, and is the

---

[83] "If anyone says that it is an abuse to celebrate masses in honour of the saints and for obtaining their intercession with God [...] let him be accursed." Sess. 22. cap. 5.

occasion of innumerable masses, services, penances, vows, pilgrimages, and macerations. It is necessary therefore to enquire what is the sentiment of the communion of Rome upon this, and we shall then compare it with the Scripture.

The church of Rome asserts:

- That God pardons our guilt wholly, and yet reserves part of the punishment, namely temporal pains.[84]

- That it is neither agreeable to the justice nor goodness of God that he should pardon our sins without satisfaction.

- That the pains which remain to be endured, after the guilt and the eternal punishment are remitted, are the same in respect of sense and intenseness, as those which the sinner ought to suffer in the prison of hell, wanting only the eternal duration.[85]

- That men can truly and properly satisfy for this punishment of sin, and that they do so, both in this life, and after death in Purgatory.

- That the souls of such as die in the fear and grace of God, have to undergo these temporal pains for many ages in that Purgatory; and that they receive relief by the suffrages, and prayers of the living, and by the sacrifice of the mass.

- That the church has authority to relax these pains, which relaxations are called *indulgences*; and that some of these may be given for many thousands of years.

- That there is a treasure of these indulgences, made up of the satisfactions of Jesus Christ, and those of the saints, which can be applied to those who are obliged to bear the punishment of their sins, after the trespass has been remitted to them in the sacrament of penitence.

---

[84] Conc. Trid. Sess. 14. c. 12. and 8. Sess. 25.
[85] Bell. l.4 *de poenit.* C. 1.

- That it is needful that a person should confess his sins in the ear of a priest, and that this confession is necessary to salvation.

Such are the sentiments of the Romish church: but what saith the Scripture?

It assures us that God freely forgives us all our offences, and that we are justified freely by his grace, through the redemption that is in Christ Jesus, and that we have the remission of sins through the blood of Christ, according to the riches of his grace.[86] But would God pardon us freely if he exacted a satisfaction at our hand; and if we should endure part of the punishment which we have merited?

It declares that God remembers not our iniquities; that he casts them behind his back, and into the depth of the sea; that he blots them out, and does not impute them; that sinners who repent and change their life become white as snow; and that none of all the sins which the just man has committed shall be imputed to him.[87] But if God should still punish sins, how can it be said that he does not impute them any more; that he blots them out and remembers them no more? It testifies that "There is no condemnation to them who are in Christ Jesus." How could the apostle speak this language, if they were yet condemned to suffer in Purgatory during so many ages? Again, "He that believeth on the Son shall not come into condemnation, but is passed from death to life."[88] But how can this be if the faithful must burn in a fire for such a long course of time? Is this to pass from death to life, to pass from death into burning flames?

The Scripture tells us that "If our earthly habitation be destroyed, we have a house eternal in the heavens: and that when the saints are absent from the body, they are present with the Lord."[89] Is this to be present with the Lord in heaven, to descend into Purgatory? It also tells us that "the dead

---

[86] Col. 1. Eph. 1. Rom. 3.
[87] Isaiah 38:17 & 44:12, Micah 7:19, Psalm 103:2 & 132:1, Jeremiah 31:34, Ezekiel 38:21 & 33:12, etc.
[88] John 5:24
[89] John 5:24

which die in the Lord are blessed, and that they rest from their labours."[90] Could the Spirit of God speak in this strain if it were true that those who die in the Lord had to undergo suffering after their death? It further testifies that the blood of Jesus Christ cleanses us from all sin (1 John 1). If so, then we have no more need to be purged by another means. The Scripture likewise speaks of the afflictions which God appoints for his children, not as punishments, but as marks of his love, in which they ought to rejoice and glory.[91] How can this comfortable truth agree with the doctrine of Rome, that these sufferings are true punishments for past sins? It also confines the afflictions and sufferings of the faithful to this present life, as may be gathered from a variety of passages:[92] and while it often comforts us against the evils to which we are exposed here below, it never affords us the least consolation against the sufferings which shall be endured in Purgatory, although these are represented as far more grievous than those which belong to this mortal life. *In fine*, it only requires of sinners who obtain the pardon of their sins, that they confess their sins to him who is faithful and just to forgive them, and that they forsake them;[93] but it nowhere enjoins us to go and confess all our sins to a priest.

All this considered, is it not clear that the Romish church is not of the sentiments of the primitive and apostolic church? But we may here deduce yet another powerful argument to prove that the Romish religion at present is not the true Christian religion; for one of the characters of the true religion, is to calm the disquieted consciences of the faithful, and to terrify those of the wicked! But what trouble must it produce in a dying man, to tell him that it is very uncertain whether he shall go some time or other into paradise; but that the most favorable lot he can expect, is to be confined for

---

[90] Revelation 14

[91] Hebrews 12, Revelation 3, Romans 5

[92] 1 Peter 1:26, 2 Corinthians 4:17, Romans 8:18

[93] Proverbs 28, 1 John [The author's words are, *Elle n'exige des pécheurs pour obtenir le pardon*, etc. *Translator*]

ages in a burning fire, from whence he cannot be liberated but by the power of masses: O what consolation![94]

Consider yet further, if it be not intolerable pride to say that men can make true and proper satisfaction unto God: finite miserable creatures to a being infinite?

Reflect again if it be not an evident outrage against Jesus Christ to pretend to make up a treasure composed of the merits of this divine Savior, and those of the saints, and to presume to say that there is but one actual satisfaction, and that our own.[95] It is alleged that this does no injury to the merit of Jesus Christ, because it is he who has given to saints the power of satisfying. But where do they find that Christ has given to the saints this power? They may as well tell us that Jesus Christ has given power to the saints to redeem us! It is also pleaded that what is called satisfaction is, after all, nothing else than the application of the satisfaction of Christ. But who ever heard it asserted before that a work which we should perform, and a punishment which we should suffer, should be the application of the obedience and sufferings of Jesus Christ? Besides, if these human satisfactions are only the application of the merit of Jesus Christ, why should they believe it needful, to make this application of the merit and superabundant sufferings of the saints?

Let us continue the examination of the Romish religion.

---

[94] The original translation reads 'O God,' yet the obvious sarcasm combined with it may have the effect of sounding flippant to some readers in modern English. — J.W.

[95] *"Tertius autem modus videtur probabilior quod una tantum sit actualis satisfactio, et ea sit nostra, neque hinc excluditur Christus, vel ejus satisfactio nam per ejus satisfactionem habemus gratiam unde satisfacimus; et hoc modo dicitur applicari nobis satisfactio, non quod immediate ipsa ejus satisfactio tollat poenam temporalem nobis debitam, sed quod mediate eam tollat, quatenus videlicet ab ea gratiam habemus, sine qua nihil valeret nostra satisfactio."* Bellar. l. 1. cap. 10. *De Purgat.*

VIII. Of the Service in a language not understood by the People.

Compare what the apostle Paul says in his epistle to the Corinthians (1 Corinthians 14:2, 9, 19-20). "He that speaketh in an unknown tongue speaketh not unto men, but unto God;" "To speak in a language which cannot be understood, is to speak in the air: It is better to speak five words in the church which may be understood, than ten thousand in an unknown tongue; and that it is a punishment from God, when he speaks unto a people by men of other tongues and other lips"; compare, I say, this language of Paul with the declaration of the council of Trent that: "It is not expedient that divine service should be performed in a language known to the people;" subjoining anathemas against those who shall maintain that it ought to be celebrated in the vulgar tongue,[96] as also with the bull which was published on January 12th 1662 against those who should render into French the words of the service contained in the missal, accusing them of schism, disobedience, sedition, and novelty, that would spoil the beauty of the church, of a rash attempt to expose to the vulgar, the dignity of sacred mysteries, and to cause thorns to spring up in the vineyard of the Lord, which tend to choke it.

IX. Of the Merit of Works.

Compare the doctrine of the Council of Trent,[97] which teaches that: "Men truly merit eternal life, and the increase of grace and of glory by their

---

[96] "Non expedire visum est Patribus ut vulgari passim lingua celebraretur. [...] Si quis dixerit lingua tantum vulgari Missam celebrari debere, anathema sit."
Sess. 22. cap. 8. and Can. 9.

[97] "Si quis dixerit, hominis justificati opera bona ita esse dona Dei, ut non sint etiam bona ipsius justificati merita, aut ipsum justificatum bonis operibus, quae ab eo Dei gratiam et Jesu Christi meritum, cujus vivum membrum est, sunt, non vere mereri augmentum gratiae, vitam aeternam, et ipsius vitae aeternae (si tamen in gratia decesserit) consecutionem atque etiam gloriae augmentum, anathema sit." Sess. 6 cap. 32.

works," with the declaration of Scripture that "eternal life is a gift;" that "the sufferings of this present time are not worthy (have no *condignity*, to use the term of the Vulgate) to be compared with the glory that shall be revealed in us;" that we are "saved by grace; and not by works, lest any man should boast"; and when we shall have done all that is commanded us, we ought to say that we are unprofitable servants, having done what was our duty to do.[98]

X. Concerning Abstinence from certain meats; and Celibacy.

Examine whether these words of Paul to Timothy,[99] "That in the last days men shall depart from the faith, giving heed to seducing spirits and doctrines of devils, speaking lies in hypocrisy (or *by the hypocrisy of those who teach lies*) having their conscience seared with a hot iron: forbidding to marry, and commanding to abstain from meats, which God hath created to be received with thanksgiving of them which believe and know the truth;"[100] whether, I say, these words do not condemn the disciples of Saturninus, the Encratites, the Marcionites, and the Manicheans, and whether they do not also impugn those of the Roman communion, who forbid marriage to the clergy; and who enjoin abstinence on certain days of the year from certain meats; examine if those of that communion do not transgress the commandment of the apostle in these words, "Let no man judge or condemn you in respect of meat or drink, or in regard of the

---

[98] Romans 6:2-3, 8:18, Ephesians [6:8], Luke 18:8-10

[99] 1 Timothy 4:1-3

[100] It would be ridiculous to the last degree to think the common translation's faulty here, in reading, *forbidding to marry, and commanding to abstain*, in opposition to the consent of ancient and modern interpreters, as the Syriac, etc. and even of famous popish doctors, as Thomas, Cajetan, etc.

distinction of a holiday;" (Colossians 2) and, "Whatsoever is sold in the shambles eat, asking no questions for conscience sake" (1 Corinthians 10).

XI. Of Antichrist.

Examine whether that man of sin, of which the apostle speaks, be not to be found in Rome, "who opposeth and exalteth himself above all that is called God, or is worshipped; so that he sitteth as God, in the temple of God, and acts as if he were God:" claiming the power of deposing kings, and of loosing their subjects from their oath of fidelity, of canonizing saints, assuming to himself dominion over consciences, and exercising unheard of cruelties upon those who refuse to acknowledge him for the head of the church. Consider what that city is upon seven hills—that Babylon out of which the faithful should depart—spoken of in Revelation. I am certainly persuaded that when you have put together these and other things, which I do not mention, you must conclude that if the Romish church at present be christian, in regard of several doctrines, she has no pretensions to pure Christianity, but is, in many respects, become anti-Christian.

XII. Of the Paganism of the Church of Rome.

It cannot be denied that this church has adopted many things belonging to the Pagan religion. The writers of their own communion avow it.[101]

---

[101] As Lombard, Durand, Polydore Virgil, etc.

They themselves compare their grand pontiff with him who bore the same title among the Pagans.[102]

The custom of kissing the feet of the pope, which Gregory VII ordained in a council of Rome in 1076: was it not derived from the Pagans, who kissed the feet of their emperors?[103]

The custom of the priests shaving their heads and making the form of a crown had its original doubtless from the priests of ancient Egypt, being practiced by the priests of the goddess Isis.[104]

Are not the present nunneries founded upon the ruins of the vestal virgins?

When the Romanists put all their cities under the protection of a saint, or an angel, what was this but an imitation of the Pagans, who placed all their countries under the protection of their gods or goddesses; as Jupiter was the tutelary god of Crete, Juno of Argos, and Venus of Amathusa.[105]

---

[102] See *A Discourse of the Religion of the Ancient Romans*, by W. Duchoul.

☞ Our author's design, and the conciseness of his plan, did not admit of his enumerating at large the various instances of the Paganism of the Romish church, nor to illustrate particularly the instances adduced. Whoever wishes to see this subject more fully treated, and set in the most striking light, accompanied with the necessary proofs and illustrations, may consult, *The Conformity of Ancient and Modern Ceremonies*, published in English by Du Pre; and Dr. Middleton's *Letter from Rome*, demonstrating the exact conformity between popery and Paganism. (*Translator*)

[103] Caligula made Pompey Pen. kiss his feet. Sen. *de benefic*. B2 C12. And Dioclesian ordered by an edict that all sorts of persons should fall down before him and kiss his feet. Pompon. Laet. in Diocl.

[104] Herod. in *Euterp*. Juven. *Sat*. 6. Mart. ep. 1. 12. Nicol. Leonic. in varia Hist. l. 2. 21. Apul.

[105] Formerly the kingdom of France was under the protection of St. Michael, and St. Denis was its Patron. Louis XIII put all his kingdom under the protection of the B. Virgin. St. James is the patron of Spain: and had among the Pagans, their particular god and patron, St. Mark of Venice. Before the Reformation, England was under the protection of St. George; Scotland under that of St. Andrew, and Ireland under that of St. Patrick.

If all the sciences and the liberal and mechanic arts had among the Pagans their particular god and patron,[106] who knows not that in the Romish church every saint has his task and business?[107]

The holy water of the Romish church is nothing else than an imitation of the Lustral water of the Pagans.[108] Whence comes their purgatory, but from the Pagans?

Wherefore Pope Gregory, who first brought this doctrine into credit, describes it in the language of a heathen poet.[109]

---

[106] Mars was the god of battles; Minerva the goddess of war and of the sciences: Apollo was the god of poets and musicians; Diana the goddess of hunters, etc.

[107] The literati have chosen St. Catharine and St. Gregory; the divines St. Thomas; St. Luke is patron of the painters: St. Anthony of Swine herds, etc. Minutius Felix ridiculed the Pagans for the vile drudgery they put upon the gods they adored: "Sometimes," said he, "Hercules is set to empty dung; Apollo turns Admetus' cowherd; Neptune hires himself to Laomedon, to build up the walls of Troy." The same thing may be objected against those of the church of Rome, who do set their most respected saints of both sexes, to do jobs, not only sordid, but dishonorable. Witness the glorious miracles, they attribute to the holy virgin: one time they make her come down from heaven to support an errant thief on the gibbet; another time she defends to mend the gown of St. Thomas of Canterbury, that was ripped on the shoulder. Another time, to wipe off the sweat of the face of the monks of Clairvaux; at another to sing mattins for a monk, or to bleed a young man in the arm, or to perform the duty of an abbess whilst she is strolling about the country with a monk." Conformity of Cerem. p.116 [*Transl.*]

[108] "Idem ter socios pura circumtulit unda,
Spargens rore levi, et ramo felicis olivae."
Virg. Æn. vi.
Old Chorineus compass'd thrice the crew,
And dipt an olive branch in holy dew;
Which thrice he sprinkled round —
— Dryden.
So Ovid, in *Fastis*,
"Terque senem flamma, ter aqua, ter sulphure lustrat."
And he makes Iris sprinkle Juno after her visit to hell before her entrance into heaven.
"Roratis lustravit aquis, Thaumantias Iris."
Met. l. 4. fab. 15.

[109] See Greg. Dial. l. 4. c. 39. and Virgil Æn. l. 6.
Ergo exercentur poenis, veterumque malorum
Supplicia expendunt, alis panduntur inanes,
Suspensae ad ventos, aliis sub gurgite vasto,

Whence did they take the whippings and macerations, practised among them, unless from the priests of Baal, who scourged themselves until the blood came; from the priests of the goddess Cybele, or of Bellona, who were wont to cut themselves with knives and lancets?

Whence proceeded the worship of images, but from the Pagans who consecrated to their gods a variety of images both embossed and painted, who placed them in their temples, raised them upon their altars, enshrined them in a costly manner, crowned them with flowers, and smoked them with incense? Yet it must be acknowledged that there have been some Gentile nations, as the Persians, the Germans, the Libyans, the first Romans during the space of 160 years, who rejected the use of statues and images in religion: and the wisest among the Pagans have acknowledged that the service of the Deity would have been more pure and chaste without images, and that those who introduced them, had diminished the respect due to the divinity, and contributed to the increase of error.[110]

Again, whence came the canonization of saints, if it was not from the apotheoses of the Pagans?

Or, whence did they draw their processions, but from the same fertile source?[111]

Infectum eluitur scelus, aut exuritur igni,
Donec longa dies perfecto temporis orbe,
Concretam exemit labem, purumque reliquit.
For this are various penances enjoin'd,
And some are hung to bleach, upon the wind.
Some plung'd in waters, others purg'd in fires,
Till all the dregs are drain'd, & all the rust expires.
... Then are they happy, when by length of time
The scurf is worn away of each committed crime:
No speck is left of their habitual stains;
But the pure aether of the soul remains. — Dryd.

[110] Varro. Augustine, *The City of God*, Book 4 Chapter 31
[111] Baruch. 6. 3. Apul. l. 2. Tit. Liv. l. 6.
Du Choul observes that when the Pagan priests made their processions through the streets, they carried the image of Jupiter, and prepared couches or resting places in the squares, on which they placed it; "which is still practised in France in the solemn procession of Corpus Christi."

Who knows not that the ceremonies of Candlemas were borrowed from the Pagans, who, on the same month celebrated a feast in honour of Ceres and her daughter Proserpine, and who went in procession, on the day of that festival, with candles and burning torches? Durand bishop of Mande, gives us this account; and informs us that Pope Sergius instituted this feast in place of the other.[112]

Once more, whence are derived the *Agnus Deis*, which they hang about the necks of their children, unless from the ancient Pagans, who in like manner suspended at the neck of their infants, small vials or bottles, to preserve them against enchantments or sorceries; as the Cardinal Baronius owns; or from these little images of the Pagans, in which was represented the thunder of Jupiter; as a learned man of the same church would account for it.

Here we have enough, I think, to oblige us to pronounce that the Romish religion is by no means that pure Christian religion which we seek.

But let us hear, notwithstanding, whether she has anything to advance, which may cause us to alter our sentiment.

---

[112] "P. Sergius," says he, "changing for the better this manner of purifying instituted, on the same month, the feast of purification in honour of the mother of our Lord, and appointed that processions should be made at that time, and that all the people should join in them carrying wax-tapers in their hands." Div Off l 7 P. Innocent III in a sermon, on the purification, confesses that the holy father not being able to abolish entirely that custom of Pagan idolaters, ordained that in honor of the blessed virgin, they should carry lighted tapers; "and by this mean, what was formerly done in honor of Ceres, is now performed in honor of the virgin; what was for the honour of Proserpine, is turned to the honor of Mary."

REASONS

WHICH THE CHURCH OF ROME ADDUCES TO PROVE THAT SHE IS THE TRUE CHURCH.

REASON I.

The Romish church finds it to be a criminal and presumptuous boldness for any to contest with her the name of the true church; with her who denominates herself the church Catholic, in opposition to all sects whatever.

But this reason deserves very little attention. It is nothing to the purpose to enquire, whether the church of Rome assumes to herself the name of the Catholic church; but if she does so on good grounds. The Novatians claimed the title of Catholics in the time of Cyprian; the Arians did the same in the time of Constans and Valens; and the Donatists in the time of Augustine. All sorts of heretics, as Lactantius observes,[113] called their body *the Catholic church*.

In order to know whether that church justly bears this name, it is necessary to compare her doctrines with those taught by the apostles. This we have already done; and in consequence have found that there is the greatest difference between the church of Rome in the time of the apostle Paul, and the Romish church in these latter ages.

---

[113] "*Sed tamen quia singuli quisque coetus haereticorum se potissimum Christianos, et suam esse Catholicam Ecclesiam putant.*" *Inst.* lib. 4.

REASON II.

But who, say they, can doubt for a moment whether the Romish church be not the true church, since it is made evident that the bishops who at present occupy the holy See at Rome, succeed to these first bishops which the apostles had consecrated, and established in that bishopric.

This second reason is not a whit better than the first. One of the most celebrated cardinals of that church confesses that we cannot necessarily infer that the church must be where the succession is.[114] The scribes and Pharisees did sit in the seat of Moses; and the Arians formerly in the chair of the orthodox. The true succession consists not in occupying the same See, but in teaching the same doctrines. Gregory Nazianzen observed long ago, that "to be in the same mind is to be in the same See, whereas to be of contrary sentiments is to in one altogether opposite; that the one has the succession only in name, and the other in truth and reality, unless they would plead for a successor of the same kind as when disease succeeds to health, darkness to light, and the tempest to a calm."[115] It belongs then to the Romish church to show that it teaches the same doctrine that the first bishops of Rome taught, and then we might without difficulty allow it the name of the true Christian church. Tertullian reasons nearly in this manner.[116] But without this proof, we will not regard her in such a light. Moreover, the argument from succession favors the Greeks as much as those of the Romish communion, for they also plead this uninterrupted succession.

---

[114] Bell. de Not. Eccl. B4 C8

[115] Gr. Naz. laud. Athan.

[116] "*Edant ergo origines Ecclesiarum suarum, volvant ordinem Episcoporum suorum ita per successiones ab initio decurrentem, ut primus ille Episcopus aliquem ex apostolis, vel apostolicis viris [qui tamen cum apostolis, perseveraverit] habuerit authorem et antecessorem. Consignant tale quid haereticæ: sed et confinxerint nihil promovebunt; ipsa enim doctrina eorum cum apostolica comparata ex diversitate et contrarietas sua pronuntiabit; quia sunt apostoli non diversa inter se docuissent, ita et apostolici contraria apostolis non edidissent.*" Tert. de Praescr. Haeret.

REASON III.

But can it be denied, they will say that the Romish church has been a true church?

No, surely; for Paul informs us that the faith of that church was celebrated throughout all the world.[117] But it can as little be denied that the churches of Corinth, of Ephesus, of Antioch, of Alexandria, of Thessalonica, of Philippi have been true Christian churches. Would those of the church of Rome be willing from thence to conclude that these are still what they formerly were? Let the Romish church then demonstrate that she is the same now that she was at the time when Paul said that her faith was spoken of throughout the whole world. The contrary of this is very obvious at this day, and we have sufficiently proven it.

REASON IV.

But it is further urged, if it be fact that the Romish church has been once a true church, how could she possibly fall from that dignity, and lose that character? Could the pillar of truth be overthrown; or the gates of hell prevail against that church which was like the mother of the rest? Or could the promise of Jesus Christ fail of their accomplishment?

This reasoning makes full as much for the Greeks as for the Latins: it was the church of Ephesus which Paul styled *the pillar and ground of truth.*[118] How then was it possible that pillar should have been overthrown? Those who maintain the cause of the Roman church, have nothing to reply to this argument. But what may we say in answer to theirs?

---

[117] Romans 1:8
[118] 1 Timothy 3

We answer that Jesus Christ has promised that there shall always be a church in the world, which shall be the pillar of truth, against which the gates of hell shall never prevail; and that all the powers of the world and of the devil cannot hinder, but that there should be always a number of believers, who shall make a profession of his gospel. But that Jesus Christ never made a promise of preserving always one particular church, as that of Rome, or Ephesus; and accordingly it has been seen that many churches, which had been founded by the apostles, are degenerated from their primitive purity, and are no longer what they formerly were. God often transports his candlestick from one place to another, and then the places which had enjoyed a clear light are plunged in darkness, and the people which were in darkness see a great light. There was a time when Rome, Antioch, Ephesus, were pillars and supports of the truth; but to these happy times very different and deplorable times have succeeded. These flourishing churches have lost their purity; and in vain should any now seek for the Rome founded by the apostles, in that which presently subsists, and which is as remarkably corrupted, as the first was pure and holy.

REASON V.

"But, was not the Roman church regarded as the center of unity, and as the mistress of all Christian churches?"

Even although this should be granted, it would not thence follow that the Roman church had not erred, or that it had not lost its purity and glory. But the assertion is false: that church was indeed better known than others because it was in the capital of the Roman empire; yet it was never regarded as the center of communion more than the first churches of other dioceses. Gregory Nazianzen—writing to the clergy of the church of Caesarea in Cappadocia—says that it is "The mother of almost all the churches, and that it is to her they all look, as the circle inclines to the centre around which it is drawn." Gregory therefore could not consider the church of Rome as the only center of unity. When Pope Victor excommunicated the Greek churches, in the end of the second century, Irenæus bishop in Gaul highly blamed the conduct of Victor, and held communion with those churches which that Pope had excommunicated. In the third century, when Pope Stephen cut off Cyprian from his communion, on account of the dispute concerning the validity of baptism conferred by heretics, Cyprian notwithstanding was still regarded as a member of the true church. The emperors Gratian, Valentinian, and Theodosius the Great, in the year 380, proposed not only Rome, but also Alexandria, for a model of the orthodox faith, ordaining that every one should follow the religion not of Damasus, bishop of Rome, alone, but likewise of Peter, bishop of Alexandria; and what is still more, in 388, Theodosius the Great made an edict in favor of the presbyters Faustinus and Marcellinus, although they had been separated from the communion of Rome, and commanded his *Præfectus Prætorium* to defend them against all persons whatever. It appears therefore that the church of Rome was not formerly regarded, as they would have us now to believe. But we once more say, though that were true, if the church of Rome has erred, why should we regard her as the rule of our faith?

REASON VI.

"But," say they, "If Rome at present is so very different from what it was formerly, let some of the circumstances of this change be specified. Let the authors of it, and the times when it was made, be pointed out."

I answer, this demand is unreasonable. No person ever denied but that changes may have taken place insensibly in the church, the beginnings of which it may be impossible to trace out. It was an error in the primitive church that the communion should be given to infants. This practice is abolished. How this change was made, nobody can tell. It was an early error

146

in the church to put up prayers to God for the patriarchs and prophets, for the blessed virgin, and the apostles; who is he who can mark the time, specify the place, and name the inventor of such a strange opinion, or show the council wherein it was condemned, or when it first sprang up? The enemy sows the tares in the field of the Lord, in the time when men sleep, and they are not perceived until afterwards. Until an error has produced some noise and disorder in the world, nobody takes the trouble expressly to impugn it; and the falsehood of an opinion and its hurtful consequences are not always at first discerned. Wherefore, although we could not mark any circumstances of the changes which have taken place in the Romish church, this would be no reason for denying that they have really happened; since nothing more is needful than to compare the faith of the three first centuries with that which is now maintained. But after all, it is not impossible to mark the time in which the errors of Rome were admitted for articles of her faith, as also the times when she began to celebrate certain feasts, and to practice certain ceremonies.

It was not until the year 1439, in the Council of Florence under Pope Eugene IV that the doctrine of Purgatory passed into an article of faith, although we do not deny that it had before this been already received in that church.

It was only in 1415 that the people were deprived of the use of the cup, namely in the Council of Constance, whose decree on this head cannot be read without horror.[119]

---

[119] It runs thus: "Although Jesus Christ instituted and administered the venerable sacrament to his disciples under both kinds of bread and wine; and though in the primitive church the faithful received it in both kinds, nevertheless, to evite certain dangers and scandals, this custom with good reason was introduced that the ministers officiating, should receive it in both kinds, but the laity under the species of bread alone. Wherefore it ought to be accounted an erroneous opinion that the observation of that custom or law, is sacrilegious or anything unlawful; and those who obstinately maintain the contrary, ought to be banished as heretics, and punished severely by the diocesan or officials of the places they belong to."

The procession of the holy sacrament was not ordained till the fourteenth century.[120]

It was in the year 1300 that Boniface VII enjoined the first jubilee which was to be solemnized every hundredth year.[121]

In 1264 Urban IV—upon a pretended revelation of a devotee of Liege—first instituted the feast of the sacrament.[122]

It was not until about the year 1220 that Honorius III ordained the adoration of the host; and Gregory IX afterwards the ringing of the bell.[123]

In the year 1215 Innocent III in the Council of Lateran, by his own proper authority, made this decree that: "The body and blood of Jesus Christ are truly contained under the species of bread and wine in the sacrament of the altar, the bread being transubstantiated into the body, and the wine into the blood."

It was in the twelfth century that Stephen, Bishop of Autun, began to make use of the word *transubstantiation*. Though it is not certain whether it was he who lived in the year 1112, or he in 1160, yet the one or the other says that: "The oblation of bread and wine is transubstantiated into the body and blood of Jesus Christ."[124]

---

[120] Some ascribe this institution to John XXII. Others think that this procession was begun at Padua, about the year 1360.

[121] Clement VI reduced it to 50 years, Urban VI to 33, and Paul II to 25.

[122] Clement. B3. tit. 16. To this religious, whose name was Eve, Urban VI wrote a letter, in which he said, "We know, my daughter, that your soul has desired with a great desire, that a solemn feast of the body of Jesus Christ should be instituted in the church, to be celebrated by the faithful forever." This nun had two friends, one of whom, named Juliana, when at prayer saw the moon at full, having a small breach or defect in it: whereupon she received an intimation that this breach denoted the defect of a feast, yet wanting to the church. Jo. Diesteim Blaerus.

[123] The constitution of Honorius enjoins that: "The priests should often instruct the people, that at the elevation of the host, when mass is celebrated, they should kneel with respect, and that they should do the same when it is carried by the priest to the sick." Gregory IX, who succeeded Honorius in 1227, ordained that "when the body and blood of Christ should be made, and the host elevated, a bell should be rung, that all who heard it might fall upon their knees, and with clasped hands worship the host." Decret. Greg. IX, l. 3. tit. 41. c. 10.

[124] Lib. de sacr. alt. c. 13.

It was about the year 1260 that Alexander III appointed that for the time to come no person should be acknowledged for a saint unless he had first been declared such by the pope; and he decreed that the body of Edward, King of England, should be adored.

It was not until the eleventh century that they presumed to condemn those who affirmed that the Eucharist was the figure of the body and blood of Jesus Christ, which was then done in the condemnation of Berenger.[125] I omit here what was done in the year 1059, in the Council of Lateran, under Nicolas II, where it was maintained that: "The bread and wine are the true body and blood of Jesus Christ; and that his body is sensibly handled and broken by the hands of the priests, and bruised by the teeth of the faithful, not only sacramentally but in reality:" because this decision is not received with general approbation in that church.

It was one Peter, a hermit of Amiens, who—according to the common opinion, in the idleness of his retreat—invented the method of praying by turning a chapelet, or, string of beads, and by repeating as many Hail Marys as Pater Nosters, about the year 1090.[126]

In the year 963, the baptism of bells was established under John XII.[127]

The doctrine of real presence, as it is adopted in the Romish communion, was not taught before the 9th century, when Paschasius Rathbert, monk of Corbie, composed his treatise of the body and blood of Jesus Christ in the year 818. On this account Cardinal Bellarmine says that

---

[125] Pope Leo IX convened two different councils, in 1050, for this purpose. In one of these Berenger or Berengarius was condemned without being either heard, or cited. Gregory VII. got him condemned in another at Rome, in 1079; where a confession of faith was drawn up, which Berenger was obliged to subscribe.

[126] Polyd. Virg. l. 5. c. 9. de rer. Inv.

[127] The same ceremonies are used by Romanists in baptizing bells, as in the baptism of Christians. They exorcise the water, salt, and oil, made use of on the occasion; and employ the same unctions and signs of the cross. They assign them godfathers and godmothers. They pour water upon them, in name of the Father, Son, and Holy Spirit. They give them a name; and even none but a bishop is allowed to baptise them.

Paschasius was the first who wrote seriously and fully of the reality of the body and blood of Christ in the Eucharist.[128]

It was in the Second Council of Nicaea, held in 787, under Pope Adrian I that the worship of images was established.

It was Boniface IV in the seventh century, who instituted the feast of All Saints, and changed the Pantheon of the Pagans into a church in honour of the blessed virgin and the martyrs: the same that now bears the name of "Our Lady of the Rotunda."

It was in the fifth century that Mamert, Bishop of Vienne in Gaul, instituted the fast of rogations, about the year 463. As for the fast of the *Quatuor Tempora*, the first who appears to have mentioned it is Leo I, though what he says may be applied to other fasts.[129]

In the fourth century, Pope Syricius prescribed celibacy to priests, about the year 386; yet his orders as to this did not meet with ready or general obedience.

The monastic life began in the fourth century: the first foundations of it were laid in Egypt by St. Anthony, who died in the year 358. But the monks

---

[128] Anastasias of Mount Sinai contented himself with attacking the ancient modes of speaking on this subject; but Paschasius attacked the doctrine.

[129] Rogation-days were so called on account of extraordinary prayers, or litanies, used at these times for obtaining mercy. Mamertus having employed them upon the prospect of some particular calamities that threatened his diocese, they afterwards grew into a custom; and the Monday, Tuesday, and Wednesday, before Holy Thursday, are the times settled for them in the churches of Rome and England.

The fasts of Quatuor Tempora, called in England Ember days, are these observed at the four seasons or quarters of the year, being the Wednesday, Friday, and Saturday after the first Sunday in Lent; the feast of Pentecost, Sept. 14th, and Dec. 13th. The testimonies of St. Leo, referred to above, are to be found in his Sermons, many of which were delivered on the fasts at different times of the year; he insists much in them upon the obligation that Christians were under to fast, and advantages arising from the duty. There are nineteen of these upon the fast of September, in which he observes that the Ember-fasts were appointed to teach us that there is no time which ought not to be employed in the doing of good works; that this fast in September was instituted to give God thanks for the fruits of the earth, which they had just gathered in, and in us mind of bestowing a part of those things which God has given us, to the poor, by abstaining from them ourselves, etc. He died in the year 461 [*Translator*].

of these times were only laymen, who lived by the labor of their hands, and were at liberty to marry.

In the three first centuries, no trace is to be found of the primacy of the pope, of the invocation of saints and their mediation, of the worship of images, of the sacrifice of the mass, and many other errors, which the Romish church maintains with such eagerness.

Therefore it is not impossible to mark the origin of the errors of the Romish church.

REASON VII.

"But how can any presume, they will say, to call by the name of errors, doctrines which were taught by the apostles, and which may be proved by passages of Scripture?"

It is certain that those of that religion who possess the greatest candor and sincerity, confess that the doctrines of which we have spoken are not to be found in the sacred books. This is what many have avowed with regard to transubstantiation, the real presence, the sacrifice of the mass, the communion in one kind, the adoration and reservation of the eucharist, private masses, confession, indulgences, purgatory, the merit of works, the number of the sacraments, the celibacy of ecclesiastics, monastic vows, confirmation, extreme unction, and the invocation of saints. It is well known that George d'Ataida, a Portuguese divine, openly maintained and proved, in the Council of Trent, that the sacrifice of the mass had no foundation in the Scripture.

But further, it must be confessed that the passages that are adduced for establishing the sentiments of the Romish church, make so little for the proof of what they pretend to prove that one would almost think himself to be in a dream, when he reads such sort of arguments. You may judge of them by a specimen. To prove the worship of images, it is alleged that there were figures of cherubims over the ark, which however were not seen by the people: and that God caused a brazen serpent to be made; to which however no worship was given, until the time of Hezekiah, who on account of that worship caused it to be broken in pieces. They say that Jacob "worshipped the head of his staff:" although it is expressly said in the Greek that "he worshipped upon the top of his staff."[130] They produce that passage of Psalm 93, where it is said, "Worship *at*" or "*before* his footstool," which they translate thus, "Worship his footstool." By this name the holy place was called, towards which the people turned their face, in adoring the Most High. Again, to prove the communion in one kind, they tell us that the communion is called "the breaking of bread," much the same as if, from Genesis 31, where it is said that Joseph invited his brethren to eat bread, it should be concluded that he gave them nothing to drink; not considering that this was a manner of speaking common among the Hebrews. To prove transubstantiation, the only passage they produce is, "This is my body," though from the words, nothing can be concluded in favour of that doctrine. In proof of purgatory, they produce a passage from the apostle Paul, where it is declared in 2 Corinthians 3 that whosoever builds upon a good foundation, wood, hay, etc., shall be saved as by fire; although it is as clear as the day that nothing more is meant thereby, but that he shall be saved with difficulty, as a man who should make his escape through the midst of flames. So also to prove the sacrifice of the mass, they say that Melchizedeck, who was priest of the living God, offered bread and wine: as if it were not beyond all doubt that Melchizedeck offered that bread and wine to Abraham, in order to afford him some refreshment, after the battle which he had fought against the kings who had made Lot a prisoner. How very far might I go did I choose to go over all the proofs which are employed to support the rest of their doctrines?

---

[130] Hebrews 11:21

REASON VIII.

"But," says the Romish church, "We are in possession of the right of teaching these opinions; there is prescription on their side."

Is truth then to be considered in the same light as a field or a house? Can there be prescription against the word of God? Who that has the least degree of reason can entertain such sentiments? Tertullian, Cyprian, Firmilian, Augustine, spoke a very different language.[131] Were that allowed, then the Gentiles and the Jews would have good warrant to insist upon their ancient possession.

If those of the church of Rome have been for a long time in possession of their errors, certainly they ought at least to acknowledge that they have not enjoyed a peaceable possession, and that some have always been found who have protested against these errors, which is sufficient to prevent the prescription they plead.

REASON IX.

But, they will say, though we suppose the church of Rome to have erred, does all error in doctrine, and every fault in worship, deprive a particular church of the essence of the true church?

No, my brethren, a church is always a true church, as long as she errs not in things essential, or overturns not the foundation of the Christian religion and is free from idolatry; for idolatry is a spiritual adultery, which breaks the bond of communion between the creature and his Creator; and idolators shall not inherit the kingdom of heaven. But sadly has the church

---

[131] "*Veritati nemo praescribere potest non spatium temporum, non patrocinia personarum, non privilegium regionum, etc. [...] Quodcunque adversus veritatem sapit, hoc erit haeresis, etiam vetus consuetudo.*" Tert. de veland. vir. "*Consuetudo sine veritate, vetustas erroris est.*" Cypr. ad Pomp. etc.

of Rome erred, and erred even in things essential and fundamental, and it is impossible to excuse her on the head of idolatry, as we have already made evident.

REASON X.

"But," it is added, "Does she not receive all the truths contained in the Apostles' Creed, the Lord's prayer, and the commandments?"

It is true she makes a profession of receiving them; but she joins such errors with these truths as directly impugn them.

She makes the Lord's prayer to be recited to God, but she also causes the saints to be invocated. She professes not to believe, nor to put her confidence in any but in God the Father, the Son and the Holy Spirit; yet it is apparent that she also places her confidence in creatures. She professes to have no other God but one, yet she adores what is but bread, and the cross; and serves those which by nature are no gods. She rehearses as an article of her creed that Jesus Christ is ascended into heaven, and sits at the right hand of the Father, notwithstanding she believes that his body is still upon the earth, in a million of places at once. She repeats the Decalogue, but she bows down before images, contrary to what is therein expressly forbidden. She receives the Scripture, but she forbids to read it, and puts traditions on a level with it. She acknowledges Christ to be our Mediator, but she joins others with him. She owns Jesus Christ to be the Head and Husband of the church, but she bestows the same titles and honor upon the pope.[132]

Are not these errors fundamental; more especially when all are obliged under the pain of anathema, and other punishments, to receive them as

---

[132] Bell. *de Rom. Pont.* c. 1. c. 9. And in his preface, he applies to the pope the words of Isaiah, which the apostle Peter declares to have been spoken of Jesus Christ: "Behold I lay in Zion, a chief corner stone, elect and precious, and whosoever believeth on him shall not be confounded."

154

truth? These are errors which have influence on practice; and they are not such as are drawn by us as consequences, which those of the Romish communion may reject; for it is by no strained consequences that we charge that community with believing the sacrifice of the mass, the worship of images, purgatory, and the adoration of the eucharist.

REASON XI.

"But who can refuse to acknowledge that church for a true one, which has all along supported, and still supports her doctrines by such a multitude of miracles?"

But this reason strikes with as little force as the preceding:

1. Everyone knows what great cause there is to doubt the truth of the miracles of which they speak; and those who avail themselves of this pretext, perhaps doubt of them as much as those to whom they propose it.

2. But besides, the sacred writers have fortified us against this argument. Paul, when describing the man of sin, who should sit as God in the temple of God," says that "the coming of that wicked one should be "according to the working of Satan, with all power and wonders." John in Revelation 13, speaking of the beast which has two horns like a lamb, says that: "He shall do great signs, so as to cause fire to come down out of heaven upon earth in the sight of men;" and Jesus Christ declares in express terms that: "False christs and false prophets should arise, and do great signs and wonders." To this may be added what a celebrated Jesuit affirms that: "In the time of Antichrist it will be very difficult to distinguish the true miracles from the false, because these shall be in great number, very notable and very like to the true."[133] Augustine, as the writers of the Romish church themselves have observed, asserts that the miracles which the Donatists wrought were no sufficient

---

[133] A Costa de Temp. noviss. l. 2. c. 19.

proof to show that they belonged to the true church, and he bestows upon them by way of contempt, the name of *wonder-workers*, etc.[134]

REASON XII.

"But," yet again it will be said, "Does not the magnificence and external glory of the Romish church form a powerful prejudice in her favor?"

Surely not, my brethren. If we must judge of a church by that, then what account must we make of Pagan Rome in former times; and what judgment must we form of these powerful empires which at present make profession either of the Pagan or Mohammedan religion? The glory and splendor of the true church is not external; all her beauty is within. She resembles her divine Head, whose kingdom is not of this world.

REASON XIII.

"But ought not the great number of ceremonies belonging to that church persuade us of the truth of her religion?"

On the contrary, this great number of ceremonies taken partly from Judaism, and partly from Paganism, is a very strong prejudice against the religion of Rome: "If you be dead with Christ," says Paul, "to the rudiments of the world, why are ye yet subject to ordinances, as if living in the world?" (Colossians 2:20, etc.) "Touch not, taste not, handle not, which all are to perish with the using; after the doctrines and commandments of men: which things have indeed a show of wisdom in will-worship, and humility, and neglecting of the body, not in any honour to the satisfying of the flesh."

---

[134] Aug. Tract. 13. in Jo. et de unit. Eccles. c. 16, "Mirabilarios." Entret. d'Eudoxe, etc. Maimbourg. Hist. des Iconocl. p. 27.

REASON XIV.

"But will not the union of the members which compose the Romish church, prove the truth of that religion?"

It does not always hold true that external union is a mark of the true church. Satan takes care that his kingdom should not be divided. There may be union in certain things which does not deserve that name: the Sadducees and Pharisees were united together in one body, under one high priest, against Jesus Christ and his apostles; although they had a mortal hatred to one another. Who is ignorant of the schisms which have taken place in the Romish church, or the division which subsists among her different orders, although they are all joined together against us under a common head?

External union without the true doctrine can never be a mark of the church. The Arians, during their prevalence, made a boast of their unity, which was the reason of Hilary thus addressing them: "The name of peace is specious, and the opinion entertained of unity is lovely; but who can doubt whether the peace of the church be any other than the peace of Christ? The ministers who are forerunners of Antichrist, who is at hand, boast of their peace, that is, of unity in their impiety, behaving themselves not as the bishops of Christ, but as the priests of Antichrist."[135]

REASON XV

"*In fine,*" they ask, "Who can refuse to pronounce that church [to be] the true church, in whose bosom are nursed up religious of both sexes, who prefer poverty to riches, the rigour of discipline to pleasures, who despise the

---

[135] "*Speciosum quidem est nomen pacis, et pulchra est opinio unitatis; sed quis ambigat eam solam pacem esse atque evangeliorum unicam pacem esse, quae Christi est.—Imminentis Antichristi praevii ministri pace sua, id est, impietatis suae unitate se jactant, agentes se, non ut Christi episcopos, sed Antichristi sacerdotes.*" Hilar. contr. Auxent.

world, its grandeur and pomp, who deny nature its demands, who mortify the flesh and conquer it, and who live, in a word, as saints and angels?"

Many things might be said here in reply, both as to the kind of life which is led by these monks, and as to their poverty and macerations, which God does not exact at their hands. But should we travel among the Turks, we might find there religious men who pass their life in still greater austerity, and apparent piety, which yet will never persuade us of the truth of the Mahometan religion. It were easy here to enlarge upon the disorders of these pretended saints, and of the greater part of the convents. But I choose to draw a veil over these matters, and appeal concerning them to the conscience of those who employ such objections against us.

From all that we have above advanced, it follows that the church of Rome has no cause to boast of her being the true church, and that it is not with her we are to seek pure and genuine Christianity; and this is what we proposed to prove.

APPLICATION

Before I conclude this discourse, I cannot avoid making the three following reflections:

The first is that as many as are of the communion of Rome have great reason to tremble. For one cannot belong to that church without adoring as the proper person of the Son of God, the Creator and Redeemer of the world, what is in reality nothing more than bread, and consequently involving themselves in idolatry. Nor can they be in it without participating of the sacrifice of the mass, which is the highest injury that can be done to Jesus Christ our great high priest; nor without invoking the saints and angels, which is to divide the honor which is due to God alone, between him and the creature; nor without participating and approving of the worship which is given to images, which God has so expressly prohibited; nor without depriving themselves of one of the signs which God has appointed in the holy supper; nor without subscribing to human satisfactions and purgatory, which is to declare themselves not content with the blood of Jesus Christ; nor without acknowledging another head of the church than our divine Redeemer. And we leave it to themselves to examine whether those who believe and do such things have good warrant to hope for salvation, after what the Scripture has said that idolaters shall not enter into the kingdom of heaven.

The second reflection is that it must be highly unreasonable to hate those who have no faith in these doctrines.

What reason is there to hate people who cannot think of invoking any other than God, not from any contempt of the saints, or the blessed virgin, but merely because they choose to do nothing but what God has commanded them?

Why hate people who will not bow themselves before images because God has expressly forbidden them? Why hate people who do not acknowledge a purgatory, either because they can find no shadow of such a thing in the sacred books, or because they perceive that it is nothing else than an imitation of the Pagans, in whose writings, as in Virgil and Plato, the Romish doctors do not deny that it is to be found, or because they are persuaded that this doctrine serves only to trouble the consciences of believers; or *in fine*, because they know that "the blood of Jesus Christ cleanseth them from all sin," as the apostle John has taught them?

Why hold in abhorrence those who receive not the doctrine of transubstantiation because they cannot receive it without contradicting the testimony of their senses, and without opposing the light of their reason, and because they find in Scripture express passages overthrowing this opinion? We are not masters either of our senses which represent things to us, such as they see them, taste them, or handle them, and by no means such as we may perhaps wish that they should be; nor of our reason to make it believe what shocks its clearest lights; nor of our faith to oblige it to believe other things than revelation has taught us.

Why hate people who will have no other sacrifice but that alone which Jesus Christ offered upon the cross, and because they are convinced the sacrifice of the mass is injurious to that which Jesus Christ offered once for all? Ought it to be accounted worthy of blame that we should place our whole hope in the cross of our Savior, and that we should acknowledge no other propitiatory offering for our sins, than that which he presented to his Father, in the days of his flesh? Ought we to be held culpable for not choosing to assign companions to our Lord in his office of priesthood, and because we will not take it upon us to present sacrifices, which God has not required?

Once more, why hate and persecute people who refuse to adore the sacrament, but content themselves with adoring Jesus Christ in heaven, because they are persuaded that the body of this divine Savior is not in the eucharist, and so they could not adore the sacrament without being idolaters?

The third reflection which we entreat you to make is that we ought continually to bless God for his graciously enabling us to retain and carry along with us all the Christianity which was in the Roman church, and to leave her only that which she received not of the Lord. Let us be satisfied with what our divine Savior has delivered to us, and not acknowledge any other infallible judges of our faith than his apostles, which he has set upon twelve thrones, to judge the twelve tribes of his mystical Israel. Let us not be wise above what is written. If the Christian religion were the work of the human understanding, we might believe that, like other productions of men, it would be formed by little and little, and that the Scriptures in that case would not contain all that was necessary to be believed in religion; but Christianity came perfect from the hands of its author. Nothing therefore is to be added to it. Let us make continual progress in the knowledge of these holy writings, which are able to make us wise unto salvation, and perfect.

Let us not allow ourselves, at any time, to be deceived by vain words; and let us request of God continually that he suffer not our faith to fail, but that he would confirm and establish us in his truth, so that we may always keep that precious deposit, which he has committed to us, without suffering ourselves at any time to be robbed of it, being persuaded that he is powerful and faithful, to keep also what we have committed to him, even to that last day of his Son Jesus Christ. Amen.

APPENDIX

To show that we do not impute to the Church of Rome principles which she does not avow, we shall subjoin here, the Bull of Pope Pius IV concerning the form of the profession of faith.

The BULL and CREED of PIUS IV

Containing an epitome of the whole doctrine of popery.

"PIUS bishop, and servant of the servants of God, to all present and to come. The duty of our apostolical office obliging us to cause to be executed without delay, to the honor and glory of the Lord Almighty, what it pleased him to inspire into the holy fathers assembled in his name, to serve for the direction of his church; and the Council of Trent having decreed that henceforth all those who shall have the charge of cathedral and metropolitan churches, and those who shall be admitted to curacies, canonries, and all other ecclesiastical benefices, having the care of souls, shall be obliged to make profession of the orthodox faith, and to swear to continue forever in the obedience of the Romish church: it being also our will that the same thing should be observed by all those who shall reside in monasteries, convents, religious houses, and other regular places or orders, under any name or title whatsoever, and that for this end one and the same profession of faith should be presented to them. We, of our full apostolical power, and according to the decree of the said council, order and expressly command all those to whom it may appertain in whatever part of the world they may be, to publish, solemnly swear, keep, and observe the form of oath annexed to these presents, and no other, under the pains ordained by the same council, against the contraveners, and that they make this profession of faith in the form following:

"I do with a firm faith believe and profess all and every one of those things, which are contained in that Creed, which the holy Roman church uses, that is to say:

1. I believe in one God, the Father Almighty, Maker of heaven and earth, and of all things visible and invisible.

2. And in one Lord, Jesus Christ, the only begotten Son of God, begotten of his Father before all worlds; God of God, Light of Light, very God of very God; begotten, not made, being one substance with the Father, by whom all things were made.

3. Who for us men, and for our salvation, came down from heaven, and was incarnate by the Holy Ghost of the Virgin Mary, and was made man.

4. And was crucified also for us, under Pontius Pilate, suffered and was buried.

5. And the third day rose again according to the Scriptures.

6. And ascended into heaven, and sits on the right hand of the Father.

7. And he shall come again with glory to judge both the quick and the dead, whose kingdom shall have no end.

8. And I believe in the Holy Ghost, the Lord and giver of life, who proceeded from the Father and the Son, who, with the

Father and the Son together, is worshiped and glorified, who spake by the prophets.

9. I believe one catholic and apostolic church.

10. I acknowledge one baptism for the remission of sins.

11. I look for the resurrection of the dead.

12. And the life of the world to come. Amen.

13. I most firmly admit and embrace apostolical and ecclesiastical traditions, and all other observations and constitutions of the same church.

14. I do admit the holy Scriptures in the same sense that holy mother church does, whose business it is to judge of the true sense and interpretation of them; and I will interpret them according to the unanimous consent of the fathers.

15. I do profess and believe that there are seven sacraments of the new law truly and properly so called, instituted by Jesus Christ, our Lord, and necessary to the salvation of mankind, though not all of them to every one, namely: baptism, confirmation, eucharist, penance, extreme unction, orders, and marriage, and that they do confer grace; and that of these, baptism, confirmation, and orders, may not be repeated without sacrilege. I do also receive and admit the received and approved rites of the catholic church in her solemn administration of the above-named sacraments.

16. I do embrace and receive all and everything that has been defined and declared by the holy Council of Trent concerning original sin and justification.

17. I do also profess that in the mass there is offered unto God a true, proper, and propitiatory sacrifice for the quick and the dead; and that in the most holy sacrament of the eucharist there is truly, really, and substantially, the body and blood, together with the *soul* and *divinity* of our Lord Jesus Christ, and that

there is a conversion made of the whole substance of the wine into the blood; which conversion the catholic church calls *transubstantiation.*

18. I confess that under one kind only, whole and entire, Christ and the true sacrament is taken and received.

19. I do firmly believe that there is a purgatory; and that the souls kept prisoners there, do receive help by the suffrages of the faithful.

20. I do likewise believe that the saints, reigning together with Christ, are to be worshiped and prayed unto; and that they do offer prayers unto God for us; and that the relics are to be held in veneration.

21. I do most firmly assert that the images of Christ, and of the blessed virgin, the mother of God, and of other saints ought to be had and retained; and that due honor and veneration ought to be given to them.

22. I do affirm that the power of indulgences was left by Christ in the church, and that the use of them is very beneficial to Christian people.

23. I do acknowledge the holy catholic and apostolic church to be the mother and mistress of all churches; and I do promise and swear true obedience to the bishop of Rome, the successor of St. Peter, the prince of the apostles, and the vicar of Jesus Christ.

24. I do undoubtedly receive and profess all other things which have been delivered, defined, and declared by the sacred canons and ecumenical councils, and especially by the holy synod of Trent; and all things contrary thereunto, and all heresies condemned, rejected, and anathematized by the church, I do likewise condemn, reject, and anathematize.

I promise, vow, and swear to do what in me lies, that all those who depend on me, and are under my charge, shall hold, teach, and preach this catholic faith, without which none can be saved, and that with the help of God I shall firmly and constantly retain it, as I now make profession of it, to the last breath of my life. *So help me God, and his holy gospels.*"

Our will and pleasure is that these presents be read and published, in the usual manner in our apostolical chancery; and that they should be registrated and printed, that they may be known to all the world. We forbid all persons, whoever they may be, to infringe the present declaration of our will, or to venture rashly to contravene it; and if any shall dare to attempt it, let him know that he will incur the indignation of God Almighty, and of the apostles St. Peter and St. Paul.

Given at Rome, the 13th of November, the year of our Lord 1564; and the 5th of our Pontificate.

THE

EXAMINATION

OF THE

RELIGION OF THE GREEKS AND THAT OF PROTESTANTS

THE FIFTH DISCOURSE

On 1 Thessalonians 5:21: *Prove all things.*

The sacred history informs us that the prophet Elijah was so extremely afflicted, when, in a time of general corruption in Israel, he believed that he alone was a worshiper of the true God that when the Lord asked him, what he did in the cave, he answered him, "I have been exceeding jealous for the Lord God of Hosts, because the children of Israel have forsaken thy covenant, broken down thine altars, and slain thy prophets with the sword, and I only am left, and they seek my life also to take it away." But the sacred writer adds that he received a very great consolation, when the Lord made him this reply: "I have reserved unto me seven thousand, which have not bowed the knee unto Baal."

My friends, the state in which the church of Israel was during the time of this prophet, has a great resemblance to that wherein the Christian church has been in the last ages. She has sometimes been reduced to such extremities that her poor Elijahs have been constrained to go and hide themselves in deserts and caves, to avoid the persecution to which the profession of the truth every moment exposed them; and from thence they have sent up to heaven these bitter complaints: "Lord, they have forsaken thy covenant, they have put to death thy servants and we only are left."[136]

But God has taken care to console his people, by informing them that he had reserved for himself a number of Christians who had not bowed the knee before the idol, and who had maintained fidelity to him in every trial. These Christians afterwards discovered themselves; for when God made them to hear that mighty voice, "Depart out of Babylon my people!" they obeyed with readiness the heavenly mandate, and formed the body of a church upon the perfect model of that of the apostles.

You are at no loss to understand, my dear brethren, that I speak to you of the Protestant and Reformed church, of which, by the grace of God, we are members. But as it becomes us to believe nothing without examination, to day let us see, whether we do not deceive ourselves, and whether indeed our religion be the true and pure Christianity.

We proved in our last sermon that we seek in vain for this pure Christianity in the Roman church. Let us enquire, if we shall find it, either in the Greek church, or in our own. These shall then be the two points of our present discourse; and by discussing them, we shall put in practice what the apostle enjoins in the words, which we have read unto you for the fifth time: *Prove all things.*

---

[136] Luther said that "It had happened to him as to the prophet Elijah, who during the idolatry of the ten tribes, and the persecution of Ahab and Jezebel, supposed himself to be alone, and desired to retire from the world, not knowing that God reserved 7000 men, and that Obadiah had preserved himself with 100 prophets who were concealed in the caves. If I may be allowed," adds he, "to compare great things with small, this appears to me to be a description of this age. For having been, I know not by what providence, forcibly drawn into the public, I have combated in such a manner these ministers of indulgences and the pontifical laws, that I thought myself to be alone. [...] But behold what they tell me [...] that God has reserved some remnant for himself, and that even at this time, there are yet some prophets preserved in some lurking place." He afterwards mentions Wesselus, otherwise called Basil of Groninga, who was surnamed, "the Light of the World."

Examination of the GREEK RELIGION.

Before entering into the examination of the religion of the Greeks, it is necessary that we should premise these two remarks.

First, that we do not here speak of those Greeks who have been gained over by the Latins; nor of those who have been brought up in the seminaries of Rome, or of Venice; nor of those who have been drawn to the Romish communion, by large promises and pensions; nor of those who having come to implore the aid of popes, have reckoned it the most effectual way to obtain to it, to submit to their yoke. But we speak of those Greeks, which the Romish church considers as schismatics, and who are, for the most part at least, subjected to the empire of the Turks.

The second remark is that when we treat of the religion of the Greeks, we mean not only to speak of the religion of the people called Greeks, but that of the whole eastern church, and of those Christians which depend on the Patriarchs of Constantinople, Alexandria, Antioch, Jerusalem, and of Russia or Muscovy; for the Muscovites have had a Patriarch for more than a century past, since Jeremias of Constantinople consecrated Job Patriarch of Russia in the year 1588.

We choose not here to give you the history at large of the separation of the eastern church from the western, and of the occasion of it. I shall content myself with giving you some short view of it.

I shall not now speak of what took place in the second century, when Pope Victor excommunicated the churches of Asia, who celebrated Easter on the 14th day of the moon, on whatever day of the week it might happen, according to the practice of the Jews. The severity of this pope was greatly blamed, and this difference was settled in the First Council of Nicaea.[137] I shall only take notice of that which chiefly divided these churches.

This began in the seventh century, partly through the pride of the Popes of Rome, who aspired to the title of universal bishops, exclusively of the other bishops, while the patriarch of Constantinople chose not to yield any of his rights, since the Council of Chalcedon in 451, had granted to the See of [the] new Rome, that is Constantinople, privileges equal to those of the ancient; partly, on account of the controversy about the procession of the Holy Spirit, which began then to be agitated, as to which, an addition had been made to the creed of Constantinople that the Holy Spirit proceeded from the Son; and partly, because in a council of Constantinople, held in 680 in a chapel of the imperial palace,[138] wherein canons were made very displeasing to the court of Rome, about the marriage of priests and deacons, the fast of the sabbath, the equality of the patriarch of Constantinople with the bishop or Pope of Rome, and several other matters.[139]

These divisions greatly increased in the ninth century, in the time of Photius, Patriarch of Constantinople, which produced a schism that continued in the ages following.[140] Attempts indeed were made in the end of

---

[137] This council ordered that they should always chuse the sabbath immediately following the 14th of the month, and if the 14th day after the new moon, should fall upon a sabbath, that they should defer it until the sabbath following, to avoid celebrating Easter on the same day with the Jews.

[138] In Trullo: which signifies a vault raised in the form of a dome, which the Italians call a *Cuppola*.

[139] In the 13th canon, the council declared that: "If anyone be found fit to be ordained a sub-deacon, deacon, or priest, he should not be deprived of that honor on account of his being married, and that he should not be required to quit his wife; and this canon was made in opposition to the Roman church. The 4th expressly forbid to fast on the sabbath, contrary to the practice of Rome at that time. The 67th enjoined abstinence from blood, and things strangled. The 36 declared the See of Constantinople to be equal to that of Rome."

[140] Photius, having been established Patriarch of Constantinople, instead of Ignatius, who had been deposed and shut up in a close prison, on account of some crimes laid to his charge, Nicolas I. Pope of Rome declared himself his enemy, and as did also Adrian II, who procured his condemnation in a council of Constantinople, held in 869, and which is called the Eighth Universal Council. He was anathematized in it as

the eleventh century[141] to reunite the Greek church with the Latin, not only in the council of Bari (a city of Italy) held in 1097 or 1098 under Pope Urban II in which Anselm of Canterbury disputed against the Greeks; but by other methods too long here to relate: from whence it appears that nothing was left untried in order to reduce the Greeks again under the yoke of the Roman Pontiff, but without any success; and the schism subsisted in the thirteenth century, notwithstanding the pains of Innocent III, who wrote a letter himself to the Patriarch of Constantinople in 1198, wherein he explained to him the reason why the Roman church called herself the church universal, and threatened to proceed against him, if he did not render the obedience which was due to her. Gregory XI also wrote in 1231 to the Patriarch Germanus; and Gregory X for the same purpose, convened the Second Council of Lyon in 1274, whither Michael Paleologus, emperor of the East, sent ambassadors, who came in his name tamely to offer submission to the pope: which however did not put an end to the schism, because Andronicus, the son of this Michael, entertained very different sentiments from his father. It is true another council was held under Pope Eugene II at Ferrara, and continued at Florence in 1438, and the year following, wherein

---

a tyrant, a schismatic, an adulterer, a parricide, a forger of lies; and according to the account of Nicetas, in his *life of Ignatius*, the bishops subscribed the condemnation of Photius, not merely with ink, but after they had dipped their pen in the blood of the Saviour. Notwithstanding he was restored in 878, and Pope John VIII received him voluntarily into fellowship. After he was replaced in his see, he held a council in Constantinople in 879, in which he presided, and wherein all former proceedings against him were annulled, and an act passed, whereby all appeals from his see to that of Rome were prohibited. Thus the council eluded the demand made by the legates of the Pope, that the churches of Bulgaria should be dependent on Rome. John VIII gave but a cold reception to his legates, and sent to the emperor Basilius, bishop Marin or Martin, to protest against what had been done in the council; and for which the bishop was detained in prison a month at Constantinople. When John understood how his legate had been treated, he proceeded anew to excommunicate Photius.

[141] In the tenth century, Silininius and Sergius, Patriarchs of, strongly supported the writings of Photius; in the following age, there were animosities between Pope Leo IX and Michel Cerularius, patriarch of Constantinople; very sharp and angry letters passed between them, and anathemas were denounced on each side.

there was some appearance of the two divided churches coming to a reconciliation, as several Greeks there made all the concessions required of them; but there were others of them who declared that the Latins were heretics, and many of those who had been gained over, upon their return to their own country, confessed that they had meanly betrayed and sold their faith: and in the year 1443, the Patriarchs of Alexandria, Antioch, and Jerusalem convened a synod at Jerusalem, wherein they treated the Council of Paris as a packed council of no authority. Thus things remained in much the same state as they were before; and these two churches to this day look upon one another with aversion.

Having made these general remarks, I proceed to what was proposed, namely, to examine the religion of the Eastern Christians.

I. It will not certainly be refused that the eastern or Greek church is to be accounted a Christian church, since it acknowledges the most holy and adorable Trinity, the satisfaction of Jesus Christ, and many other important doctrines, taught and maintained in other Christian societies.

II. It is also undeniable that the Greeks reject a part of the errors of the church of Rome.

They acknowledge not the supremacy of the pope, as appears by the writings of their authors, and in particular, from those of Nilus archbishop of Thessalonica; and in many places they excommunicate the Pope every year. They are far from believing that the Roman pontiffs have power of granting indulgences for the life to come, to dispense with perjury and incest, and to dethrone kings. They cannot endure that the church of Rome should call herself the only catholic and apostolic church.

They do not believe that the bread in the eucharist is destroyed, and that the accidents alone remain, which is an evidence that they believe not transubstantiation. The word itself is not to be found in any of their public writings, which are not supposititious, and it is very probable that Gabriel Severus, the Metropolitan of Philadelphia, who had resided a long time at Venice, was the first among them who employed that term. They do not adore the sacrament: before the symbols be consecrated, when they are carried and placed on the table, they fall upon their knees, and the Grand Duke of Muscovy lays aside his crown; but after consecration, it is a matter of public notoriety, that they pay no adoration, either in the time of communion, or after it. Neither do they approve of mass without communicants. They communicate in both kinds. They consecrate the Eucharist by prayer, and not by pronouncing certain words with a low and muttering voice. They also communicate with leavened bread, the Armenian excepted. They have no belief of purgatory. They make no images of the divinity. They make only use of paintings, and not of sculpture, or molten figures, as the Latins do. They approve not of the celibacy of priests. They know nothing of the human satisfactions of saints, to profit other men. Nor do they perform the service in a language which the people do not understand.

There are, besides, several other opinions of the Romish church which they condemn. In consideration of which it appears that the church of the East is tainted with fewer errors than that of the West, and consequently is more pure.

III. It must also be confessed that many of these Greek Christians have had errors imputed to them which they do not hold.

For example, those called Nestorians, are charged with the error condemned in the council of Ephesus in 431, namely, of believing two persons in Jesus Christ; and those called Jacobites, or Monophysites or Dioscorians, with the error condemned in the Council of Chalcedon in 451, which consisted in believing that the two natures of Jesus Christ were confounded. Yet those who have examined the matter, and who have read the liturgy of the Nestorians, the Confession of Claude, king of the Ethiopians written in 1555, and what Basilidius another king of Ethiopia is said to have written in 1634, agree in acquitting these poor people from these errors of which they have been accused.[142] How much were it to be wished that no others could be laid to their charge?

IV. But it cannot be denied that they have their errors, and these capital ones too.

In reality they pay religious worship to images. It is true that the Armenians are so far from worshipping them in any sort that they even excommunicate those who pay them religious veneration,[143] and it would seem that they have always been of the same sentiments on this head; from whence some draw an argument to prove that this veneration of images was not introduced until after the third universal council held at Ephesus in 431, for it was not until after this council that the Armenians separated from the communion of other Christians. It is also true that the Nestorians, and these denominated the Christians of St. Thomas, are of the same sentiments with the Armenians; but as for the other Greeks, they pay devotion to images with care, they bow their knees before them, and light lamps or tapers in honour of them according to the order of the Second Council of Nicaea. It is even affirmed that some of them adore them as gods, and that they never enter into a house without looking around for the image in order to salute it, after which they make the sign of the cross three times, and bowing the head, say, "Lord, have mercy on me."[144]

---

[142] Vid. Job. Ludolphi. Histor. Cum commentariis.

[143] Nicon, who died in the year 968, in the treatise he wrote concerning the Religion of the Armenians, says expressly "Venerabiles imagines non adorant, sed quod magis est eorum universalis episcopus cum reliquis, [eos] qui adorant, anathemate percutit." This is also confirmed by another named Isaac, who is supposed to have lived about the year 1150; and Niceras say that they agree in this point with the ancient Germans.

[144] This is the account Sigismond Raro gives of the Moscovites: and a late author, in a book entitled *The Religion of the Muscovites*, printed at Amsterdam in 1698, relates the same in the following manner: "When they enter into the house of another, they salute no person whatever though there were twenty *kenez*, or *princes* of the country, or ever so many other great Lords present, until they have got a view of the saints of the house; they seek for them without speaking a word, as if they were mute, and if they do not instantly discover them, they say, *Nimate Pog*, that is, "Have you no god;" and after the saint is shown to them with great respect, they make their *Puclon*, that

They also invoke the saints. The Muscovites show great devotion towards the Virgin Mary. They boast of having her image drawn by St. Luke; and say that the Virgin commanded it to be kept in the city of Moscow, with these words, "My grace and power be with this image." They likewise pay great respect to St. Andrew, whom they believe to have introduced among them the Christian religion.[145] They have a distinguished respect also for Michael the Archangel, but above all, for their St. Nicholas, bishop of Mira, of whom they report many miracles:[146] with whom their St. Sergius is associated.[147]

There are some of them who go the length to say that the Virgin Mary is the mediatrix of salvation to men, by whom God is reconciled to us; that she is worthy to be called upon, because she is the mother of God, who brought forth a God and a man at once; and because by her authority as Mother she may have great influence over her son; that she helps us in our faults and infirmities, and that she prays for and protects the whole Christian world.

---

is, they bow their heads three times, beat their breasts as often, and thrice pronounce the words, *Gospodi Pomilui*, "Lord, have pity on me."

[145] They say that this apostle—having embarked in Greece—crossed the Euxine sea, and landed in the mouth of the Borysthenes, from thence he went to Kiev, which was then the city of greatest traffic in all Russia. They add that he preached to that people, and after he had converted and baptized all Russia, he taught them the sign of the cross. These are stories invented at pleasures as the Muscovites were not converted to Christianity for many years after the death of St. Andrew.

[146] St. Nicolas was bishop of Mira in Lysia, in the beginning of the 4th century. He was apprehended during the persecution of Licinius, and sent into exile, from which he returned after the defeat of that tyrant.

It is believed that he assisted at the Council of Nicaea. He is mentioned in the liturgy of John Chrysostom. The emperor Justinian built a superb city in honor of him.

They pretend that from his tomb flows a liquor which can cure all sorts of diseases. His remains were transported in the 11th century, to Bari in Italy, where, it is said, they have wrought many miracles.

[147] Sergius was the prior of a monastery near to Moscow. The time of his death is uncertain. Possevin and Olearius say that he died in the year 1562. But the Baron of Herberstein speaks of the burial of Sergius, in his *Travels*, printed in 1549.

The above errors, which they have in common with the church of Rome, are sufficient to convince us that they are idolaters, and consequently that pure Christianity is not to be found in these eastern churches.

Besides these, they have many other opinions and practices which cannot be approved. We disapprove of the manner in which they express themselves as to the Holy Spirit, saying that he proceeds not from God the Son, but only from God the Father. For the Scripture, in very many places, calls him the Spirit of the Son; and the Son is said to have sent the Holy Spirit. We approve not of their multiplied fasts, being persuaded that they are wrong in regarding the fast as a necessary part of divine worship; in ordaining abstinence from certain meats on those days, contrary to the doctrine of the apostle Paul; and in imagining that they should suffer themselves to die of hunger or disease, rather than make use of these forbidden meats. We believe that they misunderstand the decree of the Synod of Jerusalem, with respect to abstaining from blood and things strangled, which they look upon as the meat of devils; for it is clear that that apostolic decree was only temporary. We also disapprove of the great number of their feasts, in honor of the virgin Mary, of the apostles, John Baptist, St. Mark, St. Luke, St. Athanasius, St. Basil, St. Gregory, and St. Chrysostom. "Let no man condemn you," says the apostle, "in respect of an holiday."[148]

Neither do we believe with them that there is any part of Scripture that obliges to go and confess to a priest four times a year, as is their custom, although their confession be different from that of the church of Rome. We also judge them to be mistaken, when they affirm that the signs of bread and wine in the eucharist, are, by the virtue of the Holy Spirit, so united to the body and blood of Jesus Christ, that they become the true, proper, and substantial body of Christ; in the same manner, as the food we take so unites itself to our body, as to become our body. For what foundation is there for

---

[148] Colossians 2:16

such a thought? The bread and wine are here on earth below, while the body of Jesus Christ is in heaven. How then is it possible that they should be so united? We blame them also for admitting infants to the Holy Supper, since Paul requires those who communicate to examine themselves: of which infants are incapable.

We condemn them no less for holding the opinion that the souls of the faithful, separated from their bodies, are not immediately received into heaven; but that they pass into some other place where they enjoy rest: for where does the Scripture speak of this third place? Finally, we can by no means approve of their prayers for the dead, seeing as we have neither a commandment for it in Scripture, nor can any examples be found in the canonical books of the saints having ever offered prayers for the dead.

From all which we conclude that the Greek religion is not pure Christianity.

Where then shall we find it? Shall it be in the religion of Protestants? This is what we must now examine.

Examination of the REFORMED RELIGION.

I do not suppose that you expect I should here examine all the differences which subsist among those called Protestants. I shall confine myself to speak only of that religion which we in particular profess. To judge aright of it, it is necessary that we give you a short description thereof, in order that you may yourselves see whether we do not deceive ourselves in the favourable sentiments we entertain of our belief. We shall declare to you both what we believe in common with other Christian societies, and that wherein we differ from them; and you will perceive whether in what we believe as well as in what we do not believe, we equally follow the rule which God has given us.

I. We believe that there is a God, that is to say, a Being who possesses all perfections, who has made himself known to men by the works of creation, and revealed himself much more clearly and perfectly to them in this word. I am persuaded that there is not one among you who does not approve this article. None can oppose it without renouncing his light, and doing extreme violence to himself.

II. We receive the books which contain that word, both those of the Old Testament, of which God made the Jews the keepers, and those of the New; and we are persuaded that all scripture is divinely inspired, and that the prophets, the apostles and evangelists, wrote nothing but by inspiration, or under the direction of the Holy Spirit. What persuades us of the divinity of the Scriptures is the greatness and sublimity of the mysteries which they contain; the holiness of the precepts therein delivered, the agreement of the truths which they teach with the light of conscience, the types and prophecies of the Old Testament happily accomplished under the New economy, the marvellous efficacy of the doctrine therein proposed to move and awaken the heart, to convert and to comfort souls, with many other proofs. Examine whether we have not good ground for this our belief; and endeavor to recall into your mind what we said to you in our third sermon.

III. We receive no other books but those which are acknowledged for canonical by all Christians: of these there are thirty nine in the Old Testament, reckoning every particular book separately,[149] and twenty-seven in the New. We reject the other books called Apocryphal, which were not received by the people of God, to whom the oracles were committed. Of these some are only abridgments of certain histories, full of contradictions, as the Maccabees. Some are pieces which have been annexed to the Greek version of the Septuagint. Others are inconsistent with the canonical books, as the additions to Esther and Daniel. Others contain things false, as the books of Tobit and Judith. Others have the air of fable, as the pretended

---

[149] The Jews reckoned only 22 books of Scripture, because they joined several of them together: they made only one book of the twelve lesser prophets.

history of Susanna, etc. In this are we not supported by reason? We follow the sentiments of the ancient Christian church; and if the authority of the Third Council of Carthage be objected to us, we oppose to that the Council of Laodicea; and we have even some reason to doubt of that canon of the Council of Carthage, which is not to be found in many copies.

IV. We regard the canonical books as the rule of our faith and manners. In them we are taught to know God and ourselves; what God has done for us, and what we ought to do for him; what God requires of us, and what he has promised to us. We reckon ourselves obliged to read them and meditate upon them continually, according to the commandment laid upon us therein. For this can we be condemned?

V. We refuse to admit any opinion which is not contained in these books; because we have learned of the apostle Paul that if "any should preach any other gospel besides that which hath been preached, he ought to be held accursed, were he even an angel from heaven." Can any blame us for this conduct? The primitive Christians were of the same mind, "Do not produce human reasons," said Theodoret, "For I will give credit only to divine Scripture."[150]

VI. We believe conformably to these Scriptures, that there is one God but one; that this God is the most perfect of beings, that he is a pure spirit, disengaged from all matter, that he knows all things, that he is possessed of infinite wisdom, that he is almighty, that his goodness and mercy are ineffable, that he is supremely just and perfectly holy, so that he cannot suffer sin to pass unpunished, that he is everywhere present, eternal, and necessarily existent, and that he is a being most simple, immutable, infinite, and most glorious. Are not these truths diffused through the sacred books? For this then we surely are not to be reckoned heretics.

VII. We teach that there are three in whose name we are baptised, the Father, the Son, and the Holy Spirit, which have the essence and perfections

---

[150] Theodor. In Dial. Immus.

of Divinity, but that these three are but one God, as John says expressly; that they have therefore all three the same essence, the same eternity, the same wisdom, the same goodness, power, and glory, although they be nevertheless distinguished; for it is said that the Father begat the Son, and that the Spirit proceedeth from him, but it is not said that the Son begetteth the Father, nor that the Father proceeds from the Spirit.

VIII. We are therefore persuaded that Jesus Christ is the Son of God, his proper, his only Son, and that he is "God over all blessed for ever." We can entertain no doubt of this, since the apostle Paul has so instructed us, who elsewhere says that he is "the great God and Saviour;" and that not only all things were created by him, thrones, dominions, powers, but that he himself has founded the earth, and that the heavens are his work; that it is he of whom the Father said, "Let all the angels of God worship him," and that he is Jehovah, whom Israel tempted in the wilderness. We have also learned from the apostle John that he is God, "the true God, and eternal life," that all that was made, was made by him, and that nothing was made without him; that he searches the heart and the reins; that Isaiah saw his glory, when he saw the Lord sitting upon his throne, having the seraphim before him, who cried, "Holy, holy, holy is the Lord of hosts, the whole earth is full of his glory." Finally, we have learned of Jeremiah that he is "the Lord our righteousness."[151] In this can we be accused of error?

IX. We are also persuaded of the divinity of the Holy Spirit, in whose name we are baptised, as in that of the Father and the Son. We have learned from the mouth of Peter that to lie unto the Holy Ghost is to lie unto God, and from Paul that it is this Spirit who searches the deep things of God, and who works all things; that all the diverse gifts which are in the faithful proceed from him, and that we are his temples. It is on this account that we ask, with holy Paul, no less the communion of this Spirit, than the grace of the Lord Jesus, and the love of the Father: and we fear, above all things to sin

---

[151] Romans 9:5, Titus 2:13, Colossians 1:16, Hebrews 1:6, 8-12, 1 Corinthians 10, John 1:3, 12:41, 1 John 5:20, Revelation 2:12, Jeremiah 23:6

against this Spirit, because Jesus Christ has taught us that sins against the Father, and the Son shall be forgiven, but that the sin against the Holy Ghost shall never be forgiven. Do we here advance anything which is not evidently drawn from the holy Scriptures?[152]

X. We further believe that this eternal God, Father, Son, and Holy Spirit, has determined from all eternity whatever should come to pass in the world, and that his decrees are eternal, most wise, and unchangeable. None can deny this truth, without contradicting reason, as well as the Word of God.

XI. We preach that it is God who has created all that exists without himself, both things that are seen, and things invisible; men, angels, the heavens, the earth, the stars, plants and animals, and that "of him, and through him, and for him are all things." Have you not read the very same truths in Scripture?[153]

XII. We are convinced that this same God governs and conducts all by his providence, so that nothing falls out at any time but by his permission. And have you not read the declaration of Jesus Christ that not one sparrow falls to the ground without his will; that the very hairs of our head are numbered; and that which Paul says, that we have in God life, motion. and being, and that Jesus Christ maintains all things by his all-powerful word.[154]

XIII. We teach that God created man after his own image, that he endowed him with reason that he might be capable of knowing his Creator, and rendering to him the homage which was due; that he formed him holy and innocent, that he filled his soul with light and understanding, and gave him dominion over the creatures of this lower world; but that this man, though proceeding from the hands of God in that state, truly worthy of the wisdom of his Maker, did not long continue in it, seeing as he scarce knew his Creator when he offended him, and one of the first uses he made of his

---

[152] Acts 5:3-4, 1 Corinthians 2:10-11 & 12:2 & 6, 2 Corinthians 13:13, Matthew 12
[153] Genesis 1, Acts 4:24 & 17:24, Romans 6:35
[154] Matthew 6:29-30, Acts 17:28, Hebrews 1:3

liberty was to employ it in the act of disobedience, which God had given him, not to eat of the tree of knowledge of good and evil. And of this we have information by Moses.

XIV. We believe that by this first man, sin entered into the world, and death by sin, and by that one offence the judgment or guilt is come upon all men to condemnation. These are the very expressions of Paul on this subject. We are accordingly persuaded that all men born of Adam—Jesus Christ excepted—come into the world guilty and corrupt; that they are conceived in iniquity, and being born of the flesh, they are flesh, that is, they have a nature corrupt and vicious, and that corruption of sin is universal, not peculiar to some, but common to all the human race; that we are all by nature the children of wrath, and are deserving of death. Do you not recollect, in what I have here said, the words of David, of John, and of Paul?

XV. We are convinced that sins though they are not all equal, yet are all worthy of death, and even of eternal death; since the apostle Paul has taught us that "the wages of sin is death," and since it is entirely just that an offence committed against an infinite Majesty, from whom we have our being and subsistence, should be punished with death. Nevertheless, we believe that there are none of these which God does not forgive to those to whom he is pleased to be gracious, except the sin against the Holy Spirit, which shall not be forgiven either "in this world, or in that which is to come," that is to say, never.

XVI. We consequently believe that all men being sinners and deserving death, none of them should have been happy if God, before the foundation of the world, had not chosen or elected some of them, while he has predestinated unto glory, while he has left all the rest in their corruption; and if, in the resources of his wisdom, he had not found the means of contenting his justice, and exercising his mercy; in a word, if he had not given to men a Mediator. There is nothing of this which you have not read in the Scripture.

XVII. We preach that this Mediator is the Son of God, who in the fulness of time became man, in order to save us by obeying the law, and by suffering what we deserved to suffer, and what God as God, could not have endured: and we explain the conception, birth, life, death, resurrection and ascension of this Saviour, just as they are described to us by the evangelists. You are not ignorant of these, Christians.

XVIII. We teach that Jesus Christ by his death, has satisfied the justice of God, expiated our sins, reconciled us to his Father, that he has redeemed us, procured for us the pardon of all our offences, delivered us from the curses of the law, and established the covenant of grace. Are not these truths taken from the writings of the prophets and apostles, who inform us that "Jesus Christ is come into the world to save sinners," "to give his life a ransom for many," that "he was bruised for our iniquity, and wounded for our transgressions, and that the chastisement which brings peace to us was upon him;" that "he hath redeemed us from the curse of the law, when he was made a curse for us;" that "we were redeemed by his precious blood, as of a lamb without blemish and without spot;" that in him we have the remission of sins; that he bore our sins upon the tree; that we were brought nigh by his blood; and that God has reconciled the world by him? If the doctrine of the satisfaction be not clear in the Scripture, there is certainly nothing clear in the sacred books.[155]

XIX. We believe that Jesus Christ had three offices, which had been represented under the Old Testament, and are denoted to us by the word *Christ*, as the name of *Jesus* signifies that he is our Savior. These three offices are those of prophet, priest, and king.

XX. We affirm that, as a prophet, Jesus Christ has taught us the true way to heaven, and that we cannot learn that way but in his doctrine; that he alone has the words of eternal life, and that he is the only teacher whom we ought to hear; so when he was transfigured upon the mount, with Moses and Elijah, the heavenly Father said of him, "This is my well-beloved Son, hear ye him."

---

[155] 1 Timothy 1:15 & 2:15, Matthew 20:26, Isaiah 53

XXI. We believe that he is our great High-Priest, who appeared in the end of the world, to put away sin, by the sacrifice of himself, that he offered himself but once, and not often, otherwise he must needs have frequently suffered since the foundation of the world; that his oblation is of infinite value, so that it did not need to be repeated like that of the priests of old, and that such a repetition could not possibly take place without Jesus Christ actually suffering; that by this offering he has perfected them who are sanctified, and that his blood cleanses us from all sin. But we add that after he had offered here below his sacrifice, he ascended into the heavens, that he might appear in the presence of God for us; and thus his priesthood is eternal, seeing he is always able to save to the uttermost those who come to God by him, for he ever liveth to make intercession for them; so that he stands not in need of successors, as the priests under the Old Testament, which by death were prevented from continuing always alive.

XXII. *In fine*, we say that as a king, he governs us by the scepter of his word, and by his Spirit, and that his kingdom is not a kingdom of this world, which is promoted and administered by human means, and with worldly pomp, but that it is the kingdom of heaven, wherein all is spiritual and divine. Are not all these truths explained with the utmost evidence in the holy Scripture?

XXIII. We declare with the apostle Paul that all those whom God has predestinated, and for whom he spared not his own Son, are also called, and that by this calling, God quickens them who were dead, and makes them to pass from the state of sin, to a state of grace and of righteousness; from the slavery of Satan to the liberty of the sons of God; from the kingdom of darkness to the kingdom of his Son; from death to life; and that he accomplishes all these things by his Word and by his Spirit.

XXIV. We believe that man could not, by his own strength, deliver himself from that sad state into which sin had brought him, without the aid of the Spirit of God, because we have learned from Jesus Christ, the prophets, and apostles, that we are by nature dead in our trespasses, that our flesh, or carnal mind cannot be subject to the law of God; that the natural man cannot comprehend things divine and heavenly; that no man can go unto the Son, except the Father draw him; that it is God who worketh in us both to will and to do; that it is he alone who opens our hearts, to understand the things that are spoken to us, and who—taking away our heart of stone—gives us an heart of flesh, in order that we may walk in his commandments. Are not the passages to this purpose, express?[156]

XXV. We are therefore persuaded that it is God who works faith in us, which is also called the gift of God, and which is nothing else than that act of the believing soul whereby being fully persuaded of the truth of the promises of the gospel, it has its recourse solely to Jesus Christ our Savior, and goes to seek in him its righteousness and life, whereby it relies upon his merit, and unites itself so closely to him that nothing is able to separate it from him. And we reckon that it is by this faith, we receive Jesus Christ into our hearts; that we apply his righteousness, his obedience, and death; but we declare at the same time that this faith ought to operate by love, that without works it is dead, and that it is not given unto all. What is there in this which you have not often read in the holy Scripture?[157]

XXVI. We believe with Paul that God has justified those whom he has called; that is to say that he has pardoned all their sins, and has given them the right to eternal life. But we are persuaded that the only cause of our justification, is the merit of Jesus Christ (that is, the obedience which he rendered to his Father even to the death of the cross), and the grace of God; yet we say that it is necessary that we apply by faith this perfect merit of Jesus Christ. Thus we conclude with the apostle of the Gentiles that we are justified by faith without the works of the law, as we also believe with James that we ought to justify and show our faith by our works.

---

[156] Ephesians 2:1, Romans 8:7, 1 Corinthians 2:14, John 6:44, Philippians 2:13, Acts 16:14, Ephesians 6:19-20
[157] Ephesians 2 & 3, Philippians 2 & 3, James 2

XXVII. We are persuaded that God justifies none whom he does not sanctify at the same time; and that the believer being sanctified produces good works, without which none can be saved: but we are far from believing that these good works merit salvation; the greatest sufferings "are not worthy to be laid in the balance with the glory which shall be revealed in us," and we do nothing but what we are bound to do; and as Jesus Christ says, we are only unprofitable servants.[158]

XXVIII. We acknowledge for the only rule of our actions, the law of God, of which the love of God and of our neighbor is the sum. In following this law, we avoid making any pictures of God, nor do we serve him under any corporeal images, nor bow ourselves before any image, because this worship is expressly forbidden in the second commandment of this holy law.

XXIX. As we violate every day this law, we reckon that we cannot hope to obtain the pardon of our sins without repentance, which ought to be speedy, sincere, and constant; but we believe that we ought continually to demand of God the pardon of our sins for the love of his Son, that he would grant us his Spirit, and subdue our passions. This is what we daily essay [*attempt*] in our prayers.

XXX. We teach that we ought to direct prayer to God alone, seeing as we have so learned of Jesus Christ and his apostles, who have never enjoined us to pray to any other than God, as we showed some weeks ago.

XXXI. *In fine*, we are persuaded that those whom God has justified and sanctified, shall one day be glorified; that their souls, upon leaving these bodies, when their earthly tabernacle shall be destroyed, shall be raised to an eternal mansion, where they shall rest from all their labors; whereas the souls of the wicked shall be cast down to hell. As to the bodies, which are lodged

---

[158] Pope Adrian VI has the following passage: "Our merits are as a staff of a broken reed, which cannot support those who lean upon it, and which pierces the hand of him who stays himself upon it; and all of our righteousness, says Isaiah, are as filthy rags. [...] The Lord," adds he, "has therefore wisely warned us: "When ye shall have done all these things which were commanded you, say, we are unprofitable servants.""

in the grave, we believe that they shall arise at the last day, the one in glory, the other unto everlasting shame; and that this resurrection shall arrive at the end of time when Jesus Christ shall come to judge the quick and the dead. Have you not, my brethren, read these truths in the sacred writings?

XXXII. We assert that all those great benefits which Christ has acquired, and of which he will in a future day put his members in possession, are only for his church, which is nothing else than a religious and spiritual society consisting of many persons, called by the Word of God, and by the internal efficacy of the Holy Spirit, according to the settled purpose of the election of God, under the conduct of a head, even Jesus Christ, that they may believe the same truths, serve the same God, live under the same rule; that they may enjoy the same grace and privileges in this life, and the same glory in that which is to come. Is not this, Christians, the idea which the Scripture gives us of the Church?

XXXIII. We acknowledge no other head of the church but Jesus Christ; so it has no other denomination than the body of Christ. The Scripture speaks not of another. The true members of the church therefore are the faithful: for how can we account for the members and the spouse of Jesus Christ, reprobates, hypocrites, and wicked men?

XXXIV. We believe that the marks whereby the true church may be known are the pure preaching of the Word of God, the right administration of the sacraments, and the exercise of discipline. Jesus Christ has told us that his sheep hear his voice and follow him.

XXXV. As we have learned that Jesus Christ has appointed the ministry for the edification of his body, we say that ministers ought to labor to make known Jesus Christ, instruct men, administer the sacraments, and exercise discipline against those who violate the laws of our Master. But we believe that they ought to speak to the people in a language understood, as Paul has observed in 1 Corinthians 14.

XXXVI. As we know that God wills that his church should be conducted under the shadow of the higher powers, kings, and magistrates, we pay respect to these powers, we obey them in whatever is not contrary to the law of God, and we pray for them. This is what we have learned of the apostle Paul.

XXXVII. We receive the two sacraments which Jesus Christ has instituted, baptism and the holy supper, and we celebrate them as he has ordained us.

XXXVIII. We do not retrench any of the signs which Jesus Christ has established in the eucharist, and we would hold ourselves guilty of an act of treason against him, if we should do it. We use—according to his divine commandment—bread and wine, and we consider these symbols, as the memorials of the body and blood of Jesus Christ, according as he himself says to us, "Do this in remembrance of me."

XXXIX. We do not believe that the body of the Lord Jesus is in the eucharist because we have learned from the Scripture that the heavens must retain him until the restitution of all things. But we are persuaded that we partake as really and truly of Jesus Christ, as if we did actually eat with our mouths his body; and that our soul is truly nourished by that bread which came down from heaven.

XL. Finally, we teach, after the apostle, that in order to a worthy receiving of this sacrament, a man must examine himself.

Such then is our creed. Do you not discern in it pure Christianity? Surely he must be blind who does not perceive it. It is abundantly clear that we believe nothing which is not contained in the sacred books.

If we do not receive the opinions of the Romish, or of the Greek church, it is for this reason: that we do not find them in these books, but perceive therein truths contrary to these opinions. This we have endeavored to show in this and the preceding discourse.

We have also on our side the purest antiquity. We invoke not the saints nor angels: neither did the Fathers of the three first centuries invoke them. In the year 167, the Christians of the church of Smyrna wrote a letter, giving a narration of the glorious martyrdom of Polycarp their pastor, which

Eusebius has preserved. In this letter, after reciting that the Jews endeavoured to persuade the Pagans, that if they suffered the Christians to possess themselves of the body of the martyr, they would forsake Jesus Christ, in order to serve and adore Polycarp, they add these words: "They know not that it is impossible that we should either forsake Jesus Christ, who has suffered for the salvation of all those who are saved throughout the whole world, or that we should serve or religiously honor any other. For as to Jesus Christ, we adore him as he who is the Son of God, but as for the martyrs, we love them as the disciples and followers of the Lord, and that justly because of the zeal and invincible affection which they have shown for their king and master, and may God grant that we may be both the imitators of their piety, and partakers of their glory." Irenæus, who is supposed to have died in 197, positively says that: "The church does nothing by the invocation of angels."[159]

Theophilus, bishop of Antioch, who died in 180, or the year following, says that: "The law of God commands us to serve the true God alone."[160] Clement of Alexandria teaches the same truth; and Tertullian, who died in 215, asserts in his *Apologetic*: "That which we adore is one God alone, who formed from nothing this great mass of the world;" and elsewhere declares that we are forbidden to adore or venerate in any sort, any other but this God alone who claims this for himself.[161]

Origen, who died in the year 256, is express on the same subject: "It belongs to them," says he, "who have forsaken the Creator, to worship the creature; as for us, we serve and adore no creature, but the Father, the Son, and the Holy Spirit;"[162] and in another place, he says that: "We ought not to pray to creatures, who offer up prayers themselves, seeing on the contrary they desire rather to send us to God, whom they invoke, than that we should

---

[159] Book 2 Chapter 57
[160] Lib. 2. ad Autolye.
[161] *Apol.* Chapter 17
[162] Origen in Chapter 1, Letter to the Romans

abase ourselves to them, or divide between God and them that right of our prayers, which would be to turn away from God to themselves, a part of our prayers."[163]

It is certain that in the three first centuries of Christianity, there were no temples, nor altars, nor any image, to be seen consecrated to angels, or saints, and that the fathers in those times never enjoined to make any prayer to the saints, or to the virgin.

We render no worship to images; do we not in this follow the sentiments of the most pure antiquity? It appears that the fathers in their disputes with the Pagans, reproached them for the honors which they paid to the figures and statues of their gods, which doubtless they would not have done had they themselves given a similar worship to the images of saints. During the four first centuries, the Pagans did not object to the Christians the worship of images; on the contrary, they accuse them for having neither altars, nor temples, nor graven images; and the Christians did not defend themselves by denying the charge. "The virtues," says Origen, "are our images." The greater part of the fathers (as Tertullian, Clemens of Alexandria, Origen) have even condemned painting, as an art either unlawful, or useless. And who knows not what passed in the council of Eliberis or Elvira, in the year 305, where it was ordained that there should be no paintings on the walls of churches; or that which Epiphanius bishop of Salamis did in 374, who tore asunder a curtain, which he found hanging upon the porch of a certain church, colored and having an image painted on it; or, *in fine*, what was transacted in the council of Constantinople, convened in the year 754, which declared that to worship images would be to renew the error of the Pagans.

We do not believe in transubstantiation; but did the ancient fathers believe it? Those who explained the words: *This is my body*, as being the

---

[163] Origen, *Contra Celsum*, Book 5

same with: *This is the figure of my body*, as Tertullian[164] and Augustine[165] did. Those who said that what is distributed at the holy table is bread, the matter of which after we have taken and eaten, is subject to the same natural accidents, and passes as our ordinary food, as Origen. [166] Those who termed the eucharist a sacrament, a sign, a type, an antitype, a symbol, an image, the resemblance of the body and blood of Jesus Christ, as might be made appear from many passages, which it would be too tedious to produce. Those who affirmed that when Christ says, "Except ye eat the flesh and drink the blood of the Son of man," he uses a figure which evinces the necessity of communicating in the passion of our Lord, and that to believe in Christ is to eat him.[167] Those who assert that our Saviour made an exchange of names, giving to his body the name of the symbol, and to the symbol the name of body, as Theodoret.[168] Those who taught that the bread is not properly the body of Jesus Christ, nor the cup his blood; but that they are so called because they contain in them the mystery or the sacrament of his body and blood, as that bishop of Hermiana speaks, who was present at the fifth general council, about the middle of the sixth century.[169] There would be no end, did I choose to cite all the passages of the ancient writers upon this subject.

We receive not the communion in one kind; and who knows not that the Christian church, for more than a thousand years, celebrated the eucharist in both kinds? Can those of the Romish communion be ignorant of what Leo I, one of their fathers, said of the Manicheans, who, the better to conceal themselves mingled in the assemblies of the Catholics, and even participated with them in the sacraments, but "who avoided absolutely to

---

[164] Tert. l. 3. *Contra Marc*, c. 40.
[165] Aug. contr. Ad in ant, c. 12,
[166] In Matth.
[167] Aug. *de Doctr. Christ*. l. 3. c. 6. & *de verb. Dom*. Ser. 33. et tract. 25 in Joàn.
[168] Dial. 1
[169] Facundus, Book 9

drink the blood of our redemption."[170] Are they unacquainted with the decree of Gelasius in the end of the fifth century? "We have," says he, "been informed that some, having taken only a portion of the sacred body, abstain from the cup of sacred blood: These are kept back, as it is said, by I know not what superstition; therefore, without doubt, they ought either to receive the sacraments entire, or to be wholly excluded from them; because the division of one and the same mystery, cannot take place without great sacrilege."

In the year 1095, Urban II held a council at Clermont in Auvergne, which made a decree that Cardinal Baronius gives us in these words that: "No person should communicate at the altar, who does not take the body separately, and the blood in like manner."[171] A proof that the church, for more than a thousand years after the ascension of Jesus Christ communicated in both kinds.

We have no faith in Purgatory; but is it not certain that neither the writings of the fathers who flourished during the first six centuries, nor the creeds and expositions of faith, nor the councils, say anything of such a Purgatory as the church of Rome teaches? It is true, some of the fathers believed that those who should appear before the tribunal of Jesus Christ at the last day should be purified and tried by a fire, which should separate the good from the evil, and consume in the good whatever might be corrupt in them. The purgatory of Origen was to follow the resurrection, and it was to

---

[170] "To cover," says he, "their infidelity, they have the confidence to be present at our mysteries; thus they join in the communion of the sacraments. The more effectually to disguise themselves, they receive, with an unworthy mouth, the body of Jesus Christ, but they absolutely shun to drink the blood of our redemption. Therefore we wish your sanctity to know this, in order that these sort of people may be manifested to you by these marks, and that they whose sacrilegious dissimulation shall be discovered, may be marked, and that being prohibited to frequent the society of saints, they may be chased from thence by the priestly authority." — Leo. Serm IV. cap. 5.

[171] Annal. [te.] XI

be only for those who had not obtained pardon of their sins in the present world, for wicked men, and for the devils themselves.

We admit not of the adoration of the cross; but did the ancients adore it? Tertullian, in his *Apologetic*, puts among the false opinions which certain Pagans entertained concerning that which Christians adored, the imagination of those who thought that they religiously worshiped the cross. Cecilius, in Minutius Felix, having objected to Octavius that some reckoned that the wretched pieces of wood of the cross were the ceremonies of Christians, Octavius replied, "As to crosses, we neither adore them, nor wish for them."

Those who worship the cross confess that the true cross was not found until the year 326 by Helena mother of Constantine; and they know how much reason there is to doubt the truth of this story, and even to account it fabulous.

We are as far from believing that the sacraments ought to be adored; but whether did the fathers adore it? Neither Justin, nor Irenaeus, nor Clemens of Alexandria, nor Tertullian, nor Origen, nor Cyprian, have spoken a word about: and Theodoret, an author of the fifth century, says, "It is the last degree of folly to adore what is eaten;" and he asks, "How is it possible that a man who is in his right senses, should call that God which he eats?"[172]

Neither do we regard the eucharist as a propitiatory sacrifice; but did the primitive writers consider it in that light? I grant that they sometimes call it a sacrifice; either because they applied this term to all acts of devotion; or because to us it supplies the place of Mosaic sacrifices; or, because it is the sacrament of the sacrifice of Jesus Christ; or, because it was the principal portion of the offerings, which the whole congregation presented on the sabbath days to God on his table, out of which they selected so much of the bread and wine, as was requisite for the holy communion, and the remainder was for the ministers and the poor.

---

[172] Theodor. in Genes. qu: 35. and in Lev. qu. 11.

Thus it appears that our belief is conform both to Scripture and antiquity. We should now enquire whether anything can be objected against our religion, which can justly hinder us from regarding it as the pure Christian religion. But this we shall refer to the following discourse.

APPLICATION.

How greatly may we wish that our life were as pure as our religion, and that our conduct were as holy as the morality which we teach you! How much to be wished that we had the same zeal, the same piety, the same charity, the same patience, the same gentleness, the same justice, the same temperance, which so eminently distinguished the first Christians, who trod underfoot all the riches of the earth, who were so detached from all the things of this world that they carried with joy all their possessions to the feet of the apostles, whose charity, which was the crown of Christian perfection, was so complete that they had all of them together but one heart and one soul, and they prayed for their very persecutors, who kindled with that noble fire which Jesus Christ sent down from heaven to set on flame the hearts of men; who rejoiced to lose everything for Christ; who gladly exposed their lives for the defence of the truth; who went to the scaffolds without being appalled; who did nothing to others but what they would that others should do to them; who had no higher pleasure than to speak of God, to think of God, to read his word, and meditate upon it day and night; than to call upon him both in their closets, and in company with their brethren; who had an uncommon ardent desire to approach the table of the Lord, and who were always ready to approach it! What joy would it afford us, my brethren, if this church, which teaches the pure religion of the apostles, could perceive such beautiful examples of its truth as the disciples of Jesus once had the consolation to behold!

But, alas! We imitate rather the Christians whose conduct the apostles have blamed: their intemperance, their violence, their impurities, their divisions and quarrels, their indifference about religion, their coldness and profanity as to its mysteries, particularly the holy eucharist. We imitate those Christians whom Paul accused of seeking their own interests rather than those of Jesus Christ, who made a god of their belly, were enemies of the cross of Christ, and who did eat unworthily the Lord's Supper. So that we may adopt the same complaint with Gregory Nazianzen, who said that time had effaced every Christian virtue, that little or nothing of it remained, and that he could only bestow on the church his tears; or that which Augustine expressed that the church abounded with Christians whose life was worse than that of Pagans or Jews. Certainly we have more reason to call our age "the dregs of Christianity" than Jerome had in his time. To confine myself to what relates only to the participation of the holy eucharist, to which we are called the next sabbath: how is it, pray, that persons prepare themselves for this solemn action?

How many are there, who, throughout this week, will not deprive themselves of any pleasure, not even of those which the church has condemned; not even of those which are most criminal?

How many who retain still their animosities and grudges? How many who even meditate this week to prosecute quarrels, or engage in lawsuits against their brethren?

How few will there be who will seriously enter into their own hearts, that they may discover whether they be in a better state than formerly, to take a strict review of their sins, and to examine if they should be ready for receiving the Son of God, and his Spirit? Who will be found to restore the property which they know does not pertain to them? How few will shut themselves up in their closets, to bewail their trespasses, to read good books, and to form new resolutions to live better for the time to come? How few will be employed in meditating upon the ineffable love of God, the infinite kindness of Jesus Christ, and the excellency of the grace which God is willing to confer upon us?

How many will come to the holy feast without any hunger or thirst, and without even employing any sort of reflection, but merely from habit and custom? How many will approach without respect, without thinking of the import of what they do?

After this, need it appear surprising that so little effect or fruit should be seen following our communions, or that there should be persons who depart from them in a worse disposition than before? Need we be surprised that so few are converted, and that there should be no appearance of amendment?

In the name of God, my brethren, let us think on the duty we are called to on the sabbath. Jesus Christ, the Angel of the covenant, the Lamb of God, the brightness of his glory, calls us to his communion-table; we ought to celebrate the memorial, not only of his death, but also of his resurrection, his ascension, and the mission of his Spirit.

He is about to give us his flesh to eat, and his blood to drink, the only food of our souls, the true bread of heaven, the fruit of the tree of life, the new wine of the heavenly kingdom. He proposes to give us his Spirit, the earnest of our inheritance, the seed of immortality, the source of joy, of holiness, and of light, the anointing which teaches us all things. Let us make lively and serious reflections on these things, and thus we shall be suitably prepared for the solemnity to which we are called.

Let us commune with ourselves and say, seeing as Christ is dead for our sins, shall it be said that we are still inclined to commit them, to crucify afresh the Lord of glory? He is risen; shall we remain always in the tomb of our vices? He is willing to give us his flesh to eat, and his blood to drink; let us therefore make ready for feeding on the flesh of this divine lamb. He calls us to the marriage; let us endeavour to have on that robe, without which no person can have any communion with him. He promises us his Spirit; let us purify our hearts for receiving this divine guest.

Above all, my dear brethren, let us pray to the Lord that he would work in us that which he commands, and that he would prepare us for receiving him himself. "Lord Jesus, we are not worthy that thou shouldst come to lodge under our roof, and we are incapable of receiving worthily thy Spirit, unless thou come thyself, by this same Spirit, to sanctify our hearts; give us therefore this Holy Spirit, who produceth in us the dispositions which thou demandest of those with whom thou art pleased to come and dwell, that so thou mayest take pleasure to establish thy throne in our souls, until that thou shalt make us sit upon thy throne." *Amen.*

A DEFENSE

OF THE

REFORMED RELIGION

THE SIXTH DISCOURSE

On 1 Thessalonians 5:21: *Prove all things.*

THE Christian religion has always been exposed to attacks, and its followers have often been obliged to make its apology and their own. The apostle Peter was the first, who, on the day of Pentecost, defended gloriously the cause of the Lord Jesus, his own, and that of his colleagues; and on that occasion he converted three thousand persons. Stephen, the first deacon and the first Christian martyr, some years after, maintained the same cause; but his discourse only irritated his hearers, who cruelly put him to death. Paul the apostle was also obliged many times to defend himself and the religion which he had embraced; and a few weeks ago, you heard him pleading before Felix, against the orator, or rather the calumniator, Tertullus. In the second century, Quadratus, bishop of Athens, presented to the emperor Hadrian who had come into that city of Greece in order to be initiated in the Eleusinian mysteries, a defence of the Christian religion;[173] wherein he

---

[173] Some doubt whether Quadratus was bishop of Athens; others believe it on the authority of Jerome and the menology of the Greeks. Of the *Apology*, which was presented in 124, we have only some fragments left: but Eusebius who has preserved them, says, in them we may perceive marks of the goodness of his understanding, and his apostolical uprightness. To show the difference between the miracles of our Saviour and the tricks of impostors, he observed that the works of our Lord continued always, because they were true. "The sick cured, the dead raised, not only appeared cured and raised, but they remained such, not only while our Savior was on earth, but they continued a long time after his departure; insomuch that some of them have reached to our time."

showed the difference between the miracles of Jesus Christ, and the signs and wonders of impostors. This, together with a letter of a proconsul of Asia, so pacified Hadrian that he wrote in favor of the Christians to the governors of his provinces.[174] Aristides, an Athenian philosopher, much about the same time, drew up another apology; and Justin Martyr afterwards addressed two of them to the emperors and the senate of Rome. The like was done by Athanagoras and Melito; and Tertullian, in the beginning of the persecution of Severus, published another, which is more excellent than any of the rest; not to mention many other writings, which may be considered as so many defenses of the religion of Christ.

My brethren, we propose this day to follow the example of these holy men of antiquity. As our religion is the same with that which was defended by the ancient fathers, so it has had also the same lot; and its friends find themselves obliged from time to time to vindicate it against its enemies, who attempt to blacken it by a thousand calumnies.

We showed in our last discourse its beauty and entire conformity to the religion of the holy Scriptures: but seeing as they oppose many things against it, which if they were true, might lead us to reject it, it is interesting to us to examine whether the charges that are directed against it are well founded. To this we are bound by the exhortation of the apostle in our text: "Prove all things."

Two sorts of accusations are brought against the Reformed religion: the one respects our doctrine; the other, the Reformation itself.

---

[174] Serenius Granianus, Proconsul of Asia, had written to the emperor that it was great injustice to grant to the clamours of the populace the blood of so many innocent persons, and to condemn people on no other ground than the name of a sect. Hadrian wrote in the following terms concerning the Christians: "If any one accuse them, and prove that they have done something contrary to the laws, in that case, let them be judged according to the desert of the offence; but if any bring an accusation against them by calumny, punish him as he deserves, and be careful to act herein with justice." This however did not put an immediate stop to the persecution; and if we credit the Greeks in this, Quadratus obtained the crown of martyrdom under Hadrian.

We shall therefore examine these two heads distinctly, and we hope you will give the same attention as in the preceding sermons; and may God by his Spirit lead us into all truth!

First, we are to consider the accusations against the doctrine of the Reformed.

1st Accusation

The first accusation on this head is that we "make God the author of sin." An accusation which, if well-founded, might justly expose us to be viewed by all as monsters unworthy to breathe; but, Lord, thou knowest well our innocence; pardon both the hatred and the calumny of those who accuse us of such a blasphemy!

If this were our sentiment, would these words be found in our Confession of Faith? "God is a being altogether just, good and merciful. He is not the author of evil, nor can the blame be imputed to him, seeing as his will is the sovereign and infallible rule of righteousness and equity; but he has admirable ways of serving himself of devils and wicked men; turning the evil done by them, and of which they are guilty, unto good."

If this were indeed our sentiment, would the Council of Trent—which has collected together with such care whatever appeared to it worthy of censure in our doctrine—have forgotten the most odious of our crimes?

How can it be possible that we should hold an opinion so horrible, which deserves all the pains of hell, we who teach on all occasions that though God permit sin, yet sin is contrary to his nature, that he condemns, detests, and punishes it both in this life, and in that which is to come; that he is not a God who takes pleasure in wickedness, but that he loves righteousness, and hates iniquity?

Our doctors have always spoken this language,[175] as those who have read their writings have fairly acknowledged. If they have made use of expressions which may appear harsh, it is certain they have said nothing stronger than may be found in Scripture, or than the assertions of those who calumniate them, whom we do not however charge with entertaining such strange sentiments.[176] If we say that God raised up Pharaoh to show in him his power, and to make his name known in all the earth, do we not speak as the Scripture has done? If we assert that God hardened the heart of Pharaoh, does not God himself say the same thing? If we say that "Herod and Pontius

---

[175] Calvin is explicit on this head, though attempts have been made to blacken him. On James 1:13 he thus writes: "He treats here of internal temptations, which are nothing else than inordinate appetites which incite us to sin. With good reason he denies that God is the author of such temptations seeing they flow from the corruption of our nature. This admonition is very necessary, because nothing is more common with men, than to transfer elsewhere the blame of the evils they commit. But chiefly then they think themselves to be exculpated, when they can make them fall upon God himself. This artifice for getting quit of the charge, we have transmitted to us from the first man, whom in this we carefully imitate. For this cause James directs us to a confession of our own guilt, that we may not substitute God in our place, as if he impelled us to sin." After explaining in what sense God hardens, and delivers up the reprobate to corrupt affections, consistently with his holiness, he adds: "It follows then that the source of sin is neither in God, nor can the blame of it be imputed to him, as if he took pleasure in evil. The conclusion is that in vain do men seek an evasion by trying to throw the blame of their vices upon God: seeking whatever is sinful proceeds from no other fountain than the perverse lust of man. *Summa est, frustrà tergiversarsi hominem qui vitiorum suorum culpam rejicere in Deum: quia non ex alio fonte proveniat quicquid est malorum, quam ex perversa hominis concupiscentia.*"

[176] Hear how Cardinal Bellarmine expresses himself: "God not only permits the wicked to commit many things evil, and not only does he leave the godly, that they may be obliged to suffer what is inflicted on them by the wicked, but he also presides over the wills themselves which are evil, *easque regit et gubernat, torquet ac flectit; in eis visibiliter operando*, etc. for guiding and inclining them, and visibly operating on them, that though the vices properly are evil, yet they are by divine providence directed (*ordinantur*) to one evil rather than another." *De Amiss. Grat.* lin. 11. chap. 13. Thomas Aquinas says something still more strong on Romans 9, Lect. 3. alleging that men by a certain internal instinct are moved by God both to do good and evil," quoting the words of Augustine, where he says that God works in the hearts of men to incline their wills wherever he pleases, whether it be to things good, according to his mercy, or to things evil according to their deserts. *De Grat. et libero arbit.*

Pilate, with the Gentiles and the people of Israel, were gathered together to do whatever the will and counsel of God had before appointed to be done," is not this what the apostle Peter has expressly declared? When we maintain that God directs for his glory, and the salvation of his children the actions of men, even the most criminal, did not Joseph say as much to his brethren, "As for you, you thought evil against me, but God meant it for good."

Such is our doctrine; but it never came into our mind that God infuses sin into men, that he pushes them on to commit it, or that he approves it. Anathema to those who may hold such sentiments! Whoever says that God is the author of sin, let him be to us accursed!

"But is it not true," continue they, "according to your opinion, that God permits sin; that he has foreseen it from all eternity; that he has decreed to permit it; that he hinders not the permission of it, though it is in his power to hinder it; that he suffers it even to be transmitted from fathers to children, and that he preserves the faculties of sinners, without which they could not sin?" All this is true; but are not these sentiments agreeable to Scripture and reason? And are they not confirmed by experience?

Can it be denied that God permits sin? If he chooses to hinder it, could he not do so? Who can say that he has not foreseen it, he whose knowledge is infinite, as reason and Scripture both inform us? Can it be denied that he has decreed to permit it, seeing as it is certain that nothing comes to pass in time, which God has not ordained from all eternity either to do or permit? Does not Scripture teach us that we are born corrupt, and that we are conceived in sin? Finally, do we not learn from the Bible that in God, we have life, motion, and being?

I confess, we cannot satisfy ourselves fully as to the reason why God permits sin; but must we deny a truth established in Scripture, confirmed by reason and experience, because we cannot render a reason for everything? We may add that all sects of Christians—and even all who acknowledge a God and a providence—have the same difficulties to resolve.

2nd Accusation

The next accusation against us is that we "explain the Scripture by a private spirit."

This charge is as ridiculous as the first is atrocious. We indeed believe that we have need of the grace of the Spirit of God to discern the heavenly truths from so many errors which are diffused throughout the world, and those who accuse us agree with us in this; but we are far from asserting that this Spirit who instructs us, and by whom we are persuaded of the truth, is private or peculiar unto us. We hold that he is common to all the faithful, and that he teaches us nothing but the truths revealed to the apostles, and to the whole church from the beginning. What! Because all agree that nobody can see any object without the light of the sun, or of some other luminary, must we conclude from this that every individual has a particular or private sun? Who would be so foolish as to talk in this language?

3rd Accusation

We are charged in the third place with holding strange sentiments concerning predestination.

God knows whether it be so, my brethren; and we heartily wish that you yourselves should judge.

We believe that God executes nothing, and never will do anything, which he has not ordained from all eternity. Is there anything inconsistent with reason or Scripture in this sentiment? Do they not both confirm it? We also believe that God—considering all men as fallen in Adam, and not willing that all of them should perish—did choose some of them "before the foundation of the world, that they should be holy and without blame before him in love, having predestinated them to the adoption of sons by Jesus Christ, according to the good pleasure of his will" (Ephesians 1:4–5). Do you not know this to be the very doctrine of the apostle Paul? We believe, further, that he has not dealt so with all men, but that there are some of them whom he has purposed to leave in their corruption; and do you not know that the Scripture speaks of "vessels appointed unto destruction," as well as of "vessels prepared unto glory," which the divine potter, to use the similitude of Paul, has taken from the same mass? What is there in this which any can justly blame? Should it then be accounted strange that we admit a decree of election and a decree of reprobation?

"But," say they, "You believe that God chooses men without having any respect to their faith, and good works!" We grant it: for we are persuaded that when God chooses men, he does it from his mere good pleasure, without having foreseen in them anything which could engage him to appoint them to salvation; in like manner, as a potter makes of the same lump one vessel unto honor, and another to dishonor, as the apostle has taught us. But we are at the same time persuaded that God never will save us if we have not faith, or without good works. We hold faith and good works to be the consequence of our election; according to the doctrine of the same apostle, which teaches that all those whom God has predestinated are also called (Romans 8) in order to bestow faith upon them, and to put them into a state to perform good actions. We maintain that all those who "are ordained unto eternal life believe;" according to the declaration in Acts 13:48. But it is a very different thing to believe that faith and good works are the cause of our election, or the motive which induced God to choose any of the human race. We say with Paul that God has chosen us, that we should be holy, and not because he foresaw that we should be so; and thus we give the whole glory of our election to the good pleasure and mercy of God.

"But do you not believe," they ask us, "That God reprobates men without having respect to their sin, which cannot be affirmed without injury to his justice; for divine justice allows him not to punish people without any cause."

My brethren, those who charge us in this manner, either understand not our sentiment, or they are unwilling to understand it. We say: 1. That without sin God would never have reprobated any person. 2. That God will not hereafter punish men in hell, nor has he resolved to punish them in that fearful abyss, but on account of their sins. 3. But if it be enquired, why of two men, such as Jacob and Esau, of whom the one has not done more good or evil, before they were born, God has loved Jacob, and hated Esau? Why of two men, who were viewed as in the same corrupt mass, has God appointed the one to glory, and left the other in his corruption, seeing as they were both equally considered as sinners? Then we reply, in the style of Scripture, it is because God "will have mercy on whom he will have mercy, and whom he will he hardeneth." Is there anything here that can be condemned?

"But do you not say that God is the author of the damnation of men?"

We say that it is God who condemns the wicked to eternal punishment. He must renounce all claim to be a Christian who would dare to entertain a doubt whether it be God that disposes of paradise and of hell. Yet we say that men are the sole cause of their own damnation: "Thy destruction is of thyself, O Israel." We add also that God takes no pleasure in the death of the wicked, but rather that they should turn from their evil course and live.

If there are any particular writers who have maintained certain opinions on the subject of predestination which may appear contrary to the perfections of God, let it be observed that the particular opinions of some doctors ought not to be imputed to the whole body of our churches. Neither is it just to impute to these writers the consequences which may be drawn from their opinions, which they themselves disavow.

"But is it not an error to assert that the only thing which can damn men is the doubt about their predestination?" Surely, my brethren; and this is what we never asserted. We say that vice and debauchery, impenitence and incredulity, avarice and adultery, and all the works of the flesh, damn men, if they change not their conduct. We declare that a vain and false assurance of their election has destroyed and does destroy many. We maintain that such as have not any true mark of the divine election in them would act a dangerous part to presume that they were of the number of the persons predestinated to salvation; but that those who observe in themselves, after a serious examination, a true faith, a sincere repentance, and an ardent love for God, may and ought to believe that they are elected. In a word, we affirm that as there are none less capable of becoming wise than those who suppose that they are so, though they be in reality fools, so there is no person at a greater distance from salvation than he who is drowned in perdition, and yet imagines that he shall be saved; we think it would be better for him if he doubted of it.

Judge now, my friends, whether that which they impute to us be not as contrary to our genuine doctrine, as light is to darkness.

4th Accusation

Another charge is brought against us, on a subject nearly connected with the last, namely, the certainty of salvation. They accuse us with saying that a man is obliged to believe as an article of faith that his sins have been forgiven him, and that without this, he can be no true believer. But this charge is false.[177] We believe that there is a very great difference between the

---

[177] Our author has not replied to this objection in the manner that could have been wished, nor is he at all happy in the explanation he has given of the whole subject it relates to; though in the view he takes of it, he sufficiently guards against a gross perversion and dangerous abuse of the doctrine of assurance. But the doctrine itself, and even the warrant and duty of believing on the ground of the gospel declaration and promise that a person's sins *are* (nor *have* been) forgiven him, were not only generally admitted by the most eminent lights of the Reformation, but they constitute the sum, the undiscriminating character, and chief excellency of the gospel, and of that faith which is saving. The Palatine Catechism, adopted by all the reformed churches, teaches that "true faith is an assured affiance, kindled in my heart by the Holy Ghost, by which I rest upon God, making sure account that forgiveness of sins, everlasting righteousness and life, are bestowed, not only upon others but also upon me; and that freely by the mercy of God, for the merit and desert of Christ alone." Mestrezat of the Genevan church, has expressed himself with greater propriety on this subject than our author, when he says, "This faith puts us in possession of the blessings which are announced to it; and that doubts and uncertainty about salvation do not agree with the doctrine of the gospel." Sermon on 1 John 1:3 & Chapter 5..

The author's mistake here, as of many others, arises from not distinguishing between the general belief of gospel truths abstractedly considered, and the appropriating belief of the promise or offer of saving benefits in their applicableness

belief which we give to articles of faith, and that whereby we are persuaded of our salvation. We hold that a man cannot be a believer, nor be saved, [unless] he assents to or believes the truths which God has revealed to us in the Scriptures, but a man may be saved though he doubt of his salvation; as many believers do, whose faith is weak.

The truth of articles of faith is entirely independent of us. In whatever state we may be, there will always be truth in asserting that there is but one God; that Jesus Christ came into the world, etc. Therefore there can be nothing to hinder us from believing these propositions, at all times, in all places, and in all conditions. But there are times when it would be very far wrong and dangerous for persons to believe that they shall be saved; as when they live disorderly. None are bound to believe this until they are actually in the number of the faithful; before that, they ought to doubt of their salvation.

Thus you may be sensible that we are wrongfully blamed for saying that a man in *mortal sin*, as the Romish church speaks, may and ought to be assured of his salvation. It is a most atrocious calumny, for we have never said anything like it; and our public writings sufficiently justify us on this point. How should we entertain such a thought, who maintain that a man who has committed a crime ought to be assured that it shall not be forgiven

---

to the person believing; and from overlooking the distinction between the assurance that is in faith, and that which arises from sense or reflection; as if there was no difference between the certainty arising from sensible evidences of a person's being actually and previously in a gracious state, and the certainty of having pardon and salvation in the direct acts of faith. He speaks as if the only certainty about a person's own salvation that is warrantable or attainable, is that which is deduced as an inference from the former of these: and consequently that no man may claim it until he discerns such marks, and has made considerable progress in sanctification.

The subject is of great moment, for a right understanding of the gospel, and establishing the soul's peace. It has undergone particular discussions in late times. The reader may consult *Answers to the 12 Queries of the General Assembly*; Mr. Ebenezer Erskine's *Sermons on the Assurance of Faith*; some parts of Mr. Harvey's writings; the Associate Presbytery's *Act concerning the Doctrine of Grace*; Mr. Cudworth's judicious *Aphorisms concerning the Assurance of Faith*; and more lately, Mr. Anderson's *Discourses* on the same subject. [*Transl.*]

him until he has repented of it, but that if he should come to die, he could not escape eternal misery. He is not indeed obliged to believe that he is reprobated; yet he ought to be afraid of it, and should labor to assure himself of the contrary by a speedy repentance and a holy life. Neither is he obliged certainly to believe that he never had been a true believer or truly righteous, but he ought to fear that he may never have been such; he has good reason to suspect that he has been deceiving himself, taking a shadow for the substance, and an appearance of sanctification for genuine holiness.

"But is not," they will ask, "The opinion concerning the certainty of salvation, a dangerous one?" Surely not, as it is taught by us. For we hold that no person should be assured of obtaining salvation until he find in himself the marks of his election; then he can say with Paul, "I am persuaded that neither death, nor life, angels, nor principalities, nor powers, shall be able to separate me from the love of God."

Yet again they allege that this opinion tends to annihilate all fear in the world, although fear be the great restraint from committing evil. But it is a groundless allegation that it would destroy fear. 1. Take notice that we would not have any to assure himself of his salvation until he has strictly examined his heart, and found it upright before God; so you may from this infer that all those who are regenerate, and the faithful themselves in their falls, ought to fear. Now these two sorts of people make up the greater number of those who live on the earth. 2. You ought to consider that according to our views, believers are not obliged to believe that they shall be saved, except in proportion to the degrees of renovation to which they have attained; for a believer who is still in a great measure attached to the world, and whose graces are very weak and languishing, ought not to be so much assured of his salvation, as not to take care to awaken his conscience by salutary alarms as to his present state. This sort of Christians are still very numerous. It may be evident then that our doctrine about certainty does not abolish all fear.

Indeed a believer, whose life may be a continual exercise of repentance and good works, ought to be strongly assured of his salvation; but yet this certainty is not incompatible with fear. Such a one ought not to consider the punishment of hell as an evil to which he may be exposed, while he continues to live as he does; but as that into which he should infallibly fall, if he did not remain most closely attached to his God, and do that which he commands him. Thus this assurance increases his love and attachment to God: for can it be thought that the happy penitent to whom Jesus said, "Thy sins are forgiven thee," had less love to God, after that declaration, which gave her a full assurance of her salvation?

5th Accusation

We are represented as enemies to good works, and as favoring licentiousness.

But we may appeal to you, my brethren, and you can bear witness, whether any can press more earnestly the necessity of good works, or oppose vice more strenuously, than we do. We indeed reckon it intolerable that any should say that heaven may be merited by our works, as we know this doctrine of merit to be entirely contrary to scripture and the purest antiquity. We even meet with these words in the sermons of one Radolph, a fervent preacher in the eleventh century: "If we would be true Christians, let us hold fast this belief, that we cannot be justified by any of our works, but by the grace of God alone, who freely justifies the ungodly."[178] And Durand, a bishop and famous divine in the fourteenth century, refuted whatever Thomas Aquinas had advanced in favour of merit; to say nothing here of

---

[178] The same author, who is otherwise called Raoul, and was preacher to William IV. Duke of Guienne, speaks also in that sermon, in the following terms: "It is universally true that we can neither be justified, nor saved, by our free will, or by the observation of the law, or by works of any kind, but by the mercy of God only." He says further that: "When we were children of wrath and destruction, God calls us freely to be his children, and having called us, he justifies us freely, and having justified us, he glorifies us also freely." Serm. Dom. 3. *Post. Trinit.*

Thomas Waldensis, who died in the year 1430. This shows that the doctrine of the merit of good works, was not received as an article of faith, until the time of the Council of Trent.

"But does not this," it may be said, "Abate the ardor for performing good works, to deny that they merit heaven?" Not at all: is there no other way to excite our piety than by diminishing the obligation which we lie under to God? What! Is it not sufficient to engage us to perform good works, to know that it is the way that leads us to heaven?

It is alleged too that we have "abolished auricular confession, in order to authorize impiety." No, brethren; we have abolished it because we were convinced that it was neither instituted by Jesus Christ, nor known in the practice of Christians in the three first centuries. We have abolished it, on account of the great and pernicious abuses of such confession,[179] being persuaded that as to certain things which are not necessary, nor commanded by God, the abuses which they occasion oblige us to reject them. We have abolished it because of the dangerous maxims which some confessors have vented. We have abolished it from the conviction that the easiness with which pardon is expected to be obtained in confessing, leads people to a dangerous security. Cardinal Bellarmine scruples not to say that: "Persons—by suffering a little confusion before one of their fellow servants in discovering to him their sins—procure exemption from that great confusion, which without that they would have to bear at the day of judgment, before all the angels and all men;" which he confirms by a miraculous vision, tending to show that all sins, even the most horrid, are effaced in confession, as soon as the sinner utters and rehearses them.[180]

We are persuaded that this facility of obtaining absolution is productive of the greatest evils. At the same time, we hinder not those whose conscience

---

[179] See the book of Erasmus, entitled, *Exhomologesis*, or *Confession*; the bulls of P. Pius IV. and P. Gregory XV. *contra sollicitantes in confessione.* Likewise the treatise of Escobar on this subject; and the 85th book of Thuanus' *History.*

[180] *De Poenit.* B3 C12

may be burned with any crime, or who wish to have directions as to the conduct of their life, to come and open their mind to the pastors whom they judge most proper to impart some consolation to their souls, or to give them wholesome advice. Nor do we find fault with the confession practiced by some Protestant churches, for which we have great respect.

"But is it not an error to assert that all our works are mortal sins? That a man sins mortally in loving God above all things? That the holy virgin committed a mortal sin, in giving the consent which God required from her, to work in her the chief of all his wonders?"

Certainly, it is an error; but those who charge us with it advance a calumny. Nothing like this has ever proceeded from us; and we would treat as fools anyone who would speak such language. The amount of what we say is this: that in the works which are most holy, there is always some defilement of the flesh, and if God should examine them in the rigor of his justice, he might find in them matter of condemnation; but in his great goodness, he endures the imperfections of our works, and is pleased to accept our feeble efforts.

6th Accusation

"But do you not invariably maintain," say our adversaries, "that it is not possible to keep the law of God? Is not this an error?"

I grant that if we should say that it is absolutely impossible to observe the law, we would be in an error; but we only affirm that it is not possible to obey it in that extent to which we are bound. For in order to keep it perfectly, a man must necessarily be free of sin; but "If we say that we have no sin, we do lie," as the apostle John declares. "He who imagines himself to be without sin," said Augustine, "Does not exempt himself from sin, but he cuts himself off from the remission of it."[181]

---

[181] *City of God.* B14 C9

Indeed, if it were the pleasure of God, he could bestow such a measure of his Spirit as might enable us to surmount all temptations; but it is his will that we should be constantly in conflict with our corruption, and that this warfare should not terminate but at the hour of death.

7th Accusation

They go on and say, "But do you not maintain that those who have true faith can never fall away totally from grace, and the love of God; that they cannot lose their faith, nor perish eternally; and is not this an error?"

It is not, but a Scripture-truth: "This is the will of my Father, who sent me, that of these whom he hath given me I should lose none; [...] My sheep know my voice, and I know them, and they follow me; I give to them eternal life, and they shall never perish, neither shall any pluck them out of my hand; The Father who gave them me is greater than all, and none shall pluck them out of my Father's hand." These are the words of Jesus the Saviour of the world.[182] Paul also declares that the faithful are sealed by the Holy Spirit unto the day of redemption, the time of the purchased possession; that the Lord established them to the end that they may be unreproveable in the day of the Lord; and that nothing is able to separate them from the love of God; that his gifts and callings are without repentance; that he who has called us is faithful.[183] John in like manner says: "He that is born of God"—that is, who has been truly regenerated—"doth not commit sin," meaning the sin unto death, of which he had been speaking, "For the seed of God abideth in him;" also those who went out from us were not at all of us; for "If they had been of us, they had no doubt continued with us;" and "He that believeth on the Son hath eternal life."[184] *In fine*, another apostle says that saints are "kept through faith unto salvation."[185]

---

[182] John 6:38 & 10:27-28
[183] Ephesians 4:30, 1 Corinthians 1:8, Romans 8:27-28
[184] 1 John 3:9 & 2:19
[185] 1 Peter 1:5

To doubt of the perseverance of the saints is to doubt of the firmness of God's election, contrary to the apostle's assertion that those whom he predestinated, he also glorifies. All the links of the chain of salvation are inseparably connected together; therefore as it is certain that those whom God will glorify, must also be justified, called, and predestinated; it is no less certain that those whom God has predestinated, he will also glorify. To doubt of the perseverance of the saints is to doubt of the efficacy of the death of Christ, and of the virtue of his Spirit, by whom we are sealed. It is to doubt of the constancy of the love of God, which is strong as death, and a fire which many waters cannot quench. To doubt of the perseverance of the saints is to doubt the truth of the promises of God, by which he assures us that he will put his fear into our hearts, that we may not depart from him,[186] which means nothing else than that God will give us the grace to persevere in his fear, that we may always be united to him, as Augustine observes. For the promises God has made us of bestowing the grace of perseverance, differ from that given us of eternal life. God promises us eternal life under a condition, namely: that of perseverance; but he promises us the grace of perseverance without a condition, so that there can be no uncertainty as to the event.[187]

---

[186] Jeremiah 32:40

[187] It is another inaccuracy of our author—common to him with others—to represent the promise of eternal life as conditional, in the proper sense of that word. All the parts of salvation, or eternal life, are sometimes mentioned as one great and comprehensive promise, and that absolutely free, "the gift of God." The order and connection between the several parts and blessings of it, from its commencement in the first instance of grace bestowed, to its completion in glory, detract nothing from the freedom of it throughout. So that the last and crowning part of it is not more conditional to those who receive it, than the first. If by *condition* is meant anything more than this settled connection, and the prior enjoyment of certain promised privileges, which may also be viewed as duties and prerequisite qualifications in order to the enjoyment of others, neither faith, nor fear, nor perseverance, nor anything whatever in the subject, can be called the condition of the promise of eternal life. And if it means nothing more than that the promise of perseverance may be said to be conditional as well as that of eternal life strictly taken, seeing as some other gracious acts and qualities are presupposed to perseverance. [*Translator*]

8th Accusation

"But is it not strange that we should assert that a believer—even in the time when he falls into any sin—has true faith? That David continued in a state of grace when guilty of adultery and murder? Is it not impious to say that an adulterer is still the temple of the Holy Spirit?"

We affirm that the faith of saints in their sad falls is true, to distinguish it from that which is feigned, as it is the faith which had been produced before their fall by the Holy Spirit, and which is preserved by the same Spirit; and we add to this that it cannot save a man if it does not work by love. The faithful in these cases do not cease to be elect, because the election of God cannot be revoked; neither do they cease to be the children of God, because the divine adoption is also irrevocable, although they are then rebellious and disobedient children; nor is the right to the inheritance of their Father ever lost, being founded both on the election of God, and the death of Jesus Christ. A son rebelling against his father ceases not to be his son, nor does he lose his right to the inheritance while his father has not absolutely disinherited him; but that father will not give him his goods if he does not repent. We say indeed that God cannot hate his elect as he hates the reprobate; but when they render themselves unworthy of his grace, he makes them sensible of the effects of his fatherly indignation (as the Acts of the Synod of Dort express it) and he does not take his pleasure in them, until they return from their wanderings.

We also hold that God does not withdraw altogether his Holy Spirit from believers when they fall. But those who would give our sentiments an air of impiety do allow that the Holy Spirit often acts in the unbelieving, and that it is he who checks their malice, and stops the course of their corruption. Doubtless the Holy Spirit is not in the offending as he is in the holy believer; he does not diffuse in him his joy and consolation. It is on this account we say that he withdraws in a certain manner, but he does not do so absolutely. He is there as in a temple profaned and polluted, but he remains there as it were concealed; in much the same way as a king abides in his kingdom in a time of sedition, or, as the soul lodges in a body, during a fainting, or as God was still resident in his temple of Jerusalem, in the very time when it was defiled, exhibiting therein tokens of his presence. Habitual sinners and those in whom sin reigns are not the temples of the Spirit; but the faithful, who fall as David, continue to be his temples, according to the language of that holy man, "Take not thy Holy Spirit away from me." He had not therefore entirely lost him; but he only requests the Lord to restore to him the joy of his salvation.

Nor are the sins of believers to be considered as only venial and small; nor have they reason to think that God makes no account of them. They may not only be guilty of slighter offences through inadvertency, but of enormous crimes, as were the adultery of David, and the idolatry of Solomon, in the commission of which they have reason to apprehend that thereby they may be justly exposed to the effects of divine vengeance.

"But is it not an extravagance," they yet ask, "To teach that a man retains the habits of Christian graces, even in the time when he performs acts contrary to these habits?" Doubtless, it is not. As a man of the greatest bravery may be guilty of a cowardly action by surprise without ceasing to be brave, and as a prudent man may do an imprudent act without ceasing to be prudent, it is easy to conceive how a believing man may perform an unholy act, without entirely losing his faith. For otherwise Peter, in denying his Master, would have utterly lost his faith, and have become an unbeliever; but it is likely that a sin of surprise, which lasted but for a short time, should in one moment have extinguished all the light of grace in a soul so illustrious. Bernard says: "When Peter sinned, he did not lose his love, because he sinned, rather against the truth, than against charity." He lied in affirming that he was not what he truly was in heart, and yet the truth of his love immediately poured out abundance of tears to wash away that counterfeit denial. So when David sinned, neither did he lose charity, but it remained in him stunned, as it were, by the stroke of such a violent temptation. Love was not destroyed in him, but was in a manner laid asleep; but it soon awakened at the voice of the prophet who reproved him, and all of a sudden broke out in that confession, which bears the marks of the most ardent charity, "I have sinned against the Lord."[188] The same writer had just before said: "The weak flesh often offends: through the original corruption of our nature, it often grievously assaults and is assaulted. The mind—inwardly grieved on this account, and remaining a patient rather than agent—suffers the crime which is committed without; but yet it loses not charity, only charity groans and cries before God in this language: "Ah! wretched man that I am; who shall deliver me from the body of this death?" Hence the apostle says: "With my mind I serve the law of God, but with the flesh the law of sin: It is no more I that do it, but sin that dwelleth in me," etc.: Romans 7.

9th Accusation

"Do you not teach," say they, "that the faithful are righteous, by a righteousness imputed? Whence have you drawn this doctrine?"

We have drawn it from the holy Scriptures. But to prevent misapprehensions, attend, my brethren, to the sense in which we understand it. We mean nothing else by this than that we are justified because God, in his mercy, imputes to us the satisfaction of his Son, and the obedience which he gave even to the death of the cross: in consequence of which he treats us as if we ourselves had made satisfaction to his justice. This is what the Scripture teaches when it declares that God "hath made him to be sin for us, who knew no sin, that we might be made the righteousness of God in him;" and "as by the disobedience of one many were made sinners, so by the obedience of one shall many be made righteous." We cannot better explain this to those of the Romish communion than by the imputation of the pretended satisfaction of saints, which takes place among them, by the means of indulgences: for in the same manner as the works and satisfactions of saints are, in their opinion, applied by the head of their church, to whom he

---

[188] Lib. *De Nat. Amor. Div.* C6

pleases; so do we say that whatever Christ has done and suffered is imputed and applied to every believer. Is there anything strange in this?[189]

"But does not this imputed righteousness," they say, "tend to make men negligent of good works?"

Not at all. The same objection was made to the apostle Paul: "What shall we say then? Shall we continue in sin that grace may abound? God forbid;" he replied; and we may make the same reply. The remission of sins, on the contrary, is a powerful motive to determine us to the practice of good works; for how can we find in our hearts to offend him who has forgiven us so much?

To this observation, I beg you would also add the following. According to our opinion, at the same time that God grants us the remission of sins, through the imputation of the merits of Christ's death, he sanctifies us; and while we believe that the righteousness of Jesus Christ imputed is the cause of the pardon which God bestows, as well as of the felicity which he allots for us; we also believe that without the righteousness which we call inherent, which is nothing else than our sanctification, we cannot obtain the possession of salvation. Both these truths are clearly contained in the Scripture: the first, where it is said that: "In Jesus Christ we have redemption, even the forgiveness of sins;" the second, in these words: "Without holiness no man shall see the Lord."

---

[189] The same doctrine may be found in the writers of their own church. Cardinal Cajetan, in his Commentary on 2 Corinthians 5 says, "When the merit of Jesus Christ is communicated to us, then we are made the righteousness of God in Christ; because we are made righteous, not by our own proper righteousness, but by that of God in Christ, which is communicated to us, and makes us just before God by the merit, satisfaction, and reconciliation of Jesus Christ." Cardinal Contarin, in his *Treatise of Justification*, distinguishes as we do, a twofold righteousness: the one inherent, and the other that of Jesus Christ, which is given and imputed unto us. See also Albert Pighius; Andreas Vega, in his *Treatise of Justification* B15 C20, and Thomas Stapleton's *Universal Doctrine of Justification* B7 C9.

"But," they add, "Is it not true that you reckon adulterous David as righteous through this imputed righteousness, as the blessed virgin? And is not this a very gross error?"

If this be an error, my friends, we must then maintain that the sins of David were not so completely pardoned as those of the virgin: for we mean nothing else by the expression that David was just, through an imputed righteousness of Jesus Christ. This righteousness is equally imputed to all that believe, though they have not all committed sins equal in number or degree. Grant the virgin Mary to have been much more holy than David; yet were not all sins pardoned to David as well as to the virgin? The servant in the gospel who had ten thousand talents remitted to him, was he not acquitted as well as the other who owed only a hundred pence?

Thus you see, all that is needful is to explain the terms, by the ambiguity of which our adversaries avail themselves, in order to render our religion odious.

10th Accusation

We are also accused—but falsely—of destroying the liberty of man.

We hold that liberty is as essential to man as reason, but we add that he makes a bad use of this liberty, and that his will is become a slave to his passions.

"But," say they, "Is it not the same thing with taking away all liberty from man, to maintain as you do that it is impossible for a man to convert himself?"

No, my brethren: for we at the same time declare that the reason why a man is not converted is because he chooses to continue in his crimes; because his will is so habituated to, and confirmed in the love of sin, that he will never disengage himself from it, if God does not disengage him, and inspire him with a different love. It is because he makes use of his liberty, in this case, only to do evil. Thus our sentiment does not divest man of liberty.

If any are surprised that we should ascribe an impotence to man, let them hear the Scripture, which testifies that: "The carnal mind is enmity against God, and is not subject to his law, neither indeed can be;" that "The natural man receiveth not the things of the Spirit of God;" that we are "dead in our trespasses and sins," with other things to the same purpose.

But let it be attended to that this imbecility does by no means excuse man, because it is voluntary, like the impotence of one who is unable to abstain from wine, which does not excuse his drunkenness. If this impotence rendered man inexcusable, it would necessarily follow that a reasonable creature is no longer capable of acting otherwise. But this maxim would go so far as to excuse the devil himself, as to the crimes which he commits, without intermission. It may be observed every day that evil habits—when inveterate and confirmed by many repeated acts—so possess the soul that it can never disentangle itself from them. But is the man more excusable for this? Surely not.

"But do we not rob man entirely of his liberty when we say that grace acts invincibly in us, and surmounts all resistance and obstacles, which the malice of man can present?" This is indeed what we affirm, and we follow the Scripture in saying so. Does it not declare that God creates us anew? Now creation is an act which cannot be frustrated as to its effect. Does it not speak of his raising us again, of regenerating and quickening us; of his exerting on us the exceeding greatness of his power; and assert that he works in us both to will and to do; that he takes away the heart of stone and gives us a heart of flesh; that he translates us out of darkness into the kingdom of his dear Son; and that he draws us to himself? After this, how can we doubt of the efficacy of grace? Let us only attend to what our Lord teaches in the gospel of John (6:44-45), where after he had said, "No man can come unto me except the Father draw him;" which points out the inability of man, he adds: "Every man that hath heard, and learned of the Father, cometh unto me:" which shows that the act of God is so powerful that it cannot be resisted, seeing as all those on whom it is exerted come unto God.

"But does not this sentiment despoil man of his liberty, when we pretend and teach that converting grace inclines our will, and makes us will what before we did not choose?"

A person is always free when he does what he wills, and abstains from what he wills not; but the grace that regenerates us does not put us into the communion of Jesus Christ, whether we will or not; or by violence, as slaves, who are compelled by blows to do what is exacted of them. It deals with us in effecting that change in a manner agreeable to our nature, and by an act as gentle as powerful. It draws us, but it is "with the cords of a man, and with the bands of love." It converts us by enlightening our mind, and inclining our will: thus it acts invincibly, yet without constraint.

11th Accusation

We are further charged with abolishing all sorts of vows, except those of baptism.

We refuse the truth of this, my brethren; we only want that persons who vow should have the power of disposing of themselves; that the matter of their vow should be a good action, and such as cannot become evil; that what is engaged to be possible, not only at the time when the vow is made, but during the whole time they pretend to observe it; that the vow should be agreeable to the will of God, in nothing contrary to his glory, and to the end we ought to propose, of actively promoting that glory. Thus we are far from approving the vows which are recommended, and into which they frequently enter, in the Romish church.

12th Accusation

They say that we acknowledge no head.

It is true that we acknowledge no head but Jesus Christ; but this we have learned of the apostle Paul, who makes no mention of any other. If any are not content with the divinity of this apostle, we are very sorry for it; but for our part, we are fully satisfied with it and think it our glory that we do not belong to a body that chooses to have two heads, and another chief than him whom God has constituted.

13th Accusation

They accuse us with saying that: "The sacraments are empty figures, hollow signs, or vain idols." But it is easy to show that the charge is injurious. We indeed believe not that the body and blood of Jesus Christ are contained in the eucharist, for reasons assigned in another discourse; but we believe that God accompanies the sacraments with his efficacious grace, as to those who worthily partake of them. So we do not consider them only as shadows, or mere pictures, capable only of exhibiting to the view some form of that which they represent, but as figures full of efficacy, in respect of those who receive them with faith, and as the seals of God's covenant. In this manner we never doubt but that those who worthily receive the sacrament of the supper are made partakers of Jesus Christ, and of the fruits of his sacrifice, and that their souls are nourished with the flesh and blood of the Son of God, in the hope of eternal life. Are these then nothing but empty figures?

14th Accusation

We are further charged with denying the necessity of baptism. But it is a calumny. Indeed, we do not believe that baptism is so absolutely necessary as that none can be saved unless they be baptized: for we know that the grace of God is not tied to the sacraments; that God is no less merciful under the New Testament than under the Old, and as circumcision, to which baptism has succeeded, was not essential to the salvation of Jewish infants, so we have no reason to doubt but that infants born of a believing father and mother without baptism may obtain salvation. Thus our Lord, who said, "He that believeth and is baptized shall be saved," says only, "He that believeth not shall be damned" (Mark 16).

Yet we hold that as Jesus Christ has instituted baptism to be a sacrament or seal of his covenant, those who believe, being come to the years of knowledge, without having been formerly baptized, ought with a holy earnestness to desire this privilege; and Christians to whom God has granted children, ought by no means to lose the opportunity of having baptism, which is the badge of Christians, administered to them, and those who act otherwise, are very culpable in the sight of God. Many learned doctors of the Romish church have acknowledged that those who are baptized with the baptism of blood, or of the Holy Spirit, shall be saved, although they should be deprived of the baptism of water. The famous Gerson, chancellor of the University of Paris, is of our sentiments on this subject,[190] with others, which it is not necessary here to mention.

15th Accusation

They impute also to us the following assertion: that the sins into which the faithful fall after baptism, are forgiven them, through the sole simple remembrance and faith of baptism, without repentance. But we have never asserted anything like this; and the writers on whom they would fix the charge, have justified their innocence in such a manner, as should put those who calumniate them to the blush. They have remarked that those who speak of sins being effaced by the sole remembrance or recollection of baptism, do not understand by this a cold and bare remembrance, but such as is joined with faith and repentance.[191]

---

[190] "It is certain," said he, in a discourse before the Council of Constance, "that God has not so limited his saving mercy, he has not so tied it to the common laws of Christian tradition, or he restricted it to the sacrament, as that he cannot, without prejudice to that mercy, inwardly sanctify infants not yet born by the baptism of his grace, through the virtue of his Spirit." Cardinal Cajetan says, "In case of necessity, it would seem that the vow of fathers and mothers suffices for the salvation of children; as is proved from the infants who died without being circumcised." Cajetan in *Summa Thomas Aquinas* Part 1 Q68 in the 1540 and 1562 editions, but retrenched in that of 1612.

[191] Calvin, *Antidote to the Council of Trent*, Session 7 Chapter 10

16th Accusation

We are charged with despising the eucharist, and believing that it is only common bread and wine. I confess, my brethren, that we believe what the sense and reason of all mankind, and the divine Scriptures, unanimously teach us, namely: that the eucharist is truly bread and wine, in respect of substance and essential properties. Yet we have at no time said that it is nothing more than common bread and wine. We hold it to be bread and wine consecrated by the institution of our Lord, a sacrament of our religion: bread, which is the communion of the body of Christ; wine, which is the communion of his blood; bread and wine, which man cannot receive unworthily, without rendering himself guilty of the body of Jesus Christ.

17th Accusation

They charge us also with asserting that Jesus Christ despaired when on the cross, and that after his death, he suffered torments in hell, similar to those of the damned.

This is a calumny which the missionaries are continually busy in circulating; but we declare to all the world that we should be unworthy to tread the ground, or to see the light, if such were our belief. We are persuaded that our Lord always hoped in God amidst his most violent pains; and that this merciful Savior—having accomplished the work of our redemption—committed his holy soul into the hands of his Father. The Catechism, which is explained to you every sabbath, expressly asserts in Section 10 that "Jesus Christ did not cease to hope still in God in the midst of his sufferings." Indeed, there is a passage in this section which they abuse, in which the author of the Catechism proposes this question, "How could it come to pass that Jesus Christ, who is the salvation of the world, should have been (*en une telle damnation*) in such a state of damnation?" But who sees not that this is an old French word, used at that time to denote *condemnation*: of which all the books then written are a proof?[192] In the Bible of Louvain, printed there in 1550, the following words are put into the mouth of the converted thief, "Dost thou not fear God, (*toi qui es en la même damnation*) thou who art in the same damnation?" (Luke 23:40).[193] Thus the expression used by the compiler of the Catechism means no more than if he had said: "How could Jesus Christ be liable to such a condemnation?"

But he has nowhere said that Jesus Christ suffered in hell the pains of the damned; on the contrary, he shows in that very section the difference between the torment which Jesus Christ endured, and that felt by sinners whom God punishes in his wrath, for he adds: "That which was but for a time in him, is perpetual in the other, and what was as a needle to pierce him, is as a sword to wound them to death; and instead of despairing, as the wicked do whom God damns, Jesus Christ always hoped in God." Have any of our divines ever employed such expressions on this subject as are to be found in the writings of a famous Cordelier, who says that: "Jesus Christ for the deliverance of sinners, put himself in the place of all sinners, not by killing, committing adultery, stealing, and the like; but by taking upon himself the wages, the punishment and desert of sins, which are cold, heat, hunger, thirst, fear, horror of death, and of hell, despair, death, hell itself, in order to conquer hunger by hunger, horror by horror, despair by despair, and hell by hell."[194]

---

[192] See *Le grand coustumier du pays et duché de Normandie*; à Rouen, 1539

[193] The above observation of the author is equally applicable to the term *damnation* in the English language. In some places of the New Testament, the translators have employed it as equivalent to judgment or condemnation; as was also commonly done by the older theological writers in Britain, subsequent to the Reformation. It was not then appropriated, as it seems now to be in vulgar use, to the eternal state of persons; nor was it restricted to persons, but applied to doctrines, and things inanimate. In the two following passages—particularly in consequence of the ideas now affixed to the word *damned* and *damnation*—the rendering of the original, by denoting judgment, or a judgment of condemnation, would be better substituted, as answering to the import of the original terms, and the scope of the places. Romans 14:23: "He that doubteth is *damned* if he eat." 1 Corinthians 11:29: "He that eateth and drinketh unworthily, eateth and drinketh damnation to himself." [*Translator*]

[194] Ferus in Matthew 27

18th Accusation

We are next accused as enemies to the blessed virgin: a certain Jesuit is not ashamed to rank us with Pagans and Jews, and to say that, in common with all other heretics, those of our religion "contumeliously treat and vilify the Virgin, instead of praising her."[195] What a calumny! Is it to vilify her, to pronounce her the most blessed among women, for having brought into the world the Redeemer of the human race? Is it to vilify her, to celebrate her faith, her humility, purity, zeal, patience, sanctity, and various virtues? To publish the felicity which she enjoys, and to propose her as an example to be imitated, is this to vilify her?

I confess, we never bestow upon her the titles of the *queen of heaven, the gate of paradise, the ladder of Jacob, the advocate of sinners, the mediatrix of the human race*: because we are persuaded that in so doing, we would offend the Lord Jesus, by robbing him of the glory that to him alone is due, and also insult the virgin. I own likewise that we do not consecrate images to her, nor adore the images of her which others have made; but the reason why we do not, is the divine prohibition to the contrary, and because we are assured that this holy virgin, who burns with zeal for the glory of God, would not wish to be honored by a worship which he has expressly forbidden. Were it the will of God that this blessed virgin should cause her voice to be heard from the height of heaven, to which she has been raised, we would willingly take her for the judge in her own cause.

19th Accusation

Akin to this is the next charge: that we are enemies to the saints and refuse to honor them. This is a most false accusation. So far are we from hating or despising true saints, of whose sanctity either the Scripture, or any other authentic history, bears testimony that, on the contrary, we respect their memory, we praise their holy conversation and excellent actions, we

---

[195] Maiden in Luke 1:49

propose them for an example, we endeavor to imitate and follow their steps, and we have no manner of doubt, but that their happy spirits now enjoy, in the bosom of Jesus, that glory which they hoped for, and to which we all aspire. Is this to hate and despise them?

It is true that we dedicate to them no temples, chapels, festivals, or images of any kind. We adore not either their portraits or their relics; nor do we offer them any tapers or perfumes. But such honors they never demanded. They cried out with indignation against those who prostrated themselves before their persons, and who would have sacrificed to them. What would they have done, had they seen men who profess the faith, bowing their knees before an image of them? Neither in the books of the Old or of the New Testament, nor in the writings of the three first centuries, can any trace be perceived of that religious worship which is given at present to saints. On this account, we content ourselves with granting them only such honour as they themselves have desired, and such as the Scripture would have us to render them. Is this to despise them? It is indeed true that we have a sovereign contempt for many who are called saints, but who never deserved to be reckoned among the number, whose lives were either extravagant, or impious.

It is no less a calumny to represent us as enemies to the cross of Christ. So far from this, we make the cross of the Redeemer our boast, and say with Paul: "God forbid that we should glory, save in the cross of Jesus Christ." But when we thus speak of the cross of our Savior, we understand by it his death; and we deplore the blindness of the Romish church, who give unto the wood, to which Jesus was fixed, and to material figures which represent it, the glory that belongs only to the great God and our Savior, crucified for man's salvation, which they are accustomed to call their only hope, bestowing on it adoration. We are grieved to the heart to see a people baptized, and who make profession of the holy name of Jesus, worshipping with so much appearance of devotion, and so many ceremonies, stone, wood, gold or silver, the work of mortal men.

If we refrain from making the sign of the cross, as is now practiced, and as the custom was in the time of Tertullian,[196] it is for these reasons: 1. It does not appear that it had been practised before that time. 2. The Christians then only made use of that sign to testify to the Pagans that they were not ashamed of Jesus Christ crucified. At that time, the usage might be good and holy, being unaccompanied with superstition, and the opinion of merit; but now that we live in the midst of people who profess to adore Christ crucified, and to place all their glory in the infinite merit of the pains he suffered on the cross, it is no longer of any utility. 3. That which might be lawful and good, in the beginning, is degenerated into superstition; and they now ascribe to the sign of the cross, what is competent only to Jesus Christ himself, and to the Holy Spirit, the communication of which he has procured by his sufferings.

20th Accusation

It is another charge brought against us that our churches are naked and destitute of ornaments: as if the truth which is therein purely preached and the sacraments administered were not preferable to the gold and silver which shine in other places, and to the images, paintings, and tapestry, wherewith they deck and adorn them. Isidore of Damietta—blaming the excessive care of the bishop of his city to ornament and enrich its churches—says that in the time of the apostles, they had no temples, and adds that, if he had it in his choice, he would love much rather to have lived in that time when the church was crowned with the graces of heaven, although the places where they assembled had no ornaments as yet bestowed upon them, than in his own age, when they might indeed see temples decorated, and enriched with

---

[196] It appears from this writer that in his time, Christians were accustomed to make the sign of the cross on their forehead, in coming in or going out of their houses, when they dressed, washed, or placed themselves at table, in the evening, when they lighted a candle, when they lay down, or sat down, and in almost every part of their conversation.
Tertullian, *The Chaplet*, Chapter 3.

all sorts of marble, but in which the church was naked and divested of her graces.

21st Accusation

"But your religion," they sometimes tell us, "Is a mere skeleton without sap and unction; not so the Romish religion, wherein persons may find what will nourish their souls."

And who can be so incredulous as to deny that souls are excellently nourished by these devotions which are only adapted to the eyes, and have nothing to do with the heart; by these masses of which the people understand nothing, and these litanies which are repeated without anybody knowing what is said?

Oh! How well is piety nourished by seeing a priest putting himself in a variety of antic [*bizarre*] postures, and making frequent bows, sometimes to the left, and sometimes to the right? By seeing him decked out in his sacerdotal habits, and blowing his breath several times upon him who is about to receive baptism, in order to drive the devil out of him? By seeing him touch with his spittle the ears and nostrils of the baptized, or breathing upon him who receives confirmation, with a thousand things of the same nature? Do you find these to be the proper nourishment of souls? For our part, we present you with nothing of this kind; we call all this empty viands. We offer you only that heavenly pasture by which the Lord has appointed his flock to be fed, and that bread of life, which he himself has brought from heaven.

22nd Accusation

Our religion is sometimes also charged with fanaticism. But there never was an accusation worse contrived or supported, for nothing can be more opposite to fanaticism than the religion of Protestants. Do we talk of visions, revelations, extasies, or enthusiasms? Do we pretend to be workers of miracles? Do we boast of receiving revelations for supporting our sentiments, as others have done? It is well known that the Cordeliers produce the revelations and visions of St. Bridget to prove the immaculate conception, to which the Jacobins oppose the visions and revelations of St. Catherine of Siena; and those who have read the legends need not to be told that they are full of the revelations of the angelic Carmelite, of St. Hildegard, and a great number more.

23rd Accusation

"But must it not be a great presumption against your religion," they often ask, "To see the various sects it has produced?"

But would there not be as much justice in blaming the Christian religion, which the apostles established, because from among those called Christians, a swarm of frightful sects arose, as that of the Menandrians, the Carpocratians, the Basilidians, the Valentinians, the Gnostics, the Montanists, the Manichees, and others?

Or are the sects, to which we are said to have given birth, really members of our body? "They went out from you," they tell us; but this is a proof that they were not of us. Or can the church of Rome pretend that she has never begotten any sects?

It is not to our religion, which is pure and holy, that the rise and spreading of these sects ought to be ascribed, but to the licentiousness of the human mind.

24th Accusation

But they still object that there are many divisions among us. I own that it would be highly desirable to see all Protestants perfectly united. We continually offer up prayers for such a holy union; and we could bestow even our blood and life to promote it. But were there no divisions in the primitive church? Were there none formerly at Corinth? Did no schisms take place in the church, sometimes about matters of small importance, such as the day for celebrating Easter, and the validity of the baptism of heretics?

What invectives and reproaches did not Jerome and Cyril of Alexandria pour out against Chrysostom, not scrupling even to call him a Judas; a Jeconias! And what did Theophilus, bishop of Alexandria, and Epiphanius, bishop of Salamis, in Cyprus, practise against him? And at this time, are there no divisions in the bosom of the Romish church, between the Cordeliers and Jacobins, and among the Molinists, the Thomists, and Jansenists?

25th Accusation

We are blamed for having said in our Confession (Article 31) that in the days of our fathers, "the church had fallen into ruin and desolation." This they think is the same thing with saying that the church was extinct; which is contrary to the words of Jesus Christ, "The gates of hell shall not prevail against it."

But this is a misconstruction of that passage in our Confession. It was never meant by that expression that the church was extinguished, for we certainly know that this never has been, nor ever can be; we are persuaded that she shall always obtain a full and entire victory over hell. These words are only intended to point out that the church was corrupted in doctrine, worship, and manners.

26th Accusation

Finally, we are charged with having adopted the errors of several ancient heretics.

They say that, with the Messalians, we despise the sign of the cross. We have already assigned the reason of our practice as to this; nor do I know where they are informed that the Messalians despised the cross. We are associated with Eunomius because we teach that we are saved by faith without works; as if this were not the true doctrine of Paul; and as if we taught this doctrine in the same manner as Eunomius did, who held that faith without works was sufficient.[197] We are charged also with taking away free will from man, with Simon Magus; but we have proven the contrary. In like manner, they do us the honor of joining us with many other heretics, with whom we have nothing in common.

But here we might enlarge very much, were we inclined to recriminate upon those who attack us. We could, in our turn, oppose the Simonians, who boasted of things which were not written; and the Carpocratians, who gave out that Jesus Christ had delivered many things in secret to his apostles, which they had not taught to all;[198] and who also believed that the images of Jesus Christ and his apostles ought to be adored. We might object to them the Audians who represented God under the image of a corruptible man, the Angelicans who worshiped angels, the Collyridians who adored the virgin, Marcion who gave women permission to baptize and who considered fish as a most holy food, the Manicheans who abstained from the cup, the Encratites who represented marriage as no better than whoredom, and who abstained from the use of flesh, the Montanists who had their regular feasts, with innumerable more. But on this, what we have said may suffice.

I think I have now run over the most considerable objections usually brought against our doctrine, for the time permits not to produce those which are further made to our Reformation. That shall be the matter of another discourse, if the Lord will. We therefore call upon you to examine whether there be such force in any of these objections, as to make us doubt whether our religion be the most pure and most perfect of all others in the world.

---

[197] Augustine, *De Heres*. C6.54
[198] Tren. L1 C2 ad[u] 8.

APPLICATION.

But I must not conceal from you, my brethren, that there is yet another objection brought against us, which, to my great grief, I cannot answer in the most satisfactory manner. They say that our life and manners are unworthy of people who profess to be the disciples of Jesus Christ, that the same vices are to be found among us as in all places of the world, and that nothing is so rare as to see persons whose life is so exemplary, whose piety, zeal, holiness, and virtues, contribute as much to edification as the disorders of others give scandal.

What would you have me to say in order to repel this objection? I might say with propriety that, if our life be not edifying, and if our manners are not duly regulated, this is not the fault of our religion; and that as much good and holy living may be seen in our religion as in other communions. But this answer will not shut the mouths of those who accuse us. They will still say, seeing as we boast that our religion is the most pure, our life ought also to be most holy. They will insist that, since we glory in being the disciples of Christ, it is incumbent on us to make it evident by our conduct.

There is reason in this objection; and I sincerely confess that it reduces me to silence. You could help me, my brethren, to reply to it in a victorious manner; but it can only be by a change of life.

If there were no more to be found among us, the profane, covetous, ambitious; the luxurious, the debauched, the vindictive; usurers, men of ill-acquired riches, persons without charity, without zeal, without the love of God—if, on the contrary, we saw shining among us the graces and excellencies of our Divine Master, his gentleness, his charity, his mercy, his patience, his humility, his resignation to the appointments of providence, his zeal, his love for the heavenly Father, his attachment to his service, his self-denial, his fidelity, constancy, chastity, sincerity, and temperance—then indeed we should leave nothing to reproach us with, and we should effectually shame and overthrow all our enemies.

How glorious would it be for us, if we should live so as to be distinguished from all others, and that our most cruel adversaries might say: *There can be nothing laid to the charge of these people, except that they are Protestants*; as they used to say of the first Christians: *There is nothing blameable in these men, but that they are Christians.* O how many converts would our life make!

How glorious for us, if we should live as the Author of our religion; the head and finisher of our faith? If we were to follow the excellent examples of the blessed apostles, and of other holy men, who have imitated them?

What consolation would it afford us in the hour of our death, when we shall be obliged to surrender our souls into the hands of him who bestowed them, to be able to say to ourselves that we are of the number of those for whom Jesus Christ has merited heaven and immortality, and for whom he is gone to prepare a place?

But above all, what consolation in the great and last day, when Jesus Christ shall come to crown the faith and charity of his members, to hear from his mouth, a voice calling us to take a seat upon his throne, and to receive from his hand the diadem of glory, and the crown of righteousness?

My brethren, think on these things, we beseech you. Consider whether we have not the greatest reason to entreat you to think seriously upon him. And may God establish us all in his truth, and render us perfect in every good work, that so we may be found without blame even to the day of Jesus Christ: to whom, as to the Father, and the Holy Spirit, be honor, glory, dominion, and power. Amen.

A DEFENSE

OF THE

PROTESTANT REFORMATION

The Seventh Discourse.

On 1 Thessalonians 5:21.

My brethren,

We propose this day to continue the defence of our holy religion against those who attack it. In our last discourse we vindicated its doctrine against the calumnies with which they have endeavoured to blacken it. We shall now attempt to justify our Reformation. There is nothing with which we have been more reproached, than our separation from the church of Rome. As this was an open and flagrant rupture, which carried away whole kingdoms, and many states from the Roman pontiff, our adversaries never can speak of it without great heat and emotions of anger. They represent us as people who have separated themselves from the heritage of the Lord, divided from this body, and cut themselves off from the participation of his sacraments. They accuse us with having made a cruel war on the members of this divine Savior, with having overturned his altars, and torn his garments, not choosing to leave entire that seamless coat, which the Roman soldiers would not consent to have parted among them; they charge us with having renounced the promises of the true Son of God, and vented foul abuse against his spouse. If their words were hearkened to, it might be said that we have destroyed the gospel and Christianity, bound the Lord Jesus to the cross, and opened his sacred side; and that we accordingly deserve the hatred of heaven and earth, of men, angels, and of God. Who can hear, unmoved, such injurious reproaches, and who can even keep silence on such an occasion? Would we not be the most dastardly of all men, if we should allow the memory of our worthy fathers—who delivered their posterity from an insupportable yoke—to be tarnished, without avowedly undertaking their defence? And would it not also be the basest ingratitude to the goodness of God, who has dispelled, in many parts of the earth, the darkness with which almost the whole world was covered, if we did not make known the reasons which our ancestors had for quitting the Romish religion, and which hinder us still from returning to it? This—if God wills—shall make the subject of this discourse that so you, my brethren, may examine whether our fathers have been as criminal as they are represented, and if we do wrong in following their steps. And thus you shall continue to practise what the apostle enjoins upon us in the words which we have read to you for the seventh time: "Prove all things."

We think it unnecessary to demand your attention; the matter we propose to treat affects you too nearly not to oblige you to grant us a favorable hearing; and I am persuaded there is no person who will not reckon it a pleasure to learn what answer ought to be returned to the question so often proposed to us: "Why have you made a separation?" We have made it appear in the preceding discourses that we are not heretics; let us now examine whether we are not schismatics, as they are wont to call us. May God afford us the aid of his Spirit, who is a Spirit of truth and of charity! Amen.

It cannot be denied that schism is one of the greatest evils that can beset the church. Those who are authors of it cannot be too severely blamed. But we must not believe that all those who separate from a church must be schismatics. Therefore, in order to know whether our fathers have made a schism, we must enquire:

    1.   Whether it be warrantable to separate from a church?

2. What are the reasons which may warrant and induce persons to make such a separation?

3. Whether our fathers had good reasons to forsake the Romish church?

I. If we consult the holy Scripture, reason, and the practice of the first Christians, we will find that it is warrantable sometimes to separate from a church.

First, I say, if we consult the Scripture; hear, brethren, the apostle Paul on this subject; who said to the Romans: "I beseech you, mark them which cause divisions and offences, contrary to the doctrine which ye have learned; and avoid them. For they that are such serve not our Lord Jesus Christ, but their own belly; and by good words and fair speeches deceive the hearts of the simple." Again, to the Corinthians: "What fellowship hath righteousness with unrighteousness? And what communion hath light with darkness? What concord hath Christ with Belial? Or what part hath he that believeth with an infidel? And what agreement hath the temple of God with idols? For ye are the temple of the living God, as God hath said, I will dwell in them, and walk in them, and I will be their God, and they shall be my people. Wherefore come out from among them, and be ye separate, saith the Lord, and touch not the unclean thing, and I will receive you." To the Galatians he said: "If any man preach any other gospel unto you, than that ye have received, let him be accursed!" And it is well known that no communion was held among the Jews with those against whom the great *anathema* was denounced. Further, he thus wrote to his beloved Timothy: "If any teach otherwise, and consent not to wholesome words, even the words of our Lord Jesus Christ, and to the doctrine which is according to godliness, he is proud, knowing nothing, but doting about questions and strifes of words, whereof cometh envy, strife, railings, evil surmisings, perverse disputings of men of corrupt minds, and destitute of the truth, supposing that gain is godliness: from such withdraw thyself." And that you may not think the apostle Paul alone held these sentiments, attend to what the apostle John says, in his second general epistle: "If there come any unto you, and bring not this doctrine, receive him not into your house, neither bid him God speed. For he that biddeth him God speed, is partaker of his evil deeds." But above all, hear the voice from heaven, which cries, "Come out of Babylon, my people, that ye be not partakers of her sins, lest ye receive also of her plagues."[199]

It is therefore clear that the Scripture directs us to separate sometimes from the societies in the midst of which we live, and from persons with whom we may have had a strict connection and intercourse.

Secondly, reason confirms what the Scripture teaches. It informs us:

1. That we ought not to desire the communion of men, but so far as it may consist with that of God and of Jesus Christ.

2. That one ought not to remain in a society where he is in danger of having his faith and worship insensibly corrupted, because none should abide in a place or situation in which he may have reason to fear that he may lose his soul; as prudence would forbid us to go to a city where the plague killed all who frequented it.

3. *In fine*, reason teaches us that we ought to remove at a distance from a church wherein our children are brought into hazard, because we should consider ourselves as responsible for their salvation as well as our own, and it is extremely difficult to preserve children, who are susceptible of all sorts of impressions, from being corrupted, whatever care should be taken of their education.

Lastly, if we consult the conduct of the primitive Christians, we will find that they separated themselves from the Jewish church, after she was confirmed in her incredulity. And when the Arians had gained the ascendency in synods, an actual separation was made by many persons, who

---

[199] Romans 16:17-18, 2 Corinthians 6, 1 Timothy 6:3-5, Galatians 1:9, 2 John 10, Revelation 23:3

refused to have any communion with them; but choosing rather to suffer death, they proclaimed aloud with Hilary: "We never shall have peace but with those who will anathematize Arius." "I exhort you," said the celebrated bishop of Poitiers, "to beware of Antichrist. Be not taken with a foolish love for walls. No longer consider the church of God as consisting in tiles and buildings. No longer employ or urge, on such frivolous accounts, the name of peace. [...] For my part, I find more safety in the mountains, forests and lakes, in prisons and dungeons: for there the Spirit of God animated the prophets. [...] Separate yourselves then from Auxentius: he is a messenger of Satan, an enemy of Christ, an open persecutor, a destroyer of the faith."[200]

After the Synod of Seleucia, a number of people who were under the jurisdiction of Arian bishops—not choosing to forsake the true faith—established bishops of their own. The father of Gregory Nazianzen, having by surprise given the communion to Arians, those of his diocese separated from him; although they knew very well that he had not changed his own sentiments; and it is a certain fact attested by many authors that while the Arians possessed the temples and the sees of churches, the orthodox held their assemblies apart.

Wherefore Scripture, reason, and the ancient practice of Christians, authorizes us to separate in certain cases from the church to which we belong. It is from Jesus Christ alone that we must hold ourselves bound never and in no case to separate, to whom we must always say, "Lord, to whom shall we go but to thee? Thou only hast the words of eternal life." But as Ambrose said justly, "There is need to attend carefully to the faith of a church: if Jesus Christ dwell there, there we must abide; but if a people be found therein who violate the faith, or if a heretical teacher has defiled his habitation, we must withdraw from the communion of heretics, and flee from the commerce of such a synagogue. Separation ought to be made from that church which rejects the faith, and preserves not the foundations of the

---

[200] Hilar. adv. Arian.

apostolic preaching, for fear lest her communion should fix upon us some stain of perfidy."[201]

II. Having established this first principle that it is lawful and even necessary sometimes to separate from a church, we must next enquire on what occasions this separation ought to be made. It is certain none should proceed to such a rupture, except for reasons of importance. It would, for example, be a very great sin to abandon a communion for some points of mere difficulty, like those that for which a bishop of Rome (Victor) cut off the churches of Asia, tearing by this means the great and glorious body of Jesus Christ, as Irenaeus well represented to him; neither should it be done on account of scholastic questions, which consist in terms very remote from the knowledge and edification of the people; nor yet on account of personal interests or slight pretences, such as those which produced the schisms of the Donatists, the Novatians, and the Luciferians.

But at the same time, it cannot be doubted that when a church holds fast, and is confirmed in errors directly opposite to the doctrine of Jesus Christ and to the salvation of men; when she would carry people away to an idolatrous worship, and would constrain all her members to make profession of her errors, and to practise a worship forbidden of God, then separation from such a church becomes indispensably necessary, and none can refrain from it without opposing the express orders of God, and exposing to hazard their own salvation and that of their children. This is what you may collect from the passages formerly adduced from Paul and John, and that from Ambrose; and a certain famous cardinal has granted so much.[202]

III. The only enquiry therefore that remains is whether the Romish church was in that state in which a church must be supposed to be, when it

---

[201] Ambr. Comm. in Luc. l. 6. c. 9.

[202] Cardinal du Perron says that, when there is corruption in the doctrine, the sacraments, or the ceremonies universally used in the church, none can remain in the communion of that church, without partaking of her contagion. Mr. Arnaud, likewise, in the first tome of the *Perpetuity*, declares that no connection ought to be maintained with a church, which is judged to be heretical.

becomes the duty of those who have been united with her to forsake her. This is what we require you to judge of for yourselves.

For your assistance herein, recall to your mind what we delivered in our fourth sermon, wherein we showed that the church of Rome divides the worship that is due only to God, between God and his creatures, etc.[203]

In a word, that she teaches doctrines entirely opposite to those of Jesus Christ and the apostles, and practices many things which they have forbidden. Add to all these that this church will relax nothing of her old errors and superstition, but anathematizes all those who refuse to follow her decisions, depriving them of her communion, and inflicting upon them the utmost severities. These are the reasons for which our fathers separated themselves from the Romish communion. Say, whether their conduct can be blamed?

How could they think to continue in a communion in which they had reason to fear as to the salvation of themselves and of their children? How could it be supposed that they should never have abandoned a church, which they considered as mystical Babylon, out of which God had commanded them to depart? How can it be thought that they should always have remained embodied with men who taught another gospel? Or how could they possibly have lived with people who banished them, and treated them with the utmost cruelty? Examine the matter, my brethren.

That you may the better succeed in this examination, we are willing to state to you the objections which they bring against us on this head.

---

[203] Here the author recapitulates, in 12 particulars, the principal instances of idolatry, and gross corruption, charged upon that church, in the discourse referred to, which the reader can easily, if he please, consult. He mentions also, on the head of the adoration of the sacrament, the remarkable declaration of the Jesuit Coster, that if there be nothing more than bread in the eucharist, then there was never such idolatry as that of which the Romish church is guilty. [*Transl.*]

Objection 1

They say that none ought ever to separate from the church because out of the church there is no salvation.

I answer that indeed none ought at any time to separate from the true church, that is to say, from the assembly of the faithful, who make profession of a true faith; but we add that our fathers never separated themselves from this true church, out of which, we grant, persons cannot be saved. They only left a church who calls herself the true church, though, in reality, she be not.

To render this matter clear, it may be needful to make a few remarks.

1. When it is said, "Without the church there is no salvation," we do not speak of a particular church, as the Roman, the Greek, or the Protestant; but we mean the communion of the faithful, who are dispersed throughout the world, and who constantly adhere to the doctrine of Jesus Christ. In order to enter into this church, nothing more is needful than to make a sincere and firm profession of the religion of Jesus Christ, even though a person may not be acquainted with those societies in the world which may make this profession.

2. In the days of our fathers, there were in the Romish church, as there have been at all times, tares mingled with the good grain; some true subjects of Jesus Christ, and others subjects of Antichrist. But it has so fallen out that the part most pure has separated from the party impure; the good have relinquished the bad; they have left popery behind, but carried with them pure Christianity. They alone were the true church of Jesus Christ: they continued to be what they were before, only with this difference superadded: that they could no longer maintain communion with those among whom they lived, on account of their heresies, false worship, and persecuting spirit, but held their assemblies apart. Therefore it is not true that they have made a separation from the true church out of which there is no salvation, because that which they have forsaken no longer remains the true church. It might have been so denominated, so long as it contained within its pale, the faithful, who approved not, nor joined with the errors that were

taught in it; but now that these faithful are separated from it, it has no more a claim to the title.

Objection 2

They plead that, although it were true that the church of Rome had been both heretical and idolatrous, yet the love of peace should have obliged our fathers to continue in it. Charity should have kept them from abandoning their brethren, and nothing whatever ought to make men break that bond, which the apostle calls "the bond of perfectness."

It is surprising that reasonable people can make use of such language, as if the love of peace ought to prevail over the love of truth; or as if outward peace ought to be bought at the expense of that peace of soul, which constitutes the happiness of the faithful Christian, and at the expence of that eternal peace which is prepared for him. We must love that peace alone, said an ancient father, which joins us to God. "The name of peace," said Hilary, "is indeed very specious, and the mere appearance of unity has something engaging in it. But who knows not that the church and the people acknowledge no other peace than that which comes from Jesus Christ, and which he gave to his apostles after his glorious passion, and which he left with them as a deposit by his everlasting commandment, when he was about to depart from them?"

Charity, I confess, is the greatest of Christian graces; but it ought never to go unaccompanied with truth, as Paul has observed. It may very well oblige us to render to our neighbor all the duties of humanity, of which we are capable; but it cannot constrain us to remain in a church wherein our salvation cannot be promoted. On the contrary, the love which we ought to have for ourselves should determine us to love the society of those who may bring us to destruction.

I grant that when the question is only about some points of small moment, that many things must be endured for the love of peace; but how can any suppose that the desire of unity and concord could oblige our fathers to believe and receive the doctrines which essentially injured the faith, whereby we are united to Jesus Christ, and also essentially altered the worship which we owe to God?

Further, is it not impious to assert that the Romish church cannot lawfully be condemned, even though she should be heretical and idolatrous? Are heresy and idolatry then no longer condemnable, when it shall please the Romish church to authorize them? Must men still maintain respect for her, when she retains none for Jesus Christ? What! If that church had become Mahometan, and declared it to be her pleasure that we should adopt the Quran, would it still have been unwarrantable to separate from her? Who will presume to say so?

Several learned men of the Romish church have written that Rome should sometime fall into a great apostacy, during which she should abandon herself to idolatry and all manner of abominations, sacrificing to devils and false gods; and they add that it is of Rome when thus corrupted, that the voice from heaven must be understood as spoken, "Come out of her my people."[204] Therefore it is not true that people ought not to secede from the Romish church, even though she should be heretical or idolatrous, as some have been daring enough to write.

We may ask, who has given this privilege to the church of Rome, that none may at any time, or upon any pretext whatsoever, leave her communion? Has God bestowed upon her the prerogative of infallibility? Or has he instituted her the mistress of all other churches to be the perpetual centre of Christian unity, giving a commandment to all the faithful never to withdraw from her? Where will they find proofs for this? We have seen in another discourse that the Romish church has not the smallest reason to support her pretension to infallibility, and that she never has been regarded as the center of unity.

---

[204] Viegas on Revelation 18, etc.

Objection 3

"But could not your fathers," they will say, "have contented themselves with not believing the doctrines of the Romish church, without forsaking her communion? It might have been sufficient had they accommodated their external behaviour to that of others."

In this manner do these unhappy Nicodemites of the present time continue to reason, who say, they are far from holding the sentiments of the church of Rome, although they make profession of them. Strange reasoning! As if it were enough that a man consecrate his heart to God, without paying any regard to the demand he also makes of the body. Surely our celestial Husband cannot possibly allow that his spouse should only offer to him her heart, if she prostitutes her body to the world and to idols. It is his will that she should make it appear visibly to all, by the most conspicuous tokens, what she is in reality. This we shall have occasion to treat, at greater length, in the following discourse.

Further, how could it be expected that our fathers should have acknowledged the pope as the head of the church, while they were fully convinced that we have no other head but one, even Jesus Christ? Believing as they did that the host inclosed in the pyx,[205] is nothing but a wafer, and not the body of Jesus Christ, how was it possible for them, to give to that host the worship and adoration due only to God, without involving themselves in the crime of idolatry? They were persuaded that the worship of images, is severely prohibited by the Lord in his law; with what conscience then could they have fallen down before them, and paid them religious honor? They were fully assured that prayer constitutes a principal part of the service of God, and that there is no other besides him who ought to be invoked, even as there is none but him who can be the object of our faith. How could they then, without sacrilege, invoke so many creatures? They had also learned of the apostle Paul that Jesus Christ was once offered

---

[205] i. e. the box in which the consecrated wafer is kept. [*Translator*]

upon the cross, and that by this offering, he has made perfect expiation of our sins. How could they then, consistently with this, attend daily on the sacrifice of the mass?

Objection 4

They further urge: "May not persons satisfy themselves with a mere *negative* separation, as they speak in the schools, by abstaining from communion with the errors and idolatry of the Romish church?" This they think may suffice; but that they ought never to proceed the length of a *positive* separation, which consists in forming a separate society, establishing a new ministry, and condemning positively the former society with which they had been united.

There are two things we have to offer in answer to this:

1. How was it possible for any to abstain from communicating with the errors and idolatry of that church, seeing as she anathematized all those who would not fall in with her decisions; nay, hanged, burned, and broke on the wheel, whoever refused to submit to her yoke?

2. Since they plead that our fathers should not have formed a separate body from the Romish church, it must necessarily follow, either that they should always have been one body with her, or else they must have been separated from all society. It was no longer possible for them to continue always the same body with a church, who was no more the body of Jesus Christ. Should they have made the members of the Lord the members of a church impure and idolatrous? Consequently, nothing remained for them but to have lived as wandering sheep, having nothing more than an internal communion with Jesus Christ, without daring to discover it by any outward act. This is indeed the sentiment of those who attack our Reformation. They think our ancestors ought rather to have suffered the name of Jesus Christ to have fallen into oblivion upon the earth, and to have left the faith and the knowledge of God to perish in it, than to establish new pastors to instruct

men in the truth, and to form them to piety, and the fear of God. But what Christian can endure to hear this with cool indifference?

Objection 5

We ought, they say, to imitate the example of Jesus Christ and his disciples; of Simeon, of Zacharias, of Joseph, of the holy virgin, and of Elizabeth, who continued in the communion of the high priests, although Christ had reprehended their doctrine. We must imitate the example of the prophets, who never forsook the temple of Jerusalem; and that of Paul, with respect to the church of the Corinthians, in which they had on the matter divided Jesus Christ; for one said he was of Apollos, and another that he was of Paul; in which they had dishonored Christianity, while there were among them adulterers, and every unctuous persons; in which the holy Supper was profaned by the repasts at which the rich fed intemperately, while the poor were ready to die with hunger; and in which even the resurrection of the dead was denied.

For answer to this difficulty, I beg your attention to the following remarks:

1. Although there were different sects among the Jews, of which some, as the Pharisees taught many traditions that were merely the commandments of men, and others, as the Sadducees, denied the immortality of the soul, and the resurrection of the body; yet it does not appear that idolatry was practised among them; so that nothing hindered them from attending with the people in the temple, to render to God the service that he had commanded.

2. We do not find there was any law that obliged people to the observance of these traditions; and as to the false doctrines of the Sadducees, these were so peculiar to themselves that even the other doctors opposed them.

3. Remark that under the ancient economy, the temple of Jerusalem was the only place wherein sacrifice was allowed to be offered; whereas under

the New Testament God has not confined his service to any particular place: "For the hour is come, when neither in Gerizim, nor at Jerusalem, are men bound to worship, but in which the true worshippers adore God every where, in spirit and in truth."

4. The fourth and last remark is that the errors and faults of the Corinthians, which Paul reproves, were not authorised by the body of the church of Corinth. There is also great appearance that the Corinthians repented, and profited by the censure of the apostles; whereas, if they had persisted in their error, and culpable conduct; had they rejected Paul as an heretic, or persecuted him as others had done, he would doubtless have left them, renounced their communion, and would have obliged the faithful also to abandon them.

Now these remarks may make it very evident that there was a great difference between the times of Zacharias, of Joseph, of the prophets and apostles, and that wherein our reforming fathers were placed. I submit it to your judgment, my brethren. Is there any reason then for blaming our good ancestors for having done, at a time when idolatry was established, when impositions and constraint were laid on men's faith, while the service of God was not restricted to any certain place, what Jesus Christ, the apostles, prophets, and many holy men and women, had not done, in other circumstances and times, when no idolatry prevailed, wherein people were left to their liberty, and when the public worship of God had a close and necessary connection with the temple at Jerusalem.

Objection 6

But would it not have been better, say they, to have exerted themselves to the utmost, to correct what they found wrong in the church, than thus to have torn her bosom, and pulled asunder the members of her body?

And was there nothing done, it may be replied, with that view, before coming to such a rupture? How often were complaints made of the horrid corruption prevailing in the church of Rome, without any remedy being applied to it? Look into the writings of the thirteenth, fourteenth, and fifteenth centuries. It was generally acknowledged that there were great abuses and evils to be found in it. The popes themselves confessed it. Adrian delivered memorials to his nuncio for the diet of Nuremberg, bearing that for many years back, abominations had been committed in the holy place; that abuses in spiritual things, and excess in ecclesiastical mandates, prevailed; and that all things had been perverted; that the evil had been communicated from the head to the members, from the popes to inferior prelates, and that all degrees of ecclesiastics were so much gone out of the way that there had not been, for a long time past, "any one that did good, no, not so much as one." But what availed this confession? What effect followed? Those who spoke a little freely were excommunicated; and this poor Adrian, for having, with too much freedom, declared his resolution to employ himself in correcting so great an evil, died suddenly. It is said that after his death, the licentious youths affixed in the night, at the gate of his physician's house, a crown of boughs with this inscription: *To the deliverer of the country*.

After this, who could entertain the thought of healing Babylon, seeing as she would not be healed; but killed her physicians? Was there not then a necessity of leaving her?

Objection 7

But could not your fathers, they add, have done, as theirs had done before them, who never forsook the church, in which they were born, and yet were saved?

1. I answer firstly that we ought not to regulate our conduct by that of others, but only by the law of God. Our fathers ought not to have been attentive to their salvation because their fathers had been so, but because God had expressly enjoined this upon them. If their fathers had been less careful about this matter than they ought to have been, they were under no obligation to follow their example.

2. A distinction ought to be made as to times. There was a time of captivity and bondage; and there was a time in which men were called to liberty. Before the threescore and ten years, during which the Jewish people should remain in Babylon, were finished, they could not make their escape from it; but whenever they received an order from heaven to depart, they could no longer remain there, without rendering themselves ungrateful to the grace of God, who had called them to liberty. In like manner, the ancestors of our reforming fathers might remain in the church wherein they were born without however communicating with its errors, while God had not yet opened to them the way for their departure; but as soon as the Lord had lifted up his standard, and given the signal, they were no longer permitted to continue in Babylon, but they must go up to Jerusalem.

3. Further, my brethren, before the Reformation, though there were very great errors in that church, yet they had not been established for laws, as afterwards, so that there was still room to hope that she might be reclaimed from them. But as soon as matters were come to that point when there was no hope left of being able to correct abuses, when errors and human traditions were fixed as articles of faith, when anathemas were denounced against those who received not these errors, when destructive weapons were employed to force people, then how could it be thought that our fathers should have remained any longer in connection with men who would have them to believe as truths, what they were persuaded were errors, and who no longer observed with them either the natural duties of humanity or the laws of civil society?

4. Lastly, it must be remarked that, though we doubt not but those who were in the Romish church before the Reformation, and did not participate in the corruptions of that communion, were saved; yet we ought not from this to infer that persons might still be saved remaining therein;,because we must never despise the grace that God offers to us, nor tempt God, by exposing ourselves to dangers, when we may get clear of them. [Just] because some of those who are constrained to abide in a city, where the

plague makes great ravages, may possibly escape death, this ought not to be a reason for detaining those who are at liberty to remove from it.

Objection 8

"However that may be," say they, "it is not certain that the Reformation was very precipitant?"

This is like the language of the Jewish people, who said that the time was not yet come for building the house of the Lord, for which the prophet Haggai reproves them. But what prospect was there of any advantage to be gained by longer waiting? For more than three hundred years there had been a cry for Reformation, yet no Reformation appeared. Instead of that, errors and corruptions arose to their greatest height.

Objection 9

"But granting," add they, "that all the world earnestly wished for a proper and holy reformation, yet to whom did it belong to effect it, but the pope?"

But everyone knows that nothing of this kind could be expected on the part of the pope or cardinals, for no reformation could take place but one that would begin with and include them. Who is ignorant of the many evasions they made use of, in order to hinder the holding of councils? In the Council of Constance, great noise was made, and articles proposed, for a reform both of the head and of the members; but Martin V, who was then made pope, eluded this proposition. Eugene IV afterwards resisted the fathers of the Council of Basel, when they were inclined to touch the abuses of the court of Rome. It is true that Eugene was deposed, but this did not produce in the end any real advantage. Who knows not how Julius II treated with scorn the Council of Pisa; and although he had sworn before he was constituted pope that he would assemble at the end of every two years a general council for the reformation of the church in the head and members, yet he made no account of his promise; nor would he ever have convened a council at Rome, if it had not been with a view to ruin the Council of Pisa.

When Luther reckoned himself obliged, for the discharge of his duty and his conscience, to oppose the traffic of indulgences, he wrote not only to the Archbishop of Mentz, who was the Bishop of Magdeburg, and to the Bishop of Brandenburg, but also to Pope Leo X, to whom he sent his writings, making to him, at the same time, very humble and excessive submissions. But what was the effect? They would not so much as grant Luther a hearing; and as that holy man continued to exclaim against such a horrid abuse, in a short time after, Leo—not content with publishing a bull in 1518, by which he authorized and declared the validity of indulgences, affirming that, as the successor of St. Peter and the vicar of Jesus Christ, he had power to grant them for the quick and the dead—emitted against Luther his terrible bull of excommunication; giving order to Cajetan, his legate, to cause him to be apprehended and conducted to Rome; and commanding all dukes, marquises, counts, barons, and all universities, communities, and powers, under the pain of excommunication, to lend their assistance to seize Luther, and deliver him into the hands of his legate.[206] What then had he to look for from the popes? Gregory XII—who had often promised to reform many things in the church if he should ever obtain the popedom, after he was advanced to it—declared to his friends, who put him in mind of his former promises, that all he could do would be only as a drop of water in respect of the ocean.

Objection 10

But they allege that a council should have been waited for. But what hope could be entertained from councils, after what passed in the councils of Constance, Basel, and Pisa? In 1423, a council was held at Sienna, in which it was solemnly declared that the reformation of the Catholic church was

---

[206] Luth. op. to. 2. Raynald. an. 1520.

indispensably necessary, and that it ought to be proceeded in with all sincerity; but if we look into the acts of this council, we will find nothing of reformation there. On the contrary, we read of appellations given to Martin V, which cause horror in every pious mind, for he is there styled, "Most holy, most blessed, the Lord on earth, the Christ of the Lord, the Lord of the universe, the Father of kings, the Light of the world." All are acquainted with the transactions in the Council of Trent, in which the legates alone were allowed to make proposals; in which none were made, but such as had been previously concerted at Rome, in a congregation established for the purpose; and in which the votes were influenced, and often corrupted by presents, or by hopes. What would they have our fathers to have done, when they saw such a formed design, and inflexible resolution to support errors, superstitions, and abuses, for which the most refined and profound arts of a consummate policy were employed?

Objection 11

It belongs not however (they tell us) to private persons to undertake this work of reformation.

Private persons, we own, have no right to pluck up, by their private authority, what they pretend to be tares. None but God, the true father of the family, is possessed of this authority, or can communicate it to others. But though it might be pleaded here that the greater part of our Reformers were teachers, and persons in public office, who were bound to answer before God for many thousand souls, which had been committed to their care, I would only ask whether even private persons have not sufficient authority for rejecting tares, for renouncing error, and working out their own salvation, and that of their brethren? Will it be said that God has not laid an obligation on all men to save themselves, and to remove at a distance from everything contrary to faith and godliness?

I grant that God ordinarily makes use of the ministry of pastors for pulling up the noxious weeds of his mystical field; but he has not so restricted himself, as that he cannot, from time to time, and on certain occasions, incite and impel private persons to perform his work, when those who possess public authority, and who ought to eradicate the tares, are negligent of their duty, and are tares themselves.

The passage of Scripture, where the householder forbids to pluck up the tares, for fear of rooting out the wheat with them, which they sometimes object, is improperly applied to this case. It would prove with equal force that neither popes nor councils ought to stop the progress of errors and heresies [any] more than private persons, because the tares must not be plucked up until the time of the harvest, which, according to the explication of Christ, is the end of the world. Surely, persons must choose to be blind who do not perceive that the design of our Lord is to show that the wicked shall always be mixed here below with the good; that this mixture shall continue to the end of the world, and therefore men ought not to attempt the task of entirely destroying all the tares. It may be added that our Savior hereby would have us learn that when there may be danger of damaging or plucking up the wheat in pulling up the tares, we ought to wait the time when the one may be rooted out and gathered without the other. But from this passage it can never be proven that persons are not warranted to withdraw from an impure communion, and depart from Babylon; or that, when there is evident danger of wheat being corrupted, by suffering the tares to continue, they were not at liberty, or even bound in duty, to pluck them up.

Objection 12

"But it did not become a single man such as Luther to undertake so great and excellent a work."

The Emperor Constantius formerly made the same objection to Liberius, Bishop of Rome; "All the world," said he, "agrees in confessing and condemning the impiety of Athanasius. What proportion do you bear to the rest of the world that you alone should take the side of an impious man?"

"Although I were alone," replied Liberius, "that would not in the least weaken the cause of truth, for once there were only three found who resisted the commandment of Nebuchadnezzar." Besides, it is not true that Luther was alone. Although at first he entertained this apprehension, he afterwards understood that God had reserved many thousands who had not bowed the knee to Baal.

Objection 13

"But," they add, "you cannot show the mission or vocation of your Reformers."

I would have you, my brethren, to remark:

1. That though the vocation of our Reformers were not legitimate, our religion would not be less good. We establish no doctrine upon the call of our pastors; we only say that our doctrine is true, and therefore it ought to be followed. Of what consequence is it to us, by what hands the truth has been imparted to us, provided we know it? Does not truth carry its own authority along with it? If therefore the truth is on our side, have we not reason to be very well satisfied, even though our Reformers should not have had a valid mission? It is only a pitiful shift to question us as to the mission of our Reformers. If they have delivered the truth, they have been sufficiently authorized; but if they have taught errors, the most regular call in the world would have availed them nothing. Let me ask those of the Romish communion if they would choose rather to follow one of their priests who—with a legitimate call—should teach them Mahometanism, rather than a Turk, who, having attained to the knowledge of the truth, should, without such a call, teach it to them. I cannot think there is any person so destitute of sense as to say that he would rather follow a priest who would teach the Quran than a Turk who would teach the pure gospel. If so, it may be sufficient, in order to form a judgment about a religion, to examine what it teaches, without a person troubling himself about the vocation of its pastors.

2. Those of the church of Rome cannot deny that the greater part of the Reformers had a lawful calling, seeing as they had received in it the Romish church: such were Wycliffe, Jan Huss, and Jerome of Prague, Martin Luther, Philip Melanchton, Peter Martyr, Sebastian Munster, Thomas Cranmer, primate of England, John Knox, Ulrich Zwingli, and many more, who afterwards gave it to others, who succeeded them.

Objection 14

But they still ask, "How can you allow this call to be legitimate, while you maintain that the church was corrupt?"

I answer that the call of the church might pass for legitimate in a time when there was not as yet a pure society known to our fathers, and in which there was still some true believers remaining in the communion of Rome. But though the external mission of our Reformers has passed through the channel of the Romish church, yet it proceeded from a higher source, and has God himself for its author. Thus, though the organs which God made use of to call the men to the holy ministry were corrupt, the call did not fail on that account to be good in respect of God. We may reason in the same manner about this vocation as we do in reference to baptism, which is still accounted valid, although the pastors who confer it may often be infected with errors, because the baptism properly belongs to God.

Objection 15

"Yet you consider ordination as conferred in the Romish church as unlawful, seeing as you ordain anew the priests of that church, who come over to embrace your religion, and who choose to exercise the holy ministry. But if that is illegitimate, your Reformers had not a sufficient and lawful call."

I answer, if we reordain the priests of the Romish church, it is not because we think that their vocation has nothing good in it, or that it could not be allowed in cases of necessity. But it is done partly to confirm them in what is lawful in their calling, and to correct what is evil in it; partly to render their ministry more useful among our people, who might be ready to suspect that these pastors had not entirely renounced their errors; and likewise, because we know that due care is not taken in the Romish church to examine the knowledge of priests admitted to ordination. Wherefore this reordination does not prove that the calling of our Reformers was illegitimate, in a time when our fathers were unacquainted with any society more pure. When Arianism had infected almost all the East, those who had been ordained by the Arians were not always reordained; but there is reason to believe that several Arian bishops were readmitted to the orthodox church, merely upon abjuring their heresy.

Objection 16

"But did not your Reformers fall from their ministerial vocation, seeing as these did not follow out the intention of those from whom they had received it?"

On the contrary, they acquitted themselves well in it, in following the intention of God in it, from whom they had received that ministry; insofar as they taught his pure gospel, and disengaged religion from the erroneous creeds, and false worship, which had been previously established. They purified their office and calling of what had been faulty in it, and they applied it to its true and proper end. They had been called in general to preach the truth, and they did it. They had in course been ordained to preach many errors; but they desisted from doing so, as soon as they attained to the knowledge of them. Had they not good reason for acting such a part?

Objection 17

"But were there not some of your Reformers," they ask, "who had no official character at all, but what they received from a church that claimed to itself the right of choosing pastors?"

We grant it; but firstly, it need not appear surprising that persons without the clerical character should become ministers in a time when the pastors claiming a regular vocation so strangely abused it. In a time of war, every man has a right to oppose the enemy; and none would ever think of condemning the citizens, who might give the alarm, when the centinels neglected to do their duty. What call had Aedesius and Frumentius, who converted the Indians to the Christian faith? Or that poor female captive who imparted the first knowledge of the true religion to the Iberians? Who will presume to blame them? Why then should our fathers be blamed?

Neither, secondly, should it be reckoned surprising that an assembly of believers should choose to itself pastors, as the people of whom I formerly spoke, who during the persecution of the Arians, appointed to themselves bishops. If a free people who are destitute of a sovereign can choose one for themselves, there can be no reason to condemn a church that wants a pastor, when it appoints some to that office. God has bestowed sufficient power to his church to employ all the means which are conducive to her preservation, and by which she may procure the preaching of the Word, and the administration of the sacraments; and among these, the ministry is one of the most considerable. The ministry belongs to the body of the church, for whose edification it was instituted; and the faithful are the true members of the church. They have therefore the right to give to certain persons the power of instructing them and distributing to them the heavenly bread. Indeed, calls carried in this manner into effect, by the body of the church without pastors, ought not to take place except in case of absolute necessity. But necessity produces just exceptions to ordinary laws, provided these exceptions do not engage us to anything criminal, as if a person should believe himself dispensed from confessing Jesus Christ, through the peril of death, with which he may be menaced.

Objection 18

"Whether then," they yet ask, "was the call of these pastors ordinary or extraordinary?"

They think to perplex us greatly by this question. But it is very easy to reply that the call of our Reformers might be called both ordinary and extraordinary: *ordinary* in regard to those who had received ordination by the hands of pastors who had before been vested with the office; *extraordinary* in respect of those who received their function immediately from the body of the church, which was not according to ordinary rule. It was *ordinary* in respect of the functions of their ministry which were, to preach the Word and dispense the sacraments, but *extraordinary* in respect of gifts with which God endowed the Reformers.

Objection 19

"But was it not necessary," add they, "that such a mission should have been authorized by miracles?"

Answer: If our fathers had come to publish a new gospel, until then unheard of in the world, certainly it would have been needful that they should have wrought miracles in confirmation of that new doctrine. But since our doctrine is none other than that of the Old and New Testament, confirmed by so many miracles, our fathers had only to restore things to the former state in which they had been in the beginning. The reformation that was effected in the time of Josiah, Jehoshaphat, and Hezekiah was not accompanied with any miracle.

Objection 20

"But is it not evident that you have set up altar against altar; and is not this a heinous sin, for which you may be accounted schismatics?"

Was Elijah then a schismatic when he restored the altar of God which had been demolished, and set up a new one against the altars of Baal?

Objection 21

"You cannot deny however," they add, "but you are in the same situation as the Donatists were, who are accounted schismatics."

But nothing can be more absurd than this objection; as you may easily judge. The Donatists did not accuse the church from which they separated of any error. The only cause of their separation was the ordination of Bishop Cecilian, at which having been displeased, they accused Cecilian and his ordainer with having delivered up the sacred books to the Pagans to be burned, in the time of persecution. This crime was neither acknowledged, nor proven, and though it had been so, it might be considered as a personal fault, in which those who communicated with these bishops, and with the churches of which they had the charge, had no share. The separation of the Donatists, therefore, could not be justified. But our fathers did not separate from the Romish church on account of personal matters; but from regard to the great interests of the glory of God, and their own salvation. They were convinced that the religion of that church taught a number of pernicious errors, and contained practices in worship [that are] forbidden by the law of God.

The Donatists further separated themselves voluntarily from the true church, without being constrained to do so. But the church of Rome had cut off our fathers from its communion, and she anathematizes and excommunicates those who are not inclined to receive her doctrines. When the Donatists were solicited to reunite themselves to the church from which they had voluntarily separated, they were not required to abjure any doctrine, or to embrace any which they might believe to be false. But it is enjoined on those who would return to the Romish communion that they abjure their own doctrine, and admit decisions which they account unlawful.

Objection 22

To the question which they continually ask, "Where was your church before Luther and Calvin?" after what I have advanced in this, and in the preceding discourses, the answer is very easy.

1. It is certain that our religion was always contained in the Scriptures of the Old and New Testament; and this our adversaries are never able to disprove. Nor can they point out any positive article of our belief, which was not always believed in the Christian church, and which continues not still to be so. And this may be sufficient to satisfy a reasonable mind: for if our religion be the same with that of the apostles, here is enough, surely, to determine and engage us to persevere in this religion, even though we should be at a loss to know, where our church was before Luther and Calvin; and enough, surely, to show that we deserve not the name of innovators.

2. I might next retort their argument, and ask them in my turn where their church was in the time of the apostles. That is, where was that church that maintained purgatory, a sacrifice of the mass, etc.? My demand is much more reasonable than theirs, for as long as they are unable to show that their church is conformable to the apostolic, I have good reason for abstaining to join with her; but though I might not be able to show them where our church was in the latter ages, they would not on that account have just cause to blame us, if we could give them sufficient evidence that our church is conform to that of the three first ages.

3. I might also add that before Luther and Calvin, there were several churches, who were separated from Rome, as those of the Waldensians, the Albigensians, the faithful in Bohemia, and the Greek churches.

4. But I go yet a step further, and to the question, *Where was your church?*, I reply that it was in the Roman communion, as formerly the people of God were captive in Babylon.

Objection 23

"But if your church was then in the bosom of the Romish communion, as you confess, it must have been corrupted and impious, since you cannot point out that small number of your pretended faithful, who, before your Reformers, had condemned, as you now do, the assemblies of the papacy. In outward appearance at least, they acted as others did; therefore your church could not be called holy, nor consequently the true church."

But should it be deemed impossible that in certain times, there may be people who are far from approving of the abuses of their church, although they cannot be mentioned by name, especially in the times when truth is suppressed and almost extinguished, and iniquity appears to triumph?

Is it not also unreasonable to ask the names of those who have kept themselves pure under a ministry corrupt? May it not suffice to show in general that the promises of Jesus Christ are inviolable, and that he has accordingly preserved in every period a church unto himself? If the latter ages which preceded our Reformation had been ages eminently happy, and fruitful in great men, it would be a presumption against our cause if we could not name any person who had been of the same sentiments. But these were miserable ages wherein ignorance, superstition, corruption of manners, avarice and ambition had so corrupted the Christian church that some faint rays of evangelical light can scarcely be perceived across the thick darkness.

Further, on what ground is it asserted that the faithful before the Reformation must have acted the same part externally as others did? Might they not have remained under the same corrupt ministry with others, and yet have separated the good from the evil, while they were not constrained by anathemas to believe whatever was taught them, or to do whatever others did, as came afterwards to be the case in the time of our fathers, and as it is to this very day?

Besides, it would not be very difficult to discover, in every age, some who have maintained the truth, and this has been done very clearly by many of our writers. It will hardly admit of dispute that those of the three centuries were of the same sentiments with us, if we except only some opinions which are not even adopted at present, and prayer for the dead, of which however there is no trace to be found either in Scripture or in the first writers of Christianity.

In the fourth century, other errors were introduced; yet it is very evident that in this age, they were strangers to transubstantiation, the sacrifice of the mass, auricular confession, communion in one kind, the adoration of the sacrament, and purgatory, as it is now held by the Romish church. They were persuaded of the perfection of the Scripture. The doctrine of justification by faith alone was plainly taught, and the necessity of grace acknowledged. The worship of angels was condemned; nor was any religious adoration paid either to the virgin or to images.

The fifth through eighth centuries were not so pure; but still the truth had in them its famous defenders. It is alleged that in the fifth, or at least in the seventh century, there were a number of professors in the valleys of Piedmont who retained the simplicity of the gospel.

In the ninth century, when Paschasius Rathbertus invented the doctrine of transubstantiation, those who are acquainted with church history know that there were many who opposed his error, among whom were Rabanus, Archbishop of Mayence, the celebrated scholar of the Great Alcuin; Amalarius Fortunatus, who was in such high esteem with the Emperor Lewis the Meek [Louis the Pious]; Walafridus Strabo, Ratram, priest of the monastery of Corbie, afterwards an abbot, who was chosen by all the prelates of France to defend the Latin church against the Greeks; John Scotus Eriugena, a Scotchman, who was reputed a very learned and holy man; with many others whom I do not mention. It is also well known that in the same century, Gottschalk, S. Rhemry, Archbishop of Lyon, Lupus, Abbot of Ferriere, Florus, Ratram, Prudentius, and the Synods of Valence in 855, and of Langres in 859, maintained the true doctrine concerning predestination and grace.

In the tenth century, though the error of Paschasius had now made great progress, yet the truth wanted not protectors. This appears from a sermon which was read every year to the people of England, at the feast of Easter, in which it was expressly declared that the spiritual body of Jesus Christ, called the eucharist is composed of many grains, without blood, bones, or members, and without soul; that this eucharist is temporal, corruptible, bruised with the teeth, and goes forth into the draught; and that this sacrament is a pledge and a figure. This further appears from another sermon, which is ascribed to Aelfric, whom some make Archbishop of Canterbury, wherein it is affirmed that the eucharist is not the body of Jesus Christ corporally, but spiritually; that the bread is his body, in the same manner as the manna was, and the wine was his blood, even as the waters of the desert were.[207] There were also some in this age who opposed the worship of images, the universal monarchy of the pope, and other errors then established. On this account it has been said that this century resembled the days of winter, which are indeed very dusky and gloomy; but in which the light of the sun is not altogether departed; and that the errors therein disseminated, were like an inundation of waters that overflow the meadows and plains, during which however there are some places more elevated, where the herbs still retain their verdure, and where some habitations remain, wherein persons may live without danger of perishing.

In the eleventh century, all know what Berengarius, Archdeacon of Angres, did, following his bishop Bruno; and how he filled many countries with his doctrine. Nor is Berengarius to be reckoned a man of small consequence; a fragment of the history of France, from King Robert to the death of Philip, informs us that the name of Berenger was famous among the followers of divine philosophy; and Archbishop Antonine declares that he was one very distinguished for his learning. Many indeed employed their pens against him; but many also defended his doctrine. It appears also that

---

[207] Wheeloc. in *Not. in Hist.* Bedæ *Ang. Sax.* L4 C24

before him, Leutheric Abp. of Sens, who died in the year 1032, rejected the doctrine of Paschasius.

In the twelfth century, who has not heard of a Peter Waldo, who began to appear, according to the common opinion, in the year 1160? Of a Peter of Bruys, who, after he had spread the true doctrine through Languedoc, Gascoigny, and other places, for the space of twenty years, was burnt at St. Giles, in Languedoc, whose followers were called Petrobrusians? Of a Henry of Toulouse, who was harassed by the order of Pope Eugene? Of Arnold of Brescia, who was burnt alive at Rome, in 1155, under Pope Adrian, and his ashes cast into the Tiber? Or of the appearance made by the Albigensians, who, if the annals of the Romish church may be credited on the subject, had brought over near a thousand cities to their sentiments; and of whom, as Cardinal Bellarmine testifies, 100,000 were slain in France, in one single battle, in the time of Pope Innocent III?[208] Some represent these Albigensians as if they had been of the same sentiments with the Manicheans; but it is a gross calumny. Peter of Cluny—writing against them—says that it was reported that they neither believed in Jesus Christ nor the prophets nor apostles, that they spoke disrespectfully of the Old and New Testament, and that they had rejected the whole canon of the Scriptures; but he adds that he was not disposed to believe this of them, or to accuse them of things so uncertain.[209] Reinerus also—one of the most inveterate enemies of the Waldensians—bears this testimony to them: that they commonly learned all the text of the New Testament by heart, and a good part of the Old; that they had the Old and New Testament translated, and learned and taught it in the vulgar tongue. He likewise declares that they lived justly before men, and had a sound belief as to what relates to God, and the whole articles contained in the Apostles' Creed.[210]

---

[208] Annal. Baron. ad. An. 1159. Bell. B4 *De Eccles.* C18
[209] Peter of Cluny, *Contr. Petrobr.*
[210] Rein. C3–5

In the thirteenth century, the Albigensians, in a conference which they had with the legates of Innocent III, in the city of Montreal near Carcassonne, warmly maintained that the mass and transubstantiation were the invention of men, and not the ordinance of Jesus Christ, or his apostles. And Guy the Gross, Archbishop of Narbonne, made it no secret that he held an opinion concerning the sacrament of the eucharist directly contrary to transubstantiation; so that Clement IV wrote a letter to him about it, which was published.

In the fourteenth century, besides the Waldenses and Albigenses, who kept their assemblies, John Wycliffe, about the year 1370, attacked the authority of the pope, transubstantiation, the sacrifice of the mass, and the invocation of saints. Some noblemen of the highest rank in England, next to the king, embraced the doctrine of this Reformer.

In the fifteenth century, Jan Hus and Jerome of Prague in Bohemia asserted the communion under both kinds, and had many followers. Others in the same country, opposed the tenets of the church of Rome, as the Waldensians, so that according to the testimony of Dubravius, there remained nothing of the ancient Catholic religion in the city of Prague.[211] In the year 1479, in an assembly convened by the Archbishop of Mentz, the process was carried on against the famous divine of Worms, John de Wesalia, who was condemned for maintaining that God had written all his elect in the book of life, from all eternity; that their names shall never be blotted out of it, and that none of those who are not written therein, shall come to eternal life; that all these elected ones which are known to God alone, constitute the church, against which the gates of hell can never prevail; that the holy Scripture is the only rule of faith, and that Jesus Christ, when he ascended into heaven, left no vicar on earth. He was also condemned for approving the marriage of priests, and the communion under both kinds, and holding other obnoxious doctrines. Those who are

---

[211] Hist. Boh. B24

unacquainted with the history of that age, likewise know that John de Wesalia was far from being alone in these sentiments.

It is therefore false that our church existed only in imagination before Luther and Calvin.

Objection 24

Another charge against our Reformers yet remains to be considered. There is scarcely any crime which has not been imputed to them, to render them odious; they have taken occasion to say that it is very unlikely that God should have committed the care of reforming his church to persons whose life was disorderly and scandalous, from which they draw this conclusion: that without further enquiry, we ought to quit this Reformation, and betake ourselves to the communion of the Romish church.

But it may afford some comfort under such a charge:

1. That our Reformers have not been alone exposed to such calumnies. The Jews said of Jesus Christ that he was a blasphemer, a Samaritan, a friend of publicans and sinners. If the master has received such treatment, what may not his servants look for?

2. We have this as another ground of consolation: that the Reformers have found, even among their enemies, defenders of their innocence. What have they not said of Calvin, that great man, whose memory will ever be blessed among us? There is nothing which they have not attempted, in order to blacken him; the vilest calumnies have been hatched and circulated from time to time, with reference to him. But the falsehood of these accusations have been so effectually exposed that his enemies are now convinced of it, and often do him the justice which is due to him.

3. Among other great crimes wherewith they have been charged, this is one, that they were married: as if in that they had transgressed the law of God; as if the patriarchs, prophets, several of the apostles, and celebrated bishops, had not been also in the same state; and as if it were not a greater

cause of scandal, to see ecclesiastics plunged in debauchery, than to see them enter into marriage, which is "honorable in all."

4. But, my brethren, we will go a little further: [even if] it were true that our Reformers had given cause to complain of their conduct, ought their reformation to be judged by their persons? Ought we not rather to try their doctrine, and if that be true, and the very doctrine of Jesus Christ, ought it not to be embraced, even though those who publish it to us, should be wicked men? Truth can neither change its nature, nor lose its rights, on account of the vices of its ministers. Calvin and Luther were not the authors of our religion, and it was not their authority that made our fathers abandon the Romish communion. They were considered in no other light than as men whom God made use of to give information and warning to men, of their duty; nor are they, at present, considered in any other view. We are doubtless under great obligations to them for what they have done, but it is not because of their word that we believe our religion to be exclusively true; it is because we clearly perceive it to be so.

Do they tell us that it is not likely that God should have committed the care of reforming his church to persons of scandalous life? Let it be granted; and by this rule, we could fix the charge of falsehood upon those who accuse our Reformers of having lived disorderly. I will add, however, that God sometimes employs the ministry of some who have been guilty of great faults. Aaron had been an idolater, the apostle Peter denied his Lord, and Paul was a persecutor when Christ called him.

My hearers surely do not expect that I should here undertake to justify the manner in which the Reformation was effected in several kingdoms and states. This apology would carry us too far. I shall only say a word as to the manner wherein it was accomplished among us.

You should know then, my brethren, that the Reformation was introduced at a time when this city was plunged in profound superstition, and in the greatest debauchery; at a time when the clergy abused their authority, in order to take every kind of license, and to commit every sort of crimes; at a time when they availed themselves of the credulity of the people, to make them believe whatever absurdity they pleased. For you may have heard what were some of the relics, which they were here called to adore, and what methods were taken to persuade the populace to worship the blessed virgin, and to preserve in their minds the false opinion of a purgatory. I should think I abused your patience, if I were to rehearse all that our fathers have told us on this subject.

This Reformation was not accomplished all at once; the point could not be carried but by various assaults. It was however brought about by the authority of our council. God also made use of our dear allies for spreading his truth among us; and he so ordered it that at the time when the archbishop of Vienne, the metropolitan of the province, laid an interdict on the city of Geneva, and ordered it to be affixed to the most public places, the deputies of the city were in the neighbouring canton, where they were made sensible that it was high time for them to shake off the servitude under which they had groaned, and that they ought to be afraid only of the thunders of the Almighty, and despise those of men.

In the year 1532, some one had the resolution to fix up in the most public places the following words: "*A full and plenary Indulgence, and universal Pardon of all Sins by Jesus Christ.*" This was in opposition to the pretended indulgences which were then published, and scandalously sold. But in the beginning of the year 1533, God emboldened Antoine Froment to preach in one of our public squares, and there to explain these words in Matthew 8: "Beware of false prophets, which come to you in sheep's clothing, but inwardly are ravenous wolves. By their fruits ye shall know them."

In the following year, further progress was made: on February 13th, a dispute was held between Guy Furbiti, doctor of the Sorbonne, and William Farel, in presence of the council of *Two Hundred*, about the power of the church, the authority of the pope, and traditions; and the truth had a glorious triumph over error. The success of this dispute was so great in favor of the true doctrine that the people obliged Farel to preach in the beginning of March, the same year, in the church of the convent of Cordeliers de Rive.

There was another public dispute yet more solemn on May 1st 1537, which lasted a whole month, in which the truth was displayed in such a clear and convincing light, that two of the principal disputants, who then supported the cause of the Romish church, afterwards embraced the true religion.[212] In consequence of this disputation, Farel preached in July following; in the church of Magdalene, six days after, in that of St. Gervais, and at last on the 8th of August in this great church.

In fine, the council having, on the 10th of the same month, given a long hearing to Farel, was convinced by his reasons, and having examined all that had passed in the debates, and having heard also what the Augustinians, Dominicans, and Cordeliers, who were present, could advance, they ordained that the mass should be abolished. In what other way was it possible that reformation should have been accomplished?

So soon as the people had their eyes open to see the disorders of their clergy, who had kept them in ignorance, and abused their credulity in regard to relics and saints; so soon as they became acquainted with the pure gospel, and perceived in how many ways they had been constrained to violate the divine law, many with avidity embraced the truth; and even some who had the most violent prejudices against our religion, no sooner came to the knowledge of it than they loved it, and made a voluntary profession of it.

But it is time to conclude this discourse.

---

[212] These were Caroli, doctor of the Sorbonne, and a Dominican named Chapuisi; he who maintained the Theses was named James Bernard, guardian of the convent, who also came over to the side of the Reformers.

APPLICATION

Let praise forever be ascribed to the gracious protector of this state, who appeared to dispel the darkness wherein our fathers were enveloped; who inspired our allies with the design of imparting to us the knowledge of the truth, and gave to his two servants [Farel and Froment] courage to publish it openly in our streets! Blessed be God, who made our ancestors to understand the errors, whereby they were misled, and the idolatry and superstition, wherein they were detained! Blessed be his name, who has, ever since that time, raised up eminent men among us, who have maintained the cause of God. Glory be to God, who has hitherto preserved both this state and church, as by a continued miracle, and who makes us to enjoy at the same time such a delightful liberty, and such a clear and pleasing light!

Let us not, my brethren, abuse, as we too often have done, this precious liberty, and this pure and excellent light. Let us live as those who bear the name of Reformed; let everything be indeed reformed in us. Let it be evident that we are distinguished from all other people, and let it appear that we are truly the people of God. Never, never let us return back into the captivity from which the good hand of God has drawn us. Let us stand fast in the liberty wherewith Christ has made us free, but let us not live licentiously. Let us live as a people emancipated from the yoke of superstition under which our fathers bowed, but as a people subject to the sceptre of Jesus Christ, who acknowledge him for their king, and who expect from him eternal glory. Let us obey the laws of our great Legislator, and the Prince of our salvation. Let us be zealous for his glory, and his truth. Let us not suffer them, at any time, to receive any injury or assault; but let us be holy as he is holy. It is thus we will draw down upon us the continuance of his favors. He will cause his sun always to arise on us; his hand shall afford us protection; his providence shall be our wall and bulwark. He will be our light and our shield; he will give us fruitful seasons, and fill our hearts with gladness: "No good thing will he withhold from us." And at last, when Jesus Christ shall appear to judge the human race, in that day, which will be as the day of the reformation and renovation of this universe, he will bestow on us his heaven and glory. *Amen.*

EXHORTATION

TO

PERSEVERANCE

IN THE

TRUE RELIGION.

The Eighth Discourse.

On 1 Thessalonians 5:21
Hold fast that which is good.

The wise man, in the book of Proverbs, prescribes two very important duties, when he says, "Buy the truth, and sell it not." He considers all men as so many merchants, whom he exhorts to buy "the pearl of great price," namely, *the truth*. The counsel he gives them is undoubtedly highly advantageous, as there is nothing in the world that can be more useful to us than the truth. It is a divine light that dispels our darkness, secures us against error, and gives wisdom to the simple, as David expresses it in Psalm 19. It is the true bread of the soul, which the Supreme Wisdom presents upon that table, which she daily prepares before us, and to which she invites so earnestly, saying, "Come, eat of my bread." It is serviceable to us both for making an attack upon the enemies of our salvation, and for repelling all their assaults. It is at the same time our sword and our buckler. "Nothing can be done," says Paul, "against the truth." It is stronger than all other things; as was proven in the contest once maintained before Darius, according to the account given in the book of Esdras.[213] It is that which makes us free; it is that which sanctifies us.[214] It is, *in fine*, our treasure and our glory. After this, judge whether everyone ought not to endeavour to obtain possession of it. "Buy the truth." But if persons ought to use all their efforts to possess it, they must never again consent to part with it. Communicate it indeed they may, because it is a treasure which should not be locked up, and a light which ought not to be put under a bushel; but to sell it, they are strictly prohibited. One ought to sell all that he has to obtain it; but it would be better to lose all things, than to be deprived of it. For any to abandon it, is to plunge himself into dismal darkness, to bring death on his soul, and to shut the gate of heaven upon himself. Therefore, buy the truth, but on no consideration sell it.

The apostle Paul, my brethren, gives us the same exhortation, though in different terms, in the verse we have now read: "Prove," etc. For indeed, how can any buy the truth, if it be not by proving or examining what is proposed to us? And what else is the meaning of not selling the truth, if it be not "to hold fast that which is good"? Hear then, Christians, with attention, what a wise king recommends, and what a great apostle enjoins upon us; and if you have endeavored to comply with the first part of his injunction, by examining the religions professed in the world, continue to obey him in the last, by being constantly attached to that which alone is the truth: "Hold fast that which is good."

Having in the preceding discourses shown the obligation that is laid on everyone to examine the religion he professes; that amidst all the variety of religions, Christianity is alone the true; and that pure Christianity is only preserved in the Reformed religion; having also justified our doctrine and our reformation; what now remains but that, after we have thus proven all things, and discovered the purity, truth, and sanctity of our religion, we should constantly retain it, and never be so faint-hearted as to abandon it.

---

[213] 3 Esdras 4:35
[214] John 8 & 17

To treat this part of the apostolic exhortation, in a manner that may prove useful to you, we shall do these five things:

First, we shall point out the obligation which every one is under, after having tried, to reject whatever is evil, and consequently all false and corrupt religions.

Secondly, we shall then show the obligation lying upon every one to hold fast all that is good, and consequently the true religion.

Thirdly, we shall consider what is imported in this exhortation, to hold fast the true religion, and explain the duties comprehended under it.

Fourthly, we shall refute those who think that one is not always bound to quit a false religion, or that a person may be at liberty to decline making a public profession of the true religion; and we shall reply to their objections.

Fifthly and lastly, we shall set before you the motives which should engage us to persevere in the true religion, and the promises which God has made to those who persevere.

May God impress on your hearts all we are about to deliver.

I.   HEAD

1. The exhortation of the apostle to hold fast what is good, supposes that we ought to reject whatever is evil; whatever is contrary to holiness and truth; all manner of error and vice. As the same apostle says to the Romans, "The night is passed, the day is at hand, let us put off the works of darkness, and put on the armour of light." And again, to his dear Timothy, "Reject profane fables:" and elsewhere he enjoins that a man who is a heretic should be rejected, and that those who preached any other doctrine than that which had been preached, should be accursed.

Indeed, reason itself—that asserts the right of examining all that is proposed to us—also dictates to all that we ought by no means to admit anything inconsistent with its light, or opposite to revelation, or what we clearly perceive to be error. It would be to no purpose for any to try, if they were notwithstanding to take equally the good and the bad, and embrace error as well as truth. What would we say of the man who should have a large sum of gold or silver offered him in payment, and who after he had examined it, and had found in it much counterfeit money, would yet receive it all equally? Or of a man who should have good food and at the same time poison offered to him, and after he had examined them, and distinguished the one from the other, would, after all, take both without distinction? Doubtless it would be said that the first was a fool, willing to impose on himself; and that the second was insane, or that he wanted to procure his own death. The same judgment should be pronounced on those who, having examined what had been taught them, should notwithstanding receive all indiscriminately, error as well as truth.

2. All error must therefore be rejected as soon as known. If this counsel is to be followed in matters of philosophy, it ought more carefully to be put in practice in religion; for as we lately told you, it is not of great consequence to salvation although a person should mistake in philosophical speculations, but errors in the matter of religion are pernicious. They are not all equally so, I confess, but there are none of them but may be accompanied with some hurtful effect, for it is easy and natural to proceed from one error to another. The utmost attention and endeavours ought therefore to be employed in order to discover them, and when discovered, they must be rejected.

No respect is to be paid to these errors on account of their antiquity: they are not a whit the better for being old. Age or antiquity has not changed their nature.

Neither are we to regard them the more on account of the worth of those who have taught or followed them. If great men have been deceived, we are not obliged to allow ourselves to be deceived along with them; but we ought rather to do what we may suppose they themselves would have done, for if they had come to the knowledge of their errors, they would doubtless have rejected them. The ancient fathers of the church often tell us that they are never to be blindly believed in what they advance on religion; but those are always to be followed who teach the truth. "Give no credit," says Cyril, "to what I say upon my bare word, unless you find the proof of the things I speak from the divine Scriptures. For the safety and preservation of our faith depends not upon the eloquence of our language, but upon the authority of the holy Scriptures."[215] Jerome speaks nearly the same language, in many parts of his books.[216]

Thus, let it be far from us to maintain that the faithful shall reign a thousand years in Jerusalem, or that all the souls of the just, not excepting the prophets, fall under the power of malignant spirits, and that this was the reason why our Lord, when about to expire, recommended his spirit to God, under pretext that Justin Martyr has said so. Let us not give ear to the doctrine that souls, upon their departure from this life, go to a subterraneous place, where they are to remain until the day of judgment, heaven not being opened to receive the faithful until after the consummation of time; though this was the supposition of the greater part of the fathers. Let none tell us that the sacrament of the eucharist should be given to little children, as many doctors of the church, after Cyrian, have believed. Let them not affirm that Jesus Christ was insensible of pain because Hilary said so. Once more, let us not be told that all men at the last day must pass through a fire, as Hilary, Ambrose, and so many others have dreamed.[217] Whoever may have been the author of an opinion, which we know to be erroneous, it must be a rule with us to reject it, even as we would an error advanced by the most ignorant man upon earth.

Do they hold out to us the authority of councils? We are under no obligation to embrace error, because it has been maintained by numerous assemblies. Many of these, it is well known, have favored error. Where was

---

[215] Cyr. Cat. 4

[216] Jerome, *Commentary on Habbakuk*, etc.

[217] Justin Martyr, *Dialogue with Trypho*; Tertullian, *A Treatise on the Soul* C55, etc.; Cyprian, ep. 59; Hilary *On The Trinity* B10 on Psalm 53

there ever one more famous than that of Rimini in Italy, where there were 600 bishops present? Yet there is no reason to doubt of its having avowed Arianism. And who knows not the proceedings of the council convened at Ephesus in the year 449 by Theodosius the Younger? All the patriarchs were present: Juvenal, patriarch of Jerusalem, Dioscorus of Alexandria, Domnus of Antioch, Flavian of Constantinople, and Leo, bishop of Rome, by his legates. Yet this council confirmed Eutychianism, and deposed Flavian, patriarch of Constantinople, a man eminent for sanctity and orthodoxy. When we have such instances as these, why should we implicitly receive whatever councils have delivered? Nay, brethren, let us boldly reject all that they have sanctioned contrary to holy scripture.

3. Thence it clearly follows that we are bound to reject all religions, as well as all in religion, which are not agreeable to the sacred writings.

We ought not to adhere to a religion on the frivolous pretext that we were born or educated in it. If it is bad, it ought to be relinquished. Should one hesitate to leave a way, which would conduct him to hell, although from his birth he may have been engaged in it? Neither should we be attached to any religion, merely because it has the great men of the world, or the learned, for its defenders. God is pleased sometimes to reveal his secrets to little children, in preference to the wise and prudent. He caused the birth of his Son to be announced to the shepherds which fed their flocks at Bethlehem, rather than to the Jewish priests, to Herod, or Augustus.

Wherefore since we have proven that the Pagan, the Mahometan, and the modern Jewish religion, are false, let us in the most open manner reject them. Moreover, as we have also shown that pure Christianity is neither to be found in the Romish, nor in the Greek religion, these we must in like manner reject. But after rejecting what is evil, let us hold fast what is good, agreeably to the words of our text. To show that this ought to be done, was what we proposed [in the second discourse].

II.   HEAD

As it would be unreasonable and extravagant to admit all doctrines which the erring and capricious spirit of man may bring forth, so it would be folly and extravagance no less great to reject all that may be proposed or taught.

There are some who—on pretext that they have been sometimes deceived, or that others are imposed on—conclude that the best course for them is to turn skeptic, and reject all as entirely devoid of truth. But the conduct of these persons is deplorable, and they deserve as much to be blamed as the man who should refuse either to eat or drink, because sometimes he may have taken for wholesome aliment what has proven very hurtful to him, or because many persons have been deceived by taking poison. Though it be true that people are often deceived, even when they think they are in no danger of it, it does not follow that they are always deceived, or that they can never be assured that they are not under a deception. Even the Pyrrhonists themselves would not venture to assert this.

Whoever seeks for a religion that is true, with no other view than to find it, and who are less influenced by their favor for the opinions, which already have prepossessed their minds, than by the pure lights of reason and revelation, in the end shall find it, provided they do not suffer themselves to be carried away by the violence of their prejudices or passions, or the authority of their teachers or parents; but having once attained their object, it is their duty to hold it fast.

A person however must not satisfy himself with the appearance of truth only, for error often disguises itself; but when he comes to be persuaded that what is made known to him is a truth, he must not scruple to receive that truth, even though it should be opposed by men of the greatest eminence and learning in the world.

1. Following this rule, we ought to retain, firstly, whatever the fathers and the councils have delivered to us, in conformity to the writings of the

prophets, evangelists, and apostles; particularly, the four following General Councils: the first assembled at Nicaea in the year 325, the first of Constantinople in 381, that of Ephesus which met in 431, and that of Chalcedon held in 451.

We must admit the Creed, commonly called the Apostles', although it was not composed by them; as also the Nicene Creed, and that ascribed to Athanasius.[218] In the same manner are we to proceed in the use of the writings left us by the ancient doctors.

2. In prosecution of the same principle, and in consequence of the acknowledgment we have made of the Reformed religion, as the most holy and pure of any in the world, we are bound to adhere unto it, even though it should be abandoned by all those persons who are distinguished in the world, either in respect of authority or excellencies. To act otherwise in reference to it would be to love darkness rather than light, and to be careless about promoting our own salvation. It would be pouring contempt on the exhortation of the apostle, who loudly cries, "Prove all things, and hold fast that which is good."

We must proceed, in regard to religion, as the goldsmith does in proving his metals; he rejects what is of no value, and retains that which is pure; or as the learned do, in examining writings, which have been greatly corrupted and altered; they separate and reject the spurious additions, and take care to preserve whatever appears to have suffered no alteration.

The duty of holding fast what is good is particularly enjoined on pastors. As the same apostle says to his son Timothy, "Hold fast the form of sound words, which thou hast heard of me." "Keep the good thing committed to thy trust." But it is also the duty of all Christians, without exception. Everyone is bound to seek with earnestness and keep with care whatever

---

[218] Our author expresses here the common sentiments of the Reformed churches on these heads. But the reception of these creeds must be understood of the substance of the doctrine contained in them, and not every particular mode of expression. [*Translator*]

tends to enlighten his mind, to sanctify his heart, and comfort his soul; whatever may deliver him from error, preserve him from vice, and appease the agitations of his conscience. The glory of God, our own salvation, and that of our brethren, lay us under indispensable obligation to this. None can neglect this duty, without offending God, and acting the part of an enemy to himself.

If you ask, what is the import of the expression, *Hold fast what is good*, this is next to be considered.

III.   HEAD

The apostle, in these words, exhorts us to these three duties:

1. To believe all truths taught us.

2. To make a public profession of them.

3. Lastly, never to abandon or renounce them.

Whenever any truth is proposed, and we have attained a sufficient knowledge of it, we ought to receive it; nay, we cannot even hinder ourselves from assenting to it; for truth, if I may use the expression, imposes a kind of force upon our understanding.

But it is not sufficient to have received it; it is necessary that we make it known that we have received, and are persuaded of it. We must show our faith by our confession.

In fine, no consideration whatever must oblige us to depart from it. If therefore we have acknowledged the Reformed religion as the true religion of Jesus Christ, it follows that we are bound to believe all the truths which it teaches, confess them publicly, and remain invariably attached unto this profession.

The Scripture in many places prescribes these several duties with regard to the true religion. If it requires that we should "believe with the heart unto righteousness, and make confession with the mouth unto salvation," it also requires that we should hold fast our faith and confidence unto the end.

Accordingly, it condemns three sorts of persons: the *incredulous*, the *Nicodemites*, and *apostates*. The former are those who will not believe revealed truths, but wholly discard them. The second are those who believe them, but choose not to make an open profession of them. The last are those who, after they have professed them for some time, at length relinquish them.

On the other hand, it praises those who believe the gospel, those who confess Jesus Christ before men, and such as persevere unto the end. Faith, therefore, without confession is dead, being only a light without heat. But both faith and confession must be persevering, or they cannot be saving; for Jesus Christ says, "He only who endureth to the end shall be saved." Thus the apostle here calls all, "to hold fast what is good."

Those who will not believe the gospel, or receive a religion that is true, are persons who shut their eyes against the light. Those who are persuaded of the truth of a religion, and yet dare not avow it, are the *fearful* and *lukewarm*. Those who have known the truth, and abandon it, are the cowardly changelings, and the traitors to it. But those who keep the true religion in their heart, who undauntedly profess it, who conform their lives to its precepts, who account it their glory to defend it, who, instead of forsaking it, are ready to lose their life for it, are the *hot*, or fervent, for whom the kingdom of heaven is prepared.

The *first* are highly culpable in giving error the preference to truth, for their continuing in error is owing to the want of sufficient attention to the truth published to them, and their hearkening only to their prejudices. The *second* are still more criminal because they act in opposition to their light and conscience. The *third* are the most inexcusable of all, for there is nothing which can oblige them to abandon the true religion; but they prefer the world to Jesus Christ. The last are the admiration of men and angels, and the object of the love of God. The Scripture says of the first that they "are already condemned, and the wrath of God abideth upon them". Of the second, that Jesus Christ shall be ashamed of them at the great day. Of the third, that if they persist in their apostasy, Christ shall deny them, and that "there remaineth no more sacrifice" for them. But of the last, it declares that Jesus Christ shall confess them before his Father; that he will give them eternal life, and make them to sit upon his throne. Let us, my brethren, be among this happy number. Let us hold fast what is good.

The expression of our apostle denotes that this is not done without difficulty. Indeed, in adopting and holding fast a religion that is good, a man must often do violence to himself; he must withstand the prejudices of his birth, and the respect entertained for superiors and teachers; he must conquer his ambition and avarice, surmount his fears of the evils wherewith he is threatened, oppose the natural propensity to seek after riches and honors, and expose himself to a thousand disgraces, and sometimes also to punishments. Notwithstanding, he must triumph over all those obstacles, and whatever may befall him, must embrace and hold fast the truth.

IV.   HEAD

As this is a matter of very great importance, let us examine it a little more closely. Let us hear what they have to plead for themselves, who think that persons are not always obliged to quit a false religion, or that they may be excused from making a public profession of the true.

Objection 1

They say that one may continue in a false religion, and yet hold fast that which is good, because there is no religion, however false, but has some truths belonging to it, and a man may keep firm to these truths.

Answer: I might here adduce many things in reply to this; but I shall satisfy myself with making one remark, which is that good sense and reason dictate that it is not sufficient that a man retain some truths; he must also confess them, and do nothing that may afford ground to think that he does not indeed maintain them. To act otherwise is to play the hypocrite, and to "hold the truth in unrighteousness," which Paul in the strongest terms condemns, declaring that "the wrath of God is revealed from heaven," against all who are guilty of such a heinous sin.

Objection 2

They plead that if they do not forsake the false religion in which they are engaged, they have notwithstanding good intentions, and they hope that God will have some regard to these.

But where have they learned that good intention justifies men in performing actions which God has forbidden? No man ever had better intentions than Uzziah, who, fearing lest the ark, the august symbol of the divine presence, should fall, put forth his hand to hold it; yet God struck him dead on the spot, because none except the priests and Levites had a right to touch the ark. None could have better intentions than that prophet of whom we have an account in 1 Kings 13, who being deceived by another prophet, disobeyed the order God had given him, and was torn in pieces by a lion, because of his disobedience, though what he did was viewed by him as an act of obedience to God.

But further, what are these intentions on which they value themselves?

If they speak sincerely, they would say, their intention is to preserve their honours, their goods, or perhaps their life. What! Must they then for honors and worldly goods forsake the truth, and expose themselves to the danger of losing their souls? Is it not much better to share in the sufferings and reproach of Jesus Christ than to possess all the riches of the world? This is the part which Moses embraced: "He chose rather to suffer affliction with the people of God, than to enjoy the pleasures of sin for a season." Are not the everlasting honours and pleasures that are at God's right hand preferable to all the dignities of earth, and all the carnal pleasures of sin?

Others may say, "Our intention is to make known the truth to those who are ignorant of it, which we may do with greater advantage, while we are not suspected by them."

But I ask, first, is it lawful to do evil that good may come? Secondly, is it a good mean to persuade and bring others over to the side of truth, to abstain from making a public profession of it?

"Our intention," others will say, "is to advance our children, and to procure places or employments for them in the world." But do you not perceive that this is to put your children in the road that leads to death, and to render them wretched for eternity? Unhappy parents! You have no higher aim than to deliver up your children to the world, and to fix them in attachment to the earth; whereas you ought to labor to train them up for heaven, and devote them entirely to God.

Objection 3

In excuse they will also say that: "It is unreasonable to think that a God, who is distinguished for mercy, strictly required all men to make a public profession of the truth, when it is so incompatible with their interest, and the repose of their life."

But what account then will they make of the many passages contained in Scripture, exhorting us to confess Jesus Christ before men; to be always ready to give an answer to those who ask a reason of the hope that is in us, with meekness and fear; to glorify God in our bodies as well as in our spirits; to follow Jesus Christ, and not to hearken to the voice of a stranger; and not to serve two masters?[219] What would the exhortations signify to deny ourselves and renounce all, to be the disciples of Jesus Christ; to take up his cross and to follow him, and even to lay down our life for his sake?[220]

If God does not always demand a public profession, it might so fall out that those who worship the beast, might yet be "written in the Lamb's book of life," contrary to the express declaration of the apostle John: it might be possible for men "to drink the cup of the Lord, and the cup of devils," whatever Paul says to the contrary; or to have communion with God, and

---

[219] Matthew 10:32, 1 Peter 10:15, 1 Corinthians 6:20, John 10:4, Matthew 6:24
[220] Matthew 11

still walk in darkness, in opposition to the testimony of the disciple whom Jesus loved.[221] Once more, if God exacts not of his children a public confession of his truth, whence was it that he acknowledged none for his servants in Israel, but those who had not bowed the knee to Baal? Whence is it that he threatens to spew the lukewarm out of his mouth? And why does he condemn those who halt between two opinions?[222] Can we then entertain the thought that Jesus Christ is satisfied with a partial surrender of ourselves to him, and when we serve him but by halves? Will he consent to enjoy, in partnership with the devil, what he has bought with the price of his blood?

Objection 4

"Yet it cannot be denied," they add, "that God addresses himself to us in these terms, 'My son, give me thine heart.'"

Very true, my brethren, but has he not also by authority enjoined to offer our bodies "as a living sacrifice, holy, acceptable to God, which is our reasonable service"? If he has commanded us to be steadfast in the faith, it is no less his will that we should be firm and immovable in the profession of our hope. Besides, it is a very gross mistake to imagine that our heart may be right with God, while we resign our body to the world. Would any say that a spouse truly loved her husband, if she prostituted her body to others? Certainly a good tree cannot bring forth evil fruit; so a good heart, influenced by the sincere love of God, always discovers its love; and "out of the abundance of the heart, the mouth speaketh."

Objection 5

"But God demands nothing else," they will still maintain, "but to worship him in spirit and in truth."

---

[221] Revelation 13:8, 14:9-11
[222] 1 Kings 19 & 18:21, Revelation 3

Be it so; but is it to worship God in truth, for a man to give his heart to him, but his outward conduct to the world? To act in truth must surely require an agreement between the outward and inward man, and the exterior appearance should be expressive of what is within. To assume the exterior without the interior part is to be a hypocrite; whereas to lay claim to internal without external piety is to become a liar. It is not needful to enter here on a more particular application of these words of Jesus Christ, here referred to. We lately had occasion to do this, when we showed that the design of our Savior in them was to teach us that the worship which God requires of men under the gospel should be spiritual, independent of the circumstances of time, places, and persons; but nothing could be further from his meaning than the gloss some would put upon them, that God desires to be adored only with the heart.

Objection 6

But does not Paul say to the believing Romans, "Hast thou faith, have it to thyself before God?"

True; but it ought to be attended to that the apostle is there treating of things indifferent, of days and meats, about which the Jews as yet retained some scruple; and all that he means by the expression is this: if a man have to do with weak persons, who would be offended at the use of his Christian liberty, it is better to abstain from the use of some things which God has permitted, and to keep his faith in his own heart, namely that faith whereby he is assured that Jesus Christ has abolished the distinction of days and meats, than to trouble his brethren. But is there any reason to infer from this, that the apostle would have Christians to content themselves with having faith only in the heart? Does he not elsewhere declare that separation is to be made from those who consent not to wholesome words; that we must resist even unto blood, and fight the good fight, even to the end; that we ought to go forth without the camp, bearing Christ's reproach.[223]

Objection 7

"But may not God account it sufficient that we should direct our intention towards him, and refer all that worship to him which we may perform before the creature?"

If this direction of the intention be all that is requisite to render our acts of worship agreeable to God, there is no communion whatever into which we might not enter. It might be allowable to frequent the mosques of the Mahometans, and to bow the knee before the Pagan idols. How shocking is such doctrine?

Objection 8

They further ask, "Can it be unlawful to follow the example of Nicodemus, and Joseph of Arimathea, who dared not publicly to attend upon Jesus Christ, besides many others who believed in him, and yet did not openly confess him?"

I answer firstly that all these persons are charged with blame in Scripture, for the evangelist John says of them that "they loved the praise of men more than the praise of God."[224] Secondly, it does not appear that Nicodemus or Joseph connected themselves with any assembly forbidden by God, nor were they chargeable with any idolatry. And lastly, I add that neither Nicodemus nor Joseph of Arimathea always concealed their sentiments: the one opposed the resolution which the Pharisees and priests took against Jesus Christ; and the other "consented not to their deed," and both of them went and demanded the body of Jesus, and buried it with honor, whereas those against whom we reason, are ashamed of our Savior, and are afraid to declare themselves his disciples.

---

[223] 1 Timothy 6, Hebrews 13, 2 Timothy 4
[224] John 12:42

Objection 9

"But did not Paul accommodate himself to all men? "To the Jews," says he, "I became as a Jew, that I might gain the Jews; to them that are under the law, as under the law, that I might gain them that are under the law: to them that are without law as without law, that I might gain them that are without law."[225]

The apostle—it is true—accommodated himself to times, places, and persons, when things indifferent were in question, such as the observation of some Mosaic ceremonies, in the time when they were still tolerated. But when did he ever show a base complaisance for idolatry or idolaters? Or do we forget the manner in which he reproved his fellow apostle, who walked not uprightly, but compelled the Gentiles to live as the Jews? Did he not also denounce anathema against those who taught any other doctrine than that which he delivered? And does he not inculcate the duty of suffering with Jesus Christ, in order also to reign with him? *In fine*, did not the same apostle gloriously lose his life for this divine Savior, having been beheaded at Rome?

Objection 10

"But did not Elisha the prophet permit Naaman to go into the temple of Rimmon, and to bow himself there before the idol, and consequently to dissemble his religion?"

He gave him no such permission; if he had, we might consider him as a false prophet who deserved to be held in detestation.

According to the usual translation of the passage, the words of Naaman to Elisha were: "When my master goeth into the house of Rimmon to worship there, and he leaneth on my hand, and I bow myself in the house of Rimmon, when I bow down myself in the house of Rimmon, the Lord pardon thy servant in this thing." (2 Kings 5:18). And then Elisha said unto him, "Go in peace." On this we may observe:

---

[225] 1 Corinthians 9:20–21

1. That Naaman does not here ask allowance to worship the idol of Rimmon, but only that he might have the liberty of serving the king his master in the way he had been accustomed to do, namely: to support him for the sake of honor, as sovereigns sometimes make use of their favourites for such a purpose. Naaman expressly declared that he would not henceforth offer any burnt offerings or sacrifices to other gods. So that all that could be inferred from thence, would only amount to this: that those who are engaged in serving and attending the persons of princes may be allowed to accompany their masters to the ceremonies of their religion, when their office obliges them to do them some particular service. This is what Valentinian did to the Emperor Julian when he led him into the temple of Fortune; and the Elector of Saxony, a Protestant, more lately, did the like to the Emperor Charles V. But here let it be observed that it would be needful that these persons should protest against any sort of compliance on their part with the errors and ceremonies of the false religion, as Valentinian did, when he accompanied Julian into the temple of Fortune; he struck even the person who sprinkled lustral water on those who entered, because a drop of the water had fallen on him, which made him exclaim aloud that he was polluted by it. I may add that a faithful Christian ought to avoid, or wholly renounce these employments which engage him to the performance of acts contrary to his religious belief. This first answer may of itself suffice for removing every pretext from those to whom we now reply: for they desire nothing less than to be allowed to make a public profession of a false religion, and to bow the knee to a creature, although they cannot plead that any prince leans upon them when they are about to perform their homage.

2. It may be observed that Elisha, properly speaking, gave no direct answer; he only dismissed Naaman with that form of speech that was customary among the people of the east. The prophets were not always in readiness to answer those who consulted them; it might be needful for them to ask counsel at the mouth of the Lord.

If it is said that the matter in question was not difficult to decide; in this they may find themselves mistaken. For though God had nowhere, as far as I know, forbidden a servant to perform this service to his master, to sustain his hand or his body, or even to kneel down, that his master might more conveniently lean upon him; yet he had forbidden whatever had any relation to idolatry, and even intercourse with idolaters, so that Elisha might possibly be in some embarrassment. Therefore he gives him his leave by wishing him peace, which might import either that God might pardon in that matter, if it were a sin,[226] or that he might direct him as to his duty in the case.

3. The words of the original may very properly be thus rendered, "When my master went up to the house of Rimmon to worship there, and he leaned on my hand, and I bowed myself, or *worshiped*, in the house of Rimmon, seeing as I have worshipped in the house of Rimmon, the Lord, I pray, forgive thy servant in this thing." Thus Naaman asks pardon for what he had already done; not for what he meant to do. Having acknowledged the God of Israel to be the only true God, he was afraid that he might be punished for having served other gods: accordingly he beseeches the Lord to pardon him, not merely for what he had done in accompanying and supporting his prince, but in general in that he had prostrated himself in the temple of Rimmon. In this view of the matter—which is that of many of the learned—there is no manner of difficulty.

But we may further say that it is rather surprising that our Nicodemites should propose to themselves the example of Naaman the Syrian, rather than that of the three young Hebrews, who chose rather to be cast into the flames of a burning furnace than to fall down before the statue of Nebuchadnezzar;

---

[226] This manner of solving the difficulty, so far as it supposes Naaman to have requested indulgence and pardon in resolving to perform an unlawful action, or one as to which there might be just or apparent ground of scruple, or that supposes the words of the prophet to imply a prayer for pardon in such an action, can hardly be vindicated, as there is no example of such prayers in the Scripture, nor could such a manner of acting be consistent with due regard to the honor of God, or the decision the apostle, in a similar case, condemning him who eats meat offered to idols with a doubtful mind. [*Translator*]

or that of Daniel, who was willing to be thrown into the den of lions, rather than to cease from praying to his God; or the example of those illustrious men both of the Old and New Testament who have suffered for the truth, and who might have delivered themselves from their sufferings, if they had only been inclined to dissemble their religion. I might produce many examples of the same kind; but I shall only relate the behavior of the soldiers of Julian, on a certain occasion, according to the account given of it by Gregory Nazianzen. The emperor pretended a design to distribute some money among his troops; but he ordered every soldier to cast a grain of incense upon an altar, placed near to Julian, before they received the liberality of the prince. Those who were apprised beforehand of the fraud, absented themselves on the occasion; others, who had no suspicion of it, attended, and did as he desired. But what was the consequence? The soldiers, having been advertised of the stratagem, and of the motive of the act, which they had been led by surprize to commit, went to the public square, and cried out, "We are Christians; yes, in our hearts we are. We earnestly wish all the world to hear this our confession; and above all, we pray that God for whom we live and will die, may vouchsafe to hear it. Jesus Christ, our Lord! We have not renounced thee. We have not abjured the glorious confession which we made in our baptism. If our hand committed a fault, our will took no share in it. It was the artifice of the emperor, who has imposed upon us; for gold was not capable of dazzling us to such a degree. We revoke and renounce such a horrid impiety, and are even ready to wash it away with our blood."

These soldiers did yet more: they went in quest of the emperor, and said to him, "It is not your gold that we have received; it is an act of death you have pronounced against us. It was not with a view to confer honor upon us, that you made us approach your person, but in order to make us bear the marks of your infamy. Reserve your gifts and largesses for the soldiers of your own religion; offer us a sacrifice to Jesus Christ, who is our only King. Make us undergo the fire, into which we have cast incense; reduce our bodies to ashes, rather than leave any part of them for such a sacrilegious offering. Cut off the hands that have committed so great a crime as to stretch themselves on your altar; cut in pieces our feet which served us to run to such a wicked action. Distribute your gold to persons who will not have any regret for having received it. Jesus Christ is sufficient for us; he alone is to us instead of all things."

A noble answer! Worthy of men who were the soldiers of Jesus, rather than of Julian: that zealot caused them all to be put to death, except one to whom he showed favor, but who expressed his grief that Jesus Christ had not also conferred on him the honour of repairing his fault by martyrdom.

Truly, if dissimulation were allowable, and if persons were under no obligation to confess the true religion, the martyrs and confessors would have been very great fools to choose rather to die than to cast a grain of incense into the fire. But far be it from us to speak in this manner of these heroes of Christianity, whose blood was the seed of the church.

Objection 11

But is there not reason to think that the apostle Paul meant to inculcate it as a duty that everyone should submit himself to the religion of the sovereign, under whom he lives, when he says, "He that resisteth the power resisteth the ordinance of God; and that he must needs be subject to magistrates, not only for wrath, but also for conscience sake."

Surely, not. This is very far from being the mind of the apostle. If it were, then he who should live in Turkey, would be bound to embrace the Mahometan religion, and to be a Pagan when living in Japan. If that were his meaning, then Paul himself must have been very culpable for not conforming himself to the religion of Nero. The design of the apostle in these expressions is to exhort Christians to be subject to ruling powers, and to obey them in all things not contrary to the law of God, not only from the fear of punishment, but also from the motive of conscience; because the powers are ordained of God, and whatever is ordained of God, interests and obliges conscience; so, he that resists the powers, resists God himself, who hath established them. But it must not be inferred from this that magistrates must be obeyed when they command us to do things contrary to our conscience. Hear what the papal decretals have declared on this head: "If the human lord commands anything not contrary to the holy Scriptures, let the servant submit himself to his master; if he command things contrary, let him rather obey him that is Lord of the soul, than him that has authority over the body. If what the emperor commands be good, let his command in that be performed; if it be evil, reply, *We must obey God rather than men.*"

Objection 12

Some plead a passage contained in the sixth chapter of Baruch, in which, it is alleged that Jeremiah, when writing to those who should be led captive to Babylon, requires nothing more of them than that they should say in their hearts: "Lord, thou art he who ought to be adored."

It might suffice for reply that the pretended epistle of Jeremiah is not canonical; but besides, whoever reads it may see firstly that the author of that letter forbids the Jews in it "not to conform themselves in any manner whatever to strangers," which certainly would forbid them to bow the knee before the Babylonian idols; secondly, that his aim is only to exhort the Jews, when they should behold the Babylonians worshipping false gods, to detest their idolatry in their hearts before God, yet without imitating their practice, so long as they should remain captives in Babylon. But everyone may see that our Nicodemites can draw no inference from thence in their favor.

Objection 13

Finally, they ask whether we believe that all those who have forsaken the true religion shall be damned.

Far be it from us to pronounce such a terrible judgment. On the contrary, we say that all those who have denied Jesus Christ, as Peter said, and who, like that apostle, have bewailed their sin, and returned to that divine Savior, shall be saved. We are inclined to hope that the flax[227] which smokes in many, in such unhappy circumstances, shall be rekindled, and that he who, by one powerful look, recovered Peter, and caused him to weep, will bring back many such poor wanderers.

Yet we believe that those who continue in their apostasy, and abide in that state of hypocrisy and cowardice, in opposition to the light and convictions of their conscience, ought not to entertain hope of salvation.

These are the principal objections which are produced on this subject. But in order to render your conviction in regard to it more complete, I now proceed to the motives that ought to engage you to perseverance, to hold fast the true religion.

V.   HEAD

The *motives* to engage us to make a public and stedfast profession of this religion are various.

1. It is certain that there is no duty more frequently recommended in the holy Scripture than this. The single Epistle of Paul to the Hebrews is filled throughout with exhortations to perseverance: "We are," says this apostle, "the house of God, if we hold fast the confidence and the rejoicing of the hope firm unto the end." And he adds: "Take heed, brethren, lest there be in any of you an evil heart of unbelief, in departing from the living God. But exhort one another daily, while it is called, today, lest any of you be hardened through the deceitfulness of sin" (Hebrews 3:12-14). And elsewhere he says: "Let us hold fast the profession of our faith without wavering (for he is faithful that promised)" (Hebrews 10:23). "Looking diligently lest any man fail of the grace of God, lest any root of bitterness springing up, trouble you, and thereby many be defiled. Lest there be any fornicator, or profane person, as Esau, who, for one morsel of meat, sold his

---

[227] *Lumignon*, the word employed by our author, denotes the wick of a candle, or lamp, which, when going out, continues to emit a smoke though no flame may be visible. [*Transl.*]

birthright" (Hebrews 12:15, 17). "Be not carried away with divers and strange doctrines: for it is a good thing that the heart be established with grace; not with meats, which have not profited them that have been occupied therein" (Hebrews 13:9). And we shall hear in a little, the threatenings denounced by this apostle against those who fall away. Besides, how much has he said on this head, in his other epistles? How much have the other apostles of Christ spoken about it? It would behoove us to quote a great part of the holy Scriptures, if we were here to produce all that is to be found there upon this subject. "Be thou faithful unto death," said Jesus Christ to the angel of the church of Smyrna, "Hold fast what thou hast, until I come," said he to the church of Thyatira; "Remember," said he to the church of Sardis, "how thou hast received and heard, hold fast and repent." And to the church of Philadelphia, he said, "Hold that fast which thou hast, that no man take thy crown."[228] After exhortations so urgent and forcible, is there a person but must acknowledge himself to be under an indispensable obligation to hold fast what is good, or, in other words, the true religion? He must certainly be under the necessity of shaking off the yoke of Jesus Christ, and paying no regard to him as his sovereign and master, or else give obedience to him when he commands his followers to be faithful to him, and to persevere in the religion which he himself introduced and settled in the world.

2. The consideration of the relation which Jesus Christ stands in to us, should engage us inviolably to this. He is our husband, and we are his spouse; he is our prince, and we are his subjects; he is our captain and leader, and we his soldiers. Ought we not therefore to be faithful to him in all these respects: as a spouse, that we may never suffer the unchaste love of the world to take possession of our hearts; as his subjects, so as to do nothing inconsistent with his service, and may never withdraw ourselves from

---

[228] Revelation 2 & 3

obedience to him; and as his soldiers, to fight always with him even unto death.

3. We are still more strongly bound to this from the consideration of what Jesus Christ has done for us. Not only were we brought by him from nothing, but he made himself as nothing for our sakes; not only has he bestowed on us life, but he lost his own life for our salvation; he plucked us from the hand of the devil, translated us from darkness into the kingdom of his marvellous light. Neither the cruelty of his murderers, nor the formidable preparation and apparatus of his cross, nor the dread of the overwhelming load of divine wrath, nor the ignominy of the sentence and punishment he endured, could make him abandon the work of our salvation. Would it not then be ingratitude of the most atrocious kind, to fail in fidelity to this divine Savior, without whom we could not have existed at all, or would have been eternally miserable? Even if we had a thousand lives, could we employ them to better purpose than to hazard them for the love of this glorious Redeemer, who died for our offences and rose again for our justification; who was crucified and wounded for our transgressions, who intercedes for us, who instructs us by his Word, keeps us under his protection, and who must one day appear for judgment? The apostle, in the twelfth chapter to the Hebrews, makes use of this powerful motive: "Look," says he, "unto Jesus, the author and finisher of our faith, who for the joy that was set before him, endured the cross, despising the shame, and is set down at the right hand of the throne of God. For consider him that endured such contradiction of sinners against himself, lest ye be wearied, and faint in your minds. Ye have not yet resisted unto blood, striving against sin." (Hebrews 12:2-4).

4. Regard to the truth itself, which God enjoins us to keep, obliges us to this duty. Of all things in the world, this is the most precious. It enlightens the mind, regulates the passions; makes men wise, prudent, just, sober, chaste, resolute in dangers, patient in adversity. It dissipates our doubts, and our cares; establishes in our souls a perfect peace, and fills us with a joy unspeakable. Without it, all the pleasures of life would be but bitterness, at

least none of them could be tasted pure; as was asserted, by an ancient philosopher, without sufficient ground, of physics. What Solomon says of wisdom we ought here to apply to true religion; "Happy is the man that findeth wisdom, and the man that getteth understanding. For the merchandise of it is better than the merchandise of silver, and the gain thereof than fine gold. She is more precious than rubies; and all the things thou canst desire, are not to be compared unto her. Length of days is in her right hand; and in her left hand riches and honour. Her ways are ways of pleasantness; and all her paths are peace. She is a tree of life to them that lay hold upon her: and happy is every one that retaineth her." (Proverbs 3:13-18).

If so, must not that man be foolish in the highest degree, who chooses to part with this wisdom, and to forsake the true religion? Is not this to render himself voluntarily wretched?

Antiquity has praised the daughter of Pythagoras, because she could never be prevailed with to sell her father's writings, whatever advantageous offers were made her. She chose rather to continue poor than to enrich herself by selling the deposit with which her father had entrusted her. Shall it be said that we have had less zeal for the heavenly truths, than this woman had, for the works of her father? Or that we should have chosen to abandon a religion of which Jesus Christ is the author, which he has brought to us from heaven, which he sealed with his blood, and which has been confirmed by that of so many Christians, while a female Pagan had such respect for the productions of him who had given her birth?

5. The example of so many believers, both under the Old and New Testament, who chose rather to expose themselves to all sorts of suffering, than to forsake the truth, affords another powerful motive to excite us to perseverance. "Seeing we are compassed about," said Paul to the Hebrews, "with so great a cloud of witnesses, let us lay aside every weight, and the sin that doth so easily beset us, and let us run with patience the race set before us."

By this argument did Cyprian encourage the faithful in his time, exhorting them not only to imitate Jesus Christ, but also the other saints. Thus he addresses them: "Seeing as we are the soldiers of Jesus Christ, let us not think of peace, nor fly from the combat; but let us courageously follow our Lord, who marches at our head, and who teaches us patience, having first done what he would have us to do, and having endured himself what he would have us to endure. Let us imitate righteous Abel, the first martyr who suffered for righteousness. Let us imitate Abraham, the friend of God, who did not hesitate to sacrifice his son with his own hands. Let us imitate the three young Hebrews. Also Daniel, who, when they would have forced him to prostrate himself before the idol Bel, which the people and the king adored, maintained, with a holy boldness, the cause of God, saying: "I will worship none but Jehovah my Lord, who made the heaven and the earth." What did they gain over the minds of the seven Maccabees, by making them suffer cruel torments? Did they not all die with heroical constancy? And did not their mother imitate their courage and firmness? Shall not these great examples of virtue and patience awaken our zeal, and urge us to aspire to the honour of martyrdom? Do not the prophets, the apostles, and saints, who have lost their lives in the cause of righteousness, teach us to die as they have done? Jesus Christ was no sooner come into the world than infants honoured his birth by martyrdom. Though they were not yet arrived at the age fit for combat, yet they did not fail to obtain the crown. In order that it might appear that all those who suffer for Jesus Christ are innocent, innocent babes were killed for his name. God would hereby show that none should be exempted from persecution, seeing as such creatures as these suffered martyrdom. How culpable then must Christians be, if they are not willing to suffer for Jesus Christ, seeing as Christ has suffered for us. The Master of the Universe, the Son of God, endured death, to deliver us from our iniquities, and to make us the children of God; and shall not the sons of men, the slaves of sin, give their life, to preserve the glorious title of the sons of God, which Jesus Christ has procured for them?"

6. The threatenings denounced by God against them who forsake the truth, should make all take heed that they be not among the number. "He that hath ears to hear, let him hear." "Whosoever denieth me before men," saith Christ, "him will I deny before my Father" (Matthew 10:23). "It is impossible for those who were once enlightened," saith Paul, "who have tasted of the heavenly gift, and were made partakers of the Holy Ghost, and have tasted the good word of God, and the powers of the world to come; if they shall fall away, to renew them again unto repentance: seeing they crucify to themselves the Son of God afresh, and put him to an open shame" (Hebrews 6:4-6). "If we sin wilfully," says he again, "after we have received the knowledge of the truth, there remaineth no more sacrifice for sins. But a certain fearful looking for of judgment, and fiery indignation, which shall devour the adversaries. He that despised Moses' law, died without mercy, under two or three witnesses. Of how much sorer punishment suppose ye, shall he be thought worthy, who hath trodden under foot the Son of God, and hath counted the blood of the covenant, wherewith he was sanctified, an unholy thing, and hath done despite unto the Spirit of grace?" (Hebrews 10:26-29). "It had been better," says another apostle, "not to have known the way of righteousness, than after they had known it to turn from the holy commandment delivered to them" (1 Peter 2:26). "If any man," says John, "worship the beast or his image, and receive his mark in his forehead, or in his hand, the same shall drink of the wine of the wrath of God, which is poured out without mixture, into the cup of his indignation; and he shall be tormented with fire and brimstone, in the presence of the holy angels, and in the presence of the Lamb: And the smoke of their torment ascendeth up for ever and ever. And they have no rest day nor night, who worship the beast, and his image, and whosoever receiveth the mark of his name" (Revelation 13:10-11). He who is deaf to these threatenings, is not merely deaf, but dead. Who after hearing them can allow himself to be shaken by temptation? Are gibbets, wheels, poverty, misery, or any sort of disgrace on earth, comparable with these eternal torments? Surely not. Hold fast therefore, dear

Christians, the true religion, although by your attachment to it, you may have a thousand things to fear here below, and a thousand pains to endure.

7. The great promises made to those who persevere, should doubtless have influence upon your hearts. "He who confesseth me before men," says Jesus Christ, "him will I confess before my Father." What honor to be acknowledged before such a glorious person, as the Lord Jesus! And what more could be said for encouragement than is contained in his address to the churches of Asia Minor: "To him that overcometh will I give to eat of the tree of life, which is in the midst of the paradise of God; I will give him of the hidden manna; [...] a white stone, and on the stone a name written, which no man knoweth but he only who receiveth it; [...] the bright morning star; [...] and eternal life." "He shall be clothed in white robes and I will not blot out his name out of the book of life; [...] I will make him a pillar in the temple of my God, and he shall go no more out; and I will write upon him the name of my God, and the name of the city of my God, which is New Jerusalem, which cometh down from heaven from my God, and I will write upon him my new name; [...] He shall sit with me on my throne, even as I also overcame, and am set down with the Father upon his throne."[229] O great and glorious promises! After this, can there be anything that can hinder us from holding fast the true religion, and continuing in the faithful adherence to Jesus the Lord? Shall we fear the reproach of men, seeing as Jesus Christ will acknowledge us as his own, before his heavenly Father? And who would rather choose to be esteemed in the world, and at last to be disowned by Jesus Christ, to become the contempt of angels, the scorn of devils, and the abhorrence of the sovereign Judge of the universe? Should we be afraid of sufferings? What is it to suffer some present evils in comparison with the pains of hell? What is it to lose a miserable life, to enjoy a life immortal and unspeakably blessed; to possess God himself, and to be satisfied with his likeness? Should we suffer ourselves to be dazzled by the promises of

---

[229] Revelation 2 & 3

the world? What proportion is there between the promises of man and those of God; between the pleasures of a moment, and the delights that are eternal; between some vanishing honors, and a glory that will never end?

Certainly, he must be more than a fool who hesitates a moment, as to the part he ought to take with respect to true or false religion; or who allows himself to be drawn away either by threatenings or promises, while, on one side, heaven may be seen opening for those who are faithful to Christ; and, on the other, hell appears ready to swallow up cowardly apostates. O then, my dear brethren—you who have acknowledged our religion as alone the true, never forsake it, whatever any may promise to allure you, or whatever they may menace to intimidate you—hold fast that which you have received; and retain to the end that which is good.

APPLICATION.

There are six sorts of persons who ought to reflect seriously on the words we have been explaining.

1. Those who know the truth, but yet are not disposed to embrace it.

2. Those who having known it, have basely abandoned it, and who are not yet recovered from their wandering.

3. Those who, after relinquishing it, have acknowledged their fault, and given glory to God.

4. Those who have not abandoned the profession of the truth, because they have not met with solicitations to do it, or because their temporal interests hinder them from doing it.

5. Those who have forsaken a corrupt religion, and embraced one that is good.

6. Lastly, those who make profession of the truth with all their heart.

1. I begin with those who know the truth, but yet choose not to embrace it. I know not if there are any such in the assembly; but if there be,

I must take the freedom to ask them why they refuse to reduce to practice the order of the apostle in all its extent. Paul says to them, "Prove all things." This they may have done, at least in part, so far they have done well; but the same apostle also has said to them: "Hold fast that which is good." Why then should they not give prompt obedience to this command? "How long will you halt between two opinions? If the Lord be God, follow him." If Jesus Christ be the author of the religion you profess, continue therein; but if it is only in our religion that pure Christianity can be found, embrace it. "You wait," you say, "until the times be more favorable, and then you will give glory to God." Do you think then of following Jesus Christ without bearing his cross? What! Do you not know that Christ requires his disciples to deny themselves, and to be prepared for suffering? If you desire to be accounted his disciples, why do you decline to engage in the conflicts to which he calls you? Will you, for a little worldly honor, suffer almost anything; and will you suffer nothing for him, who endured such extreme torments for our salvation: torments which made him cry out, "My God, my God, why hast thou forsaken me?"

Ought you to be averse to suffer in order to reign, to possess an inheritance incorruptible, and to be eternally happy? For it is in vain to flatter yourselves with the thought that God is satisfied with the heart alone. No; my brethren, he requires you to be wholly his, or not at all. Where is the king that would acknowledge for his true subjects those who should fight under the banners of his enemies, although they should protest that they still revere him as their sovereign?

Neither say that you will declare yourselves at the hour of death, and then make a confession of the truth. Poor souls! Do you not consider how often men are unawares surprised by death? And why would you perform so late what cannot be done too soon? Why refer a work the most difficult and important, to a time when you will be subjected to the greatest infirmities? Nay; delay no longer: "Today if you will hear the voice of God, harden not your heart," for fear he should swear in his wrath that you shall never enter into his rest.

2. I address myself next to you—miserable apostates!—who have forsaken the truth, and who are not yet returned from your wanderings.

What has Jesus Christ done to you that you should thus basely forsake him? Who was it sent you into the world? Was it not he? By whom do you subsist, but by him? To whom do you owe all the good things you possess, but to him? From whom have you received the knowledge of the truth, but from him? And what expectations do you entertain as to the life to come? Dare you hope to be crowned when you have never fought, but have revolted from your general? What ground have you to think that you shall be partakers of his glory, seeing as you have never taken part in his cross? And what else can you expect to be your portion than to be denied before the heavenly Father, by him whom you have denied before men, and to drink the wine unmixed, that is poured into the cup of the wrath of God, appointed for those who receive the mark of the beast. What will you do in the last and great day, when you shall behold him whom you have abandoned, sitting in judgment on you? What will you say in your own justification? Alas! You will have nothing to answer unto him; but you must hear his terrible sentence that will condemn you to eternal pains. Then shall you cry to the mountains and to the hills, but in vain; for you still shall be delivered to the executioners of the fearful justice of the Savior. Miserable men! Will you not have pity upon yourselves? Oh! Return from such a deplorable course of wandering, while God yet spares you on the earth; while you have still the breath of life; before the gate of mercy is entirely shut on you, and God has pronounced your doom of final condemnation. "Turn ye." God would have you to turn, and to rend your heart.

3. Let me address you, who, after having been so weak as to fall before temptation, have given glory to God by acknowledging your sin. Of these, there are two sorts: the one consists of such as make a public profession of the truth, in those places where the Word of God is purely preached; the

other, of such as are not inclined to forsake the hall, where they denied their master.

As to the first, we earnestly beseech them to call to their remembrance what they have done, and to keep their sins continually before their eyes. We entreat them to watch over themselves, lest they should fall again into such a great sin, for then their last state would be far worse than the first. We charge them diligently to labour to have their passions subdued, lest they should cause them to fall a second time. We solemnly charge and beseech them to shun the occasions whereby they may be exposed to new temptations: particularly, to flee those places where their faith may be in danger of being shaken, and those companions which tend to corrupt their heart. *In fine*, we obtest and beseech them to apply with all possible earnestness to the study of sanctification; to pray God without ceasing to pardon their sins, and to establish them in his truth, so that nothing may be able to hinder them from holding fast that which is good.

With regard to the second class, who make no public profession of the true religion, but remain buried in the places where they did violence to their conscience, because they could not quit their business, their goods, and outward conveniences, we can say nothing else than that we are greatly afraid as to their condition. We consider them as lukewarm; and must liken them to those mentioned in Mathew 22, who being invited to the marriage, made no account of it, but went their way, one to his farm, another to his merchandise, and consequently were deprived of the feast.

Let them not tell me that they do no evil. Can it be said that these do no evil, who are not found with Jesus Christ, who are not willing to follow him, and who keep at a distance from the places where the Savior of the world makes his abode?

Indeed, I cannot conceal it that I have great difficulty to believe that such persons can be saved. I must say the same of those who, though already possessed of considerable property, expose themselves to new temptations, in order to acquire still more. I consider these men as the persons of whom the wise man speaks, that seek danger, and who sooner or later fall into it. It plainly appears that they are not lovers of God: so that there is greater reason to doubt than to hope well of their salvation. Wretched men! You are cumbered about many things, but one thing alone is needful for you. Be intent upon the work of your salvation, and hold fast that which is good.

4. I proceed to those who have not forsaken the truth, because they have not been solicited to do so; and because their temporal interests do not require it of them. Of this class, the number is indeed very great. To them we may very properly say with Paul, "Hold fast that which is good." But in order to this, it is needful that we exhort them to inform themselves as to the truth, to read the Word of God and to meditate upon it; to be careful to maintain a good conscience: for the same apostle tells us that some, having put away this, concerning faith made shipwreck. We would exhort them to set God always before their eyes; to combat their passions, more especially their avarice and ambition; to accustom themselves to the contempt of life, yet not to expose themselves rashly to dangers, and to train themselves to patience; *in fine*, to pray God continually to bestow faith upon them, and increase it, so that rejecting what is evil, they may always retain that which is good.

5. I now address myself to those who have quitted a false religion, and have embraced the true. Hold fast, Christians, that good part which you have chosen, and let nothing whatever prevail with you to abandon it. Give thanks to he who has translated you out of darkness, into the kingdom of his marvellous light. Continue to study the religion you have embraced: the more you know it, the more you will love it. Read and meditate on the holy Scriptures, wherein it is all contained. Carefully shun all those temptations to which you may be exposed. Make it your daily request to God that he would continue to illuminate you with clear and powerful light, and that he would establish you in his truth. Follow the maxims of that holy religion, which you now profess, and let your life be as holy as your religion is.

6. And finally, I come to address those who with all their heart, make profession of the true religion; in which number there are not a few who have boldly confessed it. Christians, continue as you have begun, always hold fast what you have received, and fight to the last the good fight, in keeping the faith. Yet be not too confident in your own strength; but "let him that thinketh he standeth, take heed lest he fall." Work out your own salvation with fear and trembling. Be afraid of your corrupt flesh: it is a treacherous foe that may cause your destruction. But if God calls you to any conflict, fail not to combat under the banners of Jesus Christ, and you shall become more than conquerors through him who loved you.

Let *all of us*, without exception, hold steadfastly the true religion, in which, by the favor of God, we have been brought up. Let us watch every one over another, and exhort one another to perseverance.

Fathers and mothers, exhort your children to this. And lest your children at any time should induce you to forsake God (for this has been the occasion of many falling), show them an example of heroic firmness, and never be such wretches as to lead them to an idol. Address them in the language of Mattathias, "Now therefore, my children, be zealous for the law, and lay down your lives for the covenant of your fathers."[230] Imitate these fathers mentioned in history, who animated their children to maintain the interests of their religion even unto blood, and who, on seeing them shed it, rejoiced that they had given birth to martyrs.

Children, never solicit your parents to revolt, in order to your advancement. And if you have fathers so unhappy as to have denied Jesus Christ, imitate them not, neither hearken to them on this subject; rather imitate that prince, of whom Gregory of Tours speaks, who, being commanded by his father to change his religion, answered that he knew very well what he owed to his father and king, but he also knew the duty he

---

[230] 1 Maccabees 2:5

owed to God. Remember the words of our Lord: "He that loveth his father or mother more than me, is not worthy of me."

Husbands, exhort your wives to perseverance, and never allow yourselves to be seduced by them. Wives, exhort, in like manner, your husbands; and if they will not perform their duty, act not as they do in this. If they should attempt to draw you to revolt, answer them, as that illustrious woman, mentioned by Jerome, who said: "I formerly was inclined to please my husband, and the world; but now I wish to please Jesus Christ."

Old men and young men, rich and poor, learned and illiterate; let us all resolve to die together, rather than abandon our holy religion. Let us be careful to walk according to the rules it prescribes. Nor should we be greatly surprised, if we see the great ones of the earth forsaking the truth; nor need we be astonished, even though we should behold all the world embracing error. If Jesus Christ should say to us, as for you, "Will you also go away?" Let us make the reply; "Lord to whom shall we go but to thee, for thou hast the words of eternal life." "We have believed, and have known that thou art the Son of God." We desire not to live but for thee, and we are ready to die for thy sake? In this way we may be able to say at the end of our course, as the apostle Paul did: "I have fought a good fight, I have finished my course, *I have kept the faith*; henceforth there is laid up for me a crown of righteousness, which the Lord the righteous Judge shall give at that day; and not to me only, but unto all them also who love his appearance." *Amen.*

FINIS